Testimonials

Here's what other mums have to say about
The Happy Mum Handbook

"It really is great to know that there is someone else out there that understands. The processes are very easy to follow too. I have done other 'self-help' stuff which has been great but is more time consuming so it is nice just to have something to refer to quickly and to have a greater awareness of why I get frustrated with some situations. My husband also found the book useful -he really is a super husband and very helpful at home and with the babies so he could relate to it too!"

Kate -Scarborough, WA, Australia

"I have loved the book and can totally relate to so many of the real life situations that are identified in the book. Just ordering the book helped start to change my mindset – I was doing something pro-active and positive to make a change and that in itself was great. I am slowly making my way through the book and am getting something out of every chapter that I read and most importantly am having loads more fun with my fabulous children."

T B , NSW (mother of 3)

"I have been struggling with the complete change in my life since my baby was born. I found it lonely, hard work and a huge shock to the system. I searched for help through friends, other mums and online. I found other mums were always trying to be happy or just talked general chit chat and not many actually talked about how hard it all is and how to cope. When I found the Happy Mum book and began to read, I actually cried cause the situations were completely what I'd been going through and it gave me hope. Now one year down the line my little one is thriving and I have the book to thank for making things a little easier."

Jenny Ervine, Northern Ireland

"I would just like to say Thank you... I have only just started reading The Happy Mum Handbook and I have already found that I'm dealing with issues more constructively. I also realise that my child's behaviour is NOT a reflection on my parenting skills. I really struggled with this before!"

Tracy -ACT (mother of one)

"I'm not a new mum at all. My son is 12 but, I when I read your book, I found a new perspective on parenting, partnering and home life that has helped me to cope with entrenched anger, stress and tiredness. I had tried other cognitive therapy self help books with a greater focus on psychology but your practical insights and examples were much more helpful for me. Thank you, Caroline."

Caroline Noonan, NSW. Australia

"I have never really read anything like this. It made me realize how much judgement I have in my life. And that my mood is determined by my 'get my life right' model. It's nice to accept myself and know I have implicit value despite my output. Quite a contrast from my corporate world existence."

Lisa, Melbourne. Australia

The Happy MUM HANDBOOK

JACKIE HALL

Disclaimer: The intent of this author is only to offer information of a general nature to help you in your quest for emotional well-being. It is not intended to be a substitute for any psychological, financial, legal, or any other professional advice. In the event you use any of the information in this book for yourself, the author and publisher assume no responsibility for your actions. If expert assistance or counselling is needed, the services of a competent medical or psychological professional should be sought.

First published 2010

© 2010 Jackie Hall

All rights reserved. Without limiting the rights under copyright restricted above, no part of this publication may be reproduced, stored in or introduced into a retrieval system, or transmitted, in any form or by any means (electronic, mechanical, photocopying, recording or otherwise), without the prior written permission of both the copyright owner and the above publisher of this book.

Designed and typeset by Palmer Higgs Pty Ltd

Illustrations by Bev Asbeit
Edited by Sandra Balonyi

ISBN: 978-0-646-54071-9

Contents

	Introduction	1

Chapter 1 Happiness 8

What is happiness? 8
Emotions and happiness 15
Mind TRACK to Happiness 17

Part A: The Mind TRACK to Happiness process — 25

Chapter 2 Step 1 – Thoughts 26

Conversations with the mind 26
How you came to think the way you do 27
Why is it difficult to change your thoughts? 30
How to change your thoughts 32
The Fountainhead Method™ 32
Using Step 1 39

Chapter 3 Step 2 – Reality 40

How are my thoughts in conflict with reality? 40
The Personal Development Model™ 43
   Self-worth: why you're worthy just the way you are! 51
   Self-worth versus self-esteem 55
Using Step 2 59

Chapter 4   Step 3 – Aim   61

    What do I want?   61
    Is what I want in conflict with reality?   61
    Be specific   62
    Why do I want it?   63
    Using Step 3   66

Chapter 5   Step 4 – Choices   67

    What options/solutions do I have?   67
    What governs our choices?   69
    Using Step 4   74

Chapter 6   Step 5 – Know your plan and action it   75

    Know your plan and action it
    Using Step 5   77
    Summary: The Mind TRACK to Happiness process   77

Chapter 7   Three common stress disorders   80

    Psychological stress   80
        Clinical depression   85
        Generalised anxiety disorder (GAD)   90
    Clinical depression and generalised anxiety disorder (GAD)   94
    The Anti-Depression Association of Australia (ADAA)   95

Part B: Applying the Mind TRACK to Happiness process to your life   97

Chapter 8   Introduction to Part B   98

Chapter 9   Behavioural and developmental challenges   100

    It's okay to be human   101
    You are their teacher of life   103
    Their behaviour doesn't determine your self-worth   105
    The first 5 years of challenges   110
    Summary: Behavioural and developmental challenges   150

Chapter 10   Anger and guilt   153

    Applying the Mind TRACK to Happiness process   153
    Summary: Anger and guilt   165

Chapter 11 — Loss of identity — 167

How did I lose my identity? — 168
Identity and self-worth — 181
Options/solutions — 186
Boredom and lost identity — 189

Chapter 12 — Time out — 195

Why isn't 'time out' my priority? — 197
What about life balance? — 214
Readjusting your idea of 'time out' — 215
The different types of time out — 216
How do I want to spend my time? — 219
Why do I want this and is this aim in conflict with reality? — 221
Summary: Time out — 230

Chapter 13 — Relationships: You and your partner — 232

The dynamics of your relationship — 233
The reality of a relationship — 237
The blame game — 238
My life has not gone to plan — 244
Strategies for communicating well with your partner — 258
How to speak effectively when communicating with your partner — 260
Common issues in marriages with young children and how to communicate for resolutions — 261
Summary: Marital/partner relationships — 269

Chapter 14 — Summary of Part B — 271

Behavioural and developmental challenges — 271
Anger and guilt — 272
Loss of identity — 273
Time out — 274
Marital/partner relationships — 275

Chapter 15 — Summary to changing your mindset — 277

The Mind TRACK to Happiness process — 278

Chapter 16 — Be the change you wish to see in the world — 283

Afterword — 285
Acknowledgements — 287

Introduction

I remember one of the lowest points of my life. I had come home from grocery shopping with my husband and my two boys, Cody (then 22 months old) and Ryan (then 6 months old). The whole experience had been a nightmare and I was feeling drained, tired and fed up, which was my usual frame of mind in those days.

I had a kitchen full of groceries begging to be put away, several dirty dishes that needed to be washed, a messy house with toys everywhere and two whiney, hungry and tired kids to tend to.

The overwhelming feeling of being in demand had gotten to me and I just needed some space. I grunted at my husband to take the kids away from me before I completely lost the plot.

He kindly respected my wishes, but they had barely been outside for two minutes before Cody was sent back inside for assaulting our chickens. As soon as he was back, so was Ryan and that was the end of my 'time out'.

In my state of mind at the time, two minutes was definitely not enough time to pull myself together, put things back into perspective and reinstate my 'rational mum' identity.

So here I was back to my messy house and whingeing children, when Cody pushed my buttons one last time before I fell apart. I clearly remember standing in the kitchen holding Ryan in my arms, screaming at Cody (and I mean literally screaming, in a high-pitched, psychotic rage) to 'SHUT UP AND STOP WHINGEING!'

I threw a loaf of bread across the room and slammed a nearby bread knife on the kitchen bench so hard that it bounced off the bench and narrowly missed Cody's head. I screamed, 'I HATE MY LIFE!' and ran out of the kitchen into my bedroom, crying uncontrollably, like a teenager having a tantrum, all with Ryan still on my hip.

Thankfully, my understanding husband came in, took Ryan without saying a word and allowed me to have my emotional breakdown by myself.

It wasn't the first time that I had ended one of my rages in tears and it wasn't the first time that I had voiced how much I hated my life. My life had become a repetitive cycle of getting angry, losing the plot, feeling guilty, crying and then hating myself for behaving this way.

I had a good cry, got up, had a shower and went back out to resume my motherly duties.

Although that day was one of many similar days at that time, it was also the day that signalled an important shift in my mindset and the very foundation for the book that you are now reading.

And, as an additional note – just to set the record straight – it was also the first and last time that I threw knives at my child's head.

You see, something extraordinary happened that day as I sat bawling in my room, falling apart. I remember vividly – sitting there on the edge of my bed – the moment when my tears were interrupted by this overpowering voice in my mind. It was so clear and I still remember its message. It said:

No one can change this for you. No one can change how you feel about your life. Only you can.

That brief and distinct message jerked me out of my misery like an electric shock. As I digested this information, those words became deeply imbedded somewhere inside me and began fuelling a new fire that had instantly started to burn within me. Whoever or whatever put those words in my head had just changed the entire course of my life, although I didn't really know it at the time.

All I knew in that moment was that I couldn't continue allowing these feelings to consume me like they were. I *was* the only one who could stop the thoughts going on in my head and I was suddenly determined that *that* was exactly what I was going to do.

I became really inspired by this new revelation. Surely life *didn't* have to be this way. Surely I *didn't* have to feel angry and guilty all the time. Surely I *didn't* have to be bored and lonely and miserable. There had to be another way I could experience motherhood. After all, no fairy godmother was going to come out and wave her magic wand and suddenly make me happy. So who else could be my advocate for change? The answer was: only *I* could.

I had to find a way to fix this emotional mess that I was in and reinvent myself. That feeling of purpose empowered me and I was suddenly more excited than I'd been in a long time. I felt alive!

In the 12 years leading up to this event, I had always had a passion for personal development, devouring endless books on improving myself and learning how to be happy. I completed many personal-development courses and even trained with an international company and travelled overseas to become one of their 'masters', as they called them. I had so much information in the area of self-improvement, but in the midst of the busyness of motherhood and the demands of two children only 16 months apart, I never really thought to apply what I'd learnt to parenting.

In hindsight, I was way too consumed with getting parenting 'right' and hating myself for doing it 'wrong' to even notice the misery that I was causing myself.

Up until that day and that specific moment, I had forgotten that happiness was something that only I could create by changing the way that I was thinking.

So, with this new vigour and determination, I became possessed. I re-read all of my favourite self-help books and began searching on the internet for answers to motherhood happiness.

What I found, though, was very little information about the emotional aspect of becoming a mum. Of course, I found loads of information about how to raise kids and general information that told me to take time out and walk away when I was angry. But there seemed to be nothing that would help me to change my thinking and actually deal with the emotions that I was feeling.

I knew that I couldn't be the only mum to feel this way so I decided right there and then that I would find a way to teach myself to think and feel differently about motherhood and then write about it so that I could teach it to other mums and they would not have to experience the self-hatred or rough transition into parenthood that I had felt.

For the next year I researched, wrote and tested many different exercises and ways of observing what I was thinking, and changed how I viewed the challenges of being a mum to two very young and energetic boys.

I initially created a workbook that contained 10 tutorials on different aspects of parenting (which have now been turned into mini e-books). Then I created the website www.selfhelpformums.com to give mums the knowledge needed to create a healthy mindset towards the challenges of parenting.

All of the learning and growing I did over that year changed the way I viewed myself and my life and this new understanding and appreciation for my life took me on a unique adventure.

You see, during this time my husband was also suffering from anxiety, having panic attacks and feeling very stressed as he worked six days a week in our own shade-sail business to support the $350,000 mortgage we had on our dream house.

One day I rang him and told him that we should sell everything, buy a caravan and go travelling while the kids were young and wanted to be with us. I said, 'What are we doing all this for – a piece of paper to say that we own something?' He said I was crazy, but by the end of the day I had convinced him to agree. Four days later our house was sold and two weeks later someone approached us to buy our business. Three months later we were in a holiday house waiting for our caravan to be finished ... and off we went.

We spent six weeks travelling before we landed jobs (and a nanny) at a remote cattle station/resort on Gibb River Road in Western Australia. We stayed there for six months and had the most unique and spiritually therapeutic experience of our lives. The kids loved it.

This time out was sorely needed in our lives as it gave us both the space to widen back and learn about ourselves and what it felt like to feel peaceful. We all loved being with each other and being around the beauty of nature – living the 'simple life'.

Being among nature and feeling so peaceful, I began to feel even more passionate about teaching people all of the knowledge that I had learnt over the previous two years and, as circumstances would have it, our time had come to leave our remote lifestyle and return to civilisation.

It was then I came across the Anti-Depression Association of Australia (ADAA) in Maleny, Queensland. I trained with them to become one of their life coaches and course facilitators and learnt their unique, simple and effective method for treating –

and in many cases curing – psychological stress, depression and anxiety.

This new training was like the icing on the cake of the knowledge and information that I had gathered from 17 years of learning about self-help.

The passion I have to share this knowledge led me to rewrite the workbook that I had created two years earlier to include the new knowledge that I had gained from travelling and from the Anti-Depression Association of Australia (ADAA) – and that has resulted in the book that you now hold in your hands – *The Happy Mum Handbook*.

This handbook incorporates the method used by the ADAA (with their permission) with the knowledge that I have gained through my own journey of motherhood and having to work my way out of minor depression and anxiety.

As a result of my experiences you now have a book that has been written by a mum who doesn't have a natural patience for the challenges of parenting; a mum who doesn't have it all figured out; and one who, everyday, has to practise the very tools that I will be teaching you so that I can maintain a healthy mindset and don't get consumed with my role as a mum of young kids.

I don't have a degree and I'm an everyday mum who has had to teach herself a constructive way to think about the challenges of parenting and apply this knowledge firsthand to her own life, so I'm not just lecturing you on what you should do. I have used the information that I will teach you right in the very thick of times where I was at my lowest and needed a way to change the way I felt.

Motherhood changes you physically, emotionally, mentally, morally and ethically. When you embark on the journey into motherhood, from the minute you find out you are pregnant, your life significantly changes and sometimes this dramatic change can bring out emotions and issues that had previously lain dormant.

It is my hope that through this book I can teach you to discover what is causing you to feel so challenged by your role and perhaps why you feel a little bit like I used to feel. My hope is that I can give you some tools that will help you to become the Happy Mum that you'd like to be.

Chapter 1

Happiness

What is happiness?

Dear Diary

My name is Jenny and I'm falling apart. I feel lost, lifeless, on auto-pilot. I have two beautiful children and I should feel blessed, but instead I could cry. In fact, now I am. I feel like I'm just a machine. I get up at dawn, prepare breakfast, change nappies, fold clothes, pick up toys, clean the house, cook dinner, service my husband (if he's lucky), get up to the kids during the night (yes, both of them) and wake up and do it all over again. I feel useless and incompetent. I'm forever arguing with my three year old and can never seem to get my six month old to sleep.

What happened to the girl I used to be who had fun, laughed all the time and loved her life? Now I feel bored, emotional and lonely.

Don't get me wrong. I love my kids and I do love being a mum, but outside of all the goo-goo, gaa-gaa warm-and-fuzzy mummyness, something is missing. A part of me feels stifled and suffocated, probably drowned by the tunes of 'Play your guitar with Murray' or 'Are you thinking what I'm thinking, B1? I think I am B2?'

Well, you wanna know what I'm thinking? I wanna get out of here. Run off to some exotic island with a book and a glass of wine ... or 10! I need to find out who I am. What do I want?

I feel like I have no life. It's all about my children. I just can't handle it anymore. I feel like everyone's slave. I'm irrational, anxious and depressed. I'm happy one minute, and then the next I'm flying off the handle and falling apart in tears. I feel guilty for stuffing up my kids' lives and I hate myself for acting this way.

No one understands me. No one cares about how I feel. It's like I'm the only mum in the world who feels this way. Everyone else seems happy. Why can't I just get it together and be a happy mum too? What's wrong with me?

Chapter 1: Happiness **9**

You've just met Jenny. Jenny is a mum whose thoughts of lost identity and unhappiness are echoed throughout the minds of mums everywhere, although rarely admitted.

Feelings of being consumed by this role as a mum: feelings of anger and guilt, feeling useless or incompetent, mourning the loss of your old life and feeling shamefully resentful of some of the aspects of your new life as a mum are all normal and common feelings shared by mums all over the world. So, if you feel at all like Jenny, believe me, you are not alone.

The lead-up to becoming a mother is both exciting and full of trepidation. Strong expectations are set based on our own childhood experiences, including how we expect to be as a parent and what sort of life we want to provide for our children.

Visions are formed in our minds of how kind, calm and selfless we will be in this role.

'I will not fall into the trap of feeling depressed or bored. It will be different for me. I will be organised but flexible, because I'm ready for the fact that there will be some adjustments to my lifestyle and I'm okay with that.'

All of these kinds of thoughts and expectations float around in our minds while we await the birth of our children and the start of our journey into the unknown.

However, once we bring our first little bundle of joy home from the hospital and we are left to our own devices, reality kicks in and the roller-coaster ride of emotions begins, along with the numerous challenges to be handled.

Lack of sleep for both you and your child, breastfeeding or finding you can't, managing the housework, healing from an unexpected caesarean, well-meaning visitors overstaying their welcome, unsupportive husbands, lack of female support, reflux, colic, mastitis, engorged breasts and many more possible unexpected experiences can add to the sudden realisation that motherhood is nothing like you'd planned. Why didn't anyone tell me about all this?

For some, though, this part is okay. Sure, there was a little adjustment time, but generally you got through it relatively unscathed. However, throw a second child into the mix (or perhaps twins) and suddenly you're dealing with an entirely different situation.

Getting up to two kids at night; dividing your attention between two equally demanding and needy children at two forever changing developmental stages; keeping up with the household chores and combining them with the initial demands of a new baby – picture all of this and you may find one very consumed and unhappy mum who feels like she has completely lost her identity.

There are, of course, those select few mothers who seem born to do this role with ease and while I don't believe they could say that they have never felt just a fraction of what Jenny does, these feelings don't generally affect them too much. It doesn't mean that they don't come across challenges with their children – it just means that they seem to handle these challenges in a different way.

So what does make these mothers handle motherhood differently from the rest of us? Why don't they feel like their identities are lost? Why don't they feel overwhelmed by the pressures of motherhood? Is it because they are better mothers? Absolutely *not*!

The *only* thing that separates a mum who is feeling overwhelmed from one who is not is simply how she *thinks* about her experiences. That's it. She is not a superhero, or a naturally skilled, lucky mum gifted with perfect children and natural parenting abilities. She has had to learn just as many new skills and 'tricks of the trade' as you or I have had to. However, you will find that she differs from a stressed mum in how she *thinks* about these challenges.

It is the aim of this book to teach you how you can think about these challenges differently in order to become a Happy Mum and to learn a solution-focussed approach to handling these challenges too.

Chapter 1: Happiness **11**

But before we delve into the mindset that creates stress and unhappiness in mums, I first want to address the fundamental desire that enticed you to pick up this handbook and read it – that is, *how* to be a Happy Mum.

It is natural for everyone to want to be happy. The term 'happiness' runs rife in our society. We are taught to want it and that our lives are less worthwhile if we don't have it. We are taught that it is found in our abilities and our achievements and that we are failing if we cannot achieve what we want to. The desire to achieve this feeling of happiness and the difficulty of achieving this feeling long term is often what makes us feel so unhappy.

So let's explore what happiness actually is and why it is so difficult to achieve.

Happiness is an emotion, not an achievement or a destination that we'll achieve permanently. Furthermore, happiness is an emotion that is usually felt when life is going the way we want it to, or when someone or something has matched our expectations or exceeded them.

Happiness is difficult to achieve long term because it is not a sustainable goal. The reality of life is that sometimes life *doesn't* go our way and sometimes our expectations are *not* met.

In motherhood this is clearly evident when comparing your pre-baby expectations with what actually happens when you bring your baby home from the hospital. There are many times in parenthood when things certainly don't go the way that we want them to or how we had planned them to, and this doesn't make us feel happy.

However, we are taught from the time we are babies how to yearn for this feeling of happiness and, more specifically, how to attach this feeling to our definition of a successful life.

It starts with an unknowing adult speaking to you (as a baby) in their cutesy voice, saying, 'Come on now. Give us a smile. There's a good girl. Show me how cute you can be ... good girl'. You just learnt how to please someone and that made you feel happy.

Then you get older and start to walk and talk. You are taught how to gain approval – that is, how to do the right thing and not do the wrong thing. The right thing means approval; the wrong thing means disapproval. Approval feels good. At school, the objectives are to achieve academic success, and you are rewarded for this success. Success is good. It makes you feel happy. Academic failure makes you feel bad. Turn on your TV and you will see endless advertisements telling you which product will make you happy and how your life will be less happy without it. Open up magazines and you will see headings splashed with words about how you can get life 'right' – right weight, right lipstick, right clothes, right house, right attitude – all with the undertone that getting these things will make you feel happy.

Everywhere we turn we are taught to rate ourselves and our lives on what we are, do or have and that these achievements will make us happy.

When you become a mother you are literally bombarded with advice and information beginning from the time you fall pregnant, when you are handed your 'bounty bag' riddled with information about how to get parenting right. Combine this with the learning you have already received about 'proper parenting' from your childhood and the opinions of other mothers, friends, society and the media and you can easily see why motherhood has suddenly become so overwhelming. There are so many ways to get parenting right: Get it right and I'll feel happy and my children will be happy. Get it wrong and I have failed everybody.

It's little wonder there are so many mums out there who are struggling with the demands of parenting. We have been conditioned throughout our entire lives that there is a right way and a wrong way of doing things and when you do it the wrong way, you are less worthwhile – your life is less worthwhile or your child's life is less worthwhile. Perhaps sometimes all three are less worthwhile!

So how do you become happy? By changing your definition of happiness. Happiness is an emotion and emotions fluctuate all the time depending on situations and how you view them. The reality is that you don't feel this emotion every time you experience an event so you cannot expect to feel happy all the time. However, you can achieve overall happiness or a happy life by understanding and accepting the reality that although life doesn't always go to plan *there is always value to be found in all of your experiences*. Everything you experience has value because of what you learn, what you receive from the experience and how this experience contributes to other people's learning. Looking at life in this way eliminates the need to label events as being either good (making me feel happy) or bad (making me feel unhappy).

Of course, you'll always strive to achieve things in life that you enjoy – and that doesn't have to change. However, be aware that success doesn't just come from life going your way; it also comes from what you learn when it doesn't.

For example, you are in a shopping centre when your toddler throws a very loud tantrum. Contrary to your initial mortified reaction, there is value in this situation.

For you, this experience is adding to your abilities as a mum – setting boundaries for your child, teaching your child how to handle his or her emotions and behave in society – and perhaps you are also learning more about patience and your own emotions, which helps you to grow as a person.

Your child is learning about how to behave in the world and what happens when he or she does behave this way, which contributes to his or her development.

The spectators of this tantrum are learning about their own reactions. Perhaps they are also learning about patience or how to handle their own children, or perhaps they are seeing themselves in you and your reaction (good or bad) and learning something about themselves.

The benefits of this one little tantrum ripple out immeasurably. Without this experience, which initially seems like a hindrance, you don't get to learn what you now know after experiencing the tantrum, and neither does your child or the people around you.

Every event you experience contributes to who you are and adds to your experience and knowledge of life and, in this case, your knowledge of parenting. It also contributes to everyone in contact with that event.

Cease rating your life by how often you feel the emotion of happiness and embrace all of life's events, including the unenjoyable ones. Instead of thinking these times are an interruption to your happy life, practise finding the value in these events and you will start to feel happier. Ironic isn't it?

Life is full of challenges and opportunities to learn. Life lessons are how to rate your life – not how often you feel an emotion.

Emotions and happiness

Now, it's highly likely that your immediate internal reaction to the example of your child having a tantrum in public may be feelings of embarrassment, anger, helplessness, or feeling judged or uncomfortably exposed in this situation.

What causes you to feel this way is the story that you tell yourself about this situation – the self-talk you have in your mind. You feel this way not because your child is having a tantrum but because of what you are *thinking* about the tantrum.

Emotions start at a thinking level. We perceive an event with our senses and the brain processes this information by accessing what it already knows, what you believe and what has happened in the past. It reasons and sorts through what the appropriate response should be to this event and creates a physical sensation in the body, which then becomes the emotion that we feel. This thinking process then determines what the appropriate action or response is, which could be crying or lashing out in anger, for example.

My husband and I have separately witnessed two similar events where two mums were reacting to their children, who were having tantrums.

I witnessed a mum reacting in a very angry way to a tantrum her son was having. Through gritted teeth and quite roughly she picked her son up off the floor and almost threw him into the trolley while speaking quite angrily to him.

My husband witnessed a woman who was completely calm and amused by her daughter's tantrum and simply said to her, 'Oh well, Santa won't be coming to you if you behave like that'.

Both mothers were in the position of trying to get shopping done with an uncooperative child and both mothers had two completely different emotions running. They would each have had two different conversations in their minds about the tantrums because their brains were accessing different beliefs and determining what the appropriate response should be.

I highlight this difference, not to say that one mother is better than the other, but to show you that emotions are felt because of how we perceive the events that are happening before us.

Sometimes the emotional rollercoaster of parenting can become a repetitive cycle of happiness, then sadness; or anger followed by guilt, regret and then intense love and elation. This is how I personally used to experience motherhood.

Emotions can also be triggered by experiences that your child is having. For example, if your child is sick you may feel helpless or upset that he or she has to go through this. Another example may be that you are sad and teary about leaving him or her in day care while you go to work. These emotions can be surprising to you and can even feel quite raw or painful to deal with.

Regardless of the situation, the emotions that you feel have been caused by how you viewed and interpreted this event in your mind. Understanding that these intense emotions are created by our thoughts can be incredibly useful for improving how we think about our experiences and thus avoiding these intense emotional reactions or, at the very least, understanding them.

Mind TRACK to Happiness

Changing how you view happiness is the foundation for building happiness into your life and I understand that although finding the value in all events is an easy concept to grasp, it is not always that easy to practise.

Take a situation where you and your baby have had zero sleep, both of you are tired and cranky, the house is messy and you have a spirited three year old running around pushing boundaries, and it can be a bit difficult to even begin seeing the value in all of this to make you feel better. It's just not enough.

Realising this from my own life, I knew that I needed to develop a simple process I could use that would help me to quickly change the way I was thinking in every moment. I didn't want to have to keep consulting some book every time I started stressing out and feeling overwhelmed. I needed something I could use in the moment to change how I felt about what was going on.

Upon reviewing how I had personally changed my own mindset and had become what I consider a Happy Mum, and combining that with the teachings of the Anti-Depression Association of Australia (ADAA), I started to put together a specific process that I could remember which would help me to change how I perceived challenges and also help me to begin to create solutions rather than feeling stuck within these challenges.

This process is made up of five distinct steps that can be used to handle every stressful situation in motherhood and in life. It's called the **Mind TRACK to Happiness** process.

The acronym 'TRACK' stands for the following five steps:

Thoughts: What am I thinking about this situation?

Reality: What is the reality that my thoughts are in conflict with?

Aim: What do I want to achieve?

Choices: What are my choices, options and solutions?

Know your plan and action it: How am I going to get what I want?

Step 1: Thoughts

Become aware of the thoughts you are having. These thoughts are actually what are causing your stress. What is the conversation that you're having with yourself about this situation? What are the opinions and views that are actually causing you to feel this way?

Step 2: Reality

How is your thinking in conflict with reality? All stress is created because of a direct conflict between what is actually happening and what our thoughts and opinions are about what is happening.

Step 3: Aim

What is my aim? What do I want right now? This is where you begin to shift your mindset from what is going 'wrong' to what the ideal is of the situation. What do I want to achieve right now?

Step 4: Choices

What are the options and solutions that I have to choose from in this moment? There are always options that you have available which will either resolve your problem or change the way you view your problem. Now that your mind is thinking about what you want, this step gets you thinking about how you can achieve it.

Step 5: Know your plan and action it

Now that you know the choices available, it's time to decide on your plan and know what you need to do to get what you want.

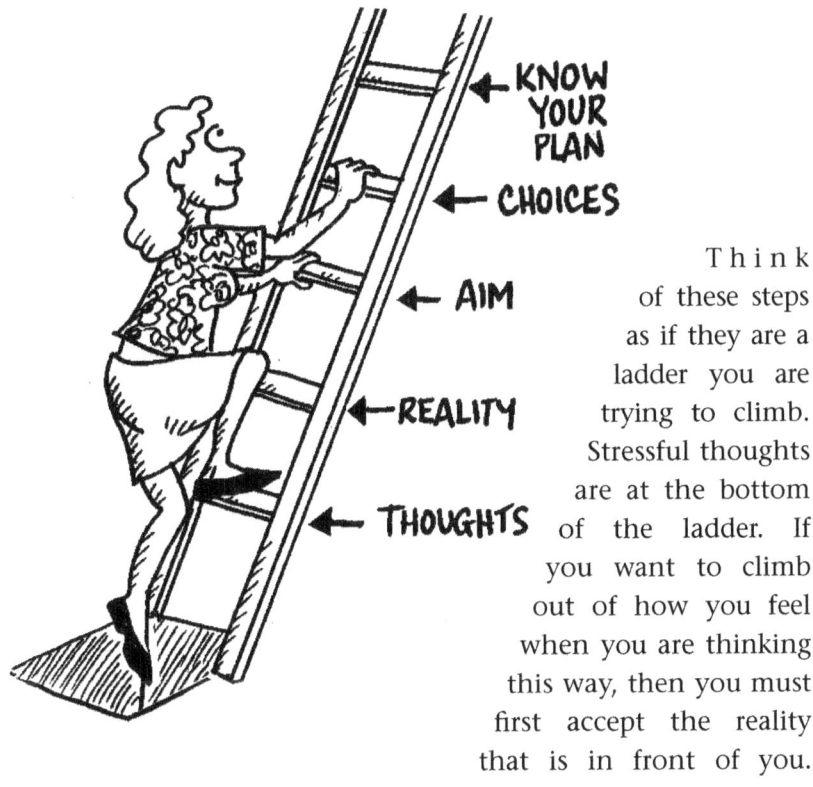

Think of these steps as if they are a ladder you are trying to climb. Stressful thoughts are at the bottom of the ladder. If you want to climb out of how you feel when you are thinking this way, then you must first accept the reality that is in front of you. Acknowledge what is actually happening and accept it so that you can take the next step, which is figuring out what you want – the ideal of the situation. Then step even higher by ascertaining how you are going to get what you want. Finally, action your plan and climb to the top of the ladder away from the stress you were feeling at the bottom of the ladder.

Using these steps as often as you can literally retrains your mind to look at what you want and how to get it, rather than staying fixed on what's not happening or what you're not getting, which keeps you at the bottom of the ladder. However, you cannot move forward until your mind becomes aligned with the current reality.

Chapter 1: Happiness

Example

My personal experience

My younger son, Ryan (16 months old at the time), was whining at me in that high-pitched shriek that kids get. I was trying to finish doing the dishes at the time and he was clinging to my leg. My older son Cody (two and a half) kept coming in after what seemed like two seconds of watching yet another video, asking me to change it, also in a similar whiney tone. The noise of their whining and my inability to 'just get the dishes done' was seemingly causing me to feel really angry. As my anger intensified I happened to catch the conversation in my mind that was really causing my anger, and realised it was not the children causing the anger in me. It went similar to this:

'I wish they'd both just leave me alone. I just want to get these bloody dishes done. It shouldn't be a hard thing to do. I just need five minutes to finish them. Why can't I just have five minutes of peace and quiet? I wish they would just go and play so I could have some time out. I never get any time out. Get off me. Why do you have to cling to me all the time? I just want some space. I can't even walk anywhere without you hanging off me. I'm so tired. I just want to sleep. I need time out, but of course, I can't. Shut up and leave me alone, Cody. This is so draining. I just want to disappear where I can sleep or relax. I don't want to do this anymore. I'm sick of dealing with these whingeing kids. I feel like everyone's slave and I never get to do anything for myself. I'm sick of this life ...'

Can you imagine how this self-talk was making me feel? Can you see how it was getting progressively worse? A couple of whingeing moments with the children suddenly meant that my whole life was a disaster. A little dramatic when you've widened back from it though, isn't it?

When you put your attention on the problem and your mind is engaged in this kind of internal monologue the problem feels worse and begins to consume you. You really do feel like your whole life is miserable, especially if this becomes your regular internal monologue.

Unknowingly at the time, I had just completed **Step 1** of the Mind TRACK to Happiness process, which is to identify your **Thoughts:** What am I thinking about this situation, which is causing my stress?

Step 2: Reality. The reason why my thoughts were causing me stress is because they were in direct conflict with the reality of what was actually happening.

The reality in this moment was that Cody and Ryan both wanted my attention and they were whingeing at me to get it. That's the reality. That's what was actually happening.

My resistance to this reality (through thinking) was what was causing the stress. They wanted something right now and I, being the one looking after them in that moment, was the one who had to help them with their needs, particularly at that age.

It doesn't mean that my life is any less worthwhile; this is just the reality of this moment. I am a mum, in this moment, at home looking after my kids and they want my attention. That's it. Any other thoughts that indulge in thinking that this reality therefore means that I'll never get the dishes done, that I've had enough of their whingeing, that I want to get away, that I'm a slave, that I'm sick of it all (and so on) is all in conflict with the reality of what is actually happening.

As you saw, this line of thinking only magnifies how badly you feel about the situation and goes on to create an emotional response – in my case, anger.

Step 3: Aim. What do I want right now? Now my first thoughts are that I just want them to stop whingeing at me so I can do the dishes. But I want to be careful that my aim is not still in conflict with reality.

The reality is that you are not in control of someone else's behaviour. If stopping their whingeing is your aim, it would be purely chance that you would achieve this aim. You could try to stop them from whingeing all you want. However, they are the ones who will decide whether they will stop or not.

So perhaps an aim that is within your control would benefit you more, such as, 'I want to stay calm and find a way that I can get the dishes done'.

In this step, when determining what your aim is, it can also be helpful to think about what your priorities are and why you want what you want. Why is it so important to get these dishes done? Is it really about getting the dishes done or is it more about you being able to do something by yourself without interruption? Are you looking to get the dishes done or are you looking for five minutes of peace? If it is the latter, then you have just found your aim.

Step 4: Choices. What are my options for dealing with this situation? Are there any solutions that I could look at? In this situation, my internal monologue might change to this:

'What does Ryan really want? This behaviour is not usual for him, so there must be something else happening for him to be doing this. Is he hungry? Is he tired? Does he just want a little attention – maybe a bit of a cuddle? Does he need a nappy change? Is he bored and does he need a game to play, or a toy to occupy him? Is what I am doing so important that I can't just stop for five minutes or so to figure out what the problem is? If it is an attention thing and what I am doing can't wait, can I stop for just a few seconds to find something to occupy him until I've finished? The same goes for Cody. Clearly he's bored with his videos and wanting something else to do. Can I play with him or give him something to do? As for how I feel personally, what can I do to feel more awake? Can I take an iron tablet or perhaps have a coffee or a Berocca to lift me up? Mental note: Organise a few hours for myself this weekend or tonight when Steve (husband) gets home, where I can do whatever I want without interruption. But right now, maybe I could put some music on to make me feel more alive and energised.'

Can you see how my mindset shifted from the problem to the solution and how much better this self-talk would have made me feel?

Finally, **Step 5: Know your plan and action it.** In this situation the natural next step is to try some of the things mentioned in Step 4. If you already know your plan all you need to do is action it. In other situations this planning and action stage requires more consideration.

One example is behaviour management. If your child is going through a stage of hitting, then at Step 4 you might research ways that other mums get their kids to stop hitting. At Step 5 you would weigh up all the options available to you for handling that behaviour and decide on the plan that you are going to use, so that every time this situation arises, you know what you need to do.

This 5-step Mind TRACK to Happiness process is designed to shift your thinking away from the problem and onto the solutions. That is the intention of this process. You might find that you have realised at Step 2, after noticing the conflict between your thoughts and reality, that you are already calmer and don't need to continue on with the rest of the process. That's great. Depending on the situation, this might happen and you probably don't need to go through the entire process each time.

Sometimes you might find that the Mind TRACK to Happiness self-talk can be as quick as:

'Oh I wish these kids would stop whingeing. I just want to get these bloody dishes done. Well, the reality is that they are whingeing, so what am I going to do about it? How about I just figure out what they need and get back to the dishes later. It's no big deal'.

We will be using this process with many different examples of challenges that arise in motherhood, both simple and complex, so you will get to see how it is used in many ways to help you to use it in your own life.

Remember that this is a skill that you are learning too and it will take some time for it to become your new habit. Be patient with yourself. Sometimes you will go back to your old habits of thought, but the more you work on creating new ones the more those habits will die off over time.

So far I have only given you a simple introductory outline of the Mind TRACK to Happiness process and only one example. In order to give you a more thorough understanding of this valuable process, I have split this book into two parts.

Part A goes into more detail about each step so that you will know exactly why you are using each step and how to use each one.

Part B then takes this process and applies it to many common challenges that mums face, such as behavioural and developmental challenges, anger and guilt, loss of identity, boredom, time management and time out, and marital/partner relationships. It is here that you will also get an opportunity to apply this process to your situation using some exercises provided for you in Part B.

By the end of this book you will be well equipped with a complete understanding of this process and enough examples to be able to implement this process into your own life with confidence. You will have a thorough understanding of the mindset needed to become a Happy Mum and you will know exactly what you need to do to achieve this.

PART A

The Mind TRACK to Happiness process

Chapter 2

Step 1 – Thoughts

Conversations with the mind

You're useless. You just aren't as good as other mums. Everyone else is able to learn how to do this. Why can't you? You must be doing something wrong. You're selfish. You're spending way too much time doing the housework. You should be spending more time with the kids. You're stuffing your kids up. Cody should be talking more. You should be getting this by now. The house is too messy. C'mon, get it together girl. You have to look like you're doing okay. Everyone thinks you're a whinger, you know.

When I first started observing the conversations in my own mind both during my angry outbursts and just in general, I was shocked with what I was saying to myself and even more so by the constant stream of judgements I made about the way I did things. I was my own worst nightmare.

Aside from the destructive thoughts about things not going my way and how annoying and frustrating that was, there were repetitive statements about me being useless, stupid, a whinger, not doing anything right, stuffing my kids up, being too impatient, not being loving enough, not giving the kids enough quality time, not teaching them enough ...

I could write a whole page of criticisms that I was using to describe my beliefs about my abilities as a mum. It was like a constant voice in my head telling me what a bad job I was doing.

Before children, I'd never considered myself to be someone who suffered from low self-esteem, but after having children and observing how I spoke to myself, it was clear that I had some serious self-esteem issues.

Mothers often feel as though they were confident before they became mums but somehow they lost their self-esteem when they had their kids.

Although it may seem as if having children caused the loss of self-esteem, what actually causes this to happen was set up long before your children arrived. In fact, it was set up when you were just a child yourself.

How you came to think the way you do

Without going into too much detail about the brain, it is relevant to write a few pages describing how we actually come to think the way we do and how we can change our thinking.

As babies we are born with 100 billion neurons. These neurons form connections with other neurons at the synapse. This is where an electric signal (the message) is passed from one neuron to the next, creating neural pathways that connect to the many different functional brain regions, with each governing everything we do from breathing and sleeping to thinking and feeling.

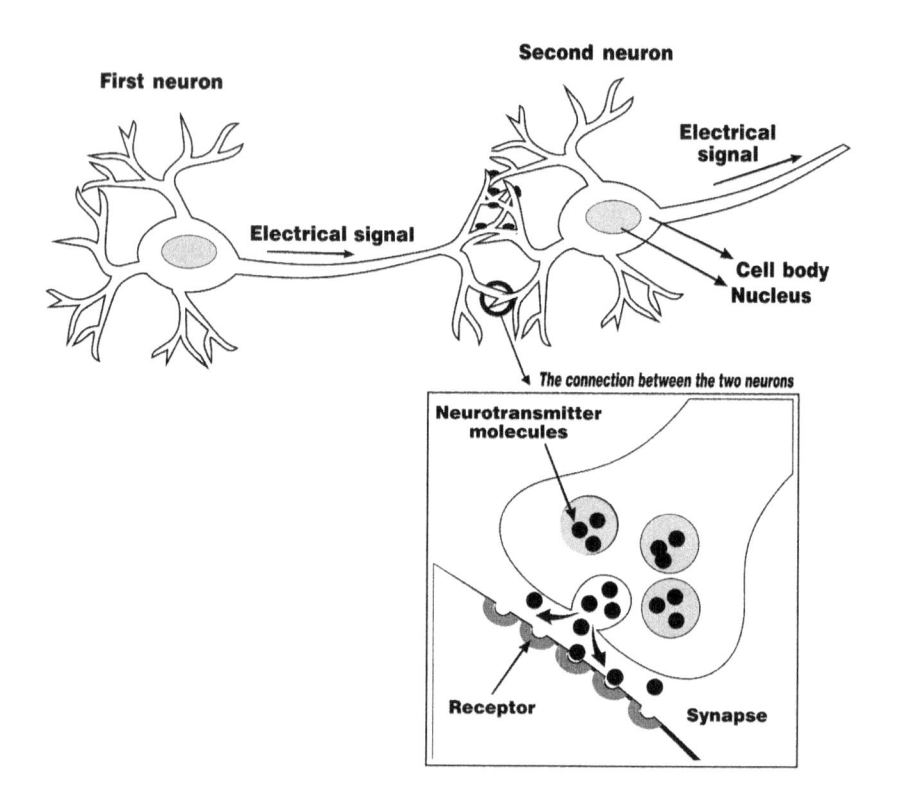

When we are born, only a relatively small portion of these synapses (connection points between neurons) have been formed and mostly they regulate the basic functions necessary for life such as breathing, heart rate, sleeping, eating, and so on.

The rest of the synapses are formed in response to our environment as we learn to function in the world (for example, walk, talk, run, jump, use a spoon) and understand it (perceive what we sense and respond to). This is why we can adapt to the surroundings and experiences that we are raised in and this is why each person develops slightly differently.

The environment that you were raised in differed from everyone else's environment. It even differs among siblings because they tend to experience family-related events at different ages and stages of brain development.

The synapses and the neuronal pathways are strengthened through continuous environmental exposure and repetition, meaning that the majority of our brains are developed in response to how we are raised and the environment we grow up in.

Furthermore, children have a significant number of certain types of neurons – called mirror neurons – which mimic the behaviour we observe around us. By experiencing events, behaviour and emotions happening in our environment and mirroring these over time to strengthen some neural pathways more than others, we begin to form what becomes our personality complete with our unique construction of behaviours, feelings, attitudes, thoughts and beliefs.

In summary, your brain developed as a child in response to what you learnt through your observations, experiences and environment, which has created the behaviours, beliefs and personality that you now have as an adult and also dictates how you now perceive events and challenges.

We have learnt to behave the way we currently do from our surroundings and we think the way we have been taught to think.

If you have been taught to believe that a certain event is wrong and learnt that the appropriate response is anger followed by the experience of this anger being effective in getting what you want, then that is how you are likely to automatically react over time.

However, if you have been taught to behave and experience consequences differently, then you will have different beliefs and therefore may respond differently. Herein lies the difference between a naturally calm mother and one who is not. It's not because the calm mother is a better person; it's only because she has learnt to think and react differently.

When you feel stressed or emotional, it is never the events that are causing you to feel this way – it is the thoughts that you have about those events and your thoughts are habitual thoughts that were created long before the event occurred.

The most sobering part of all of this, which can be used as further motivation to change your thoughts and learn how to handle life's challenges, is that if you have learnt all these beliefs and behaviours from childhood (primarily from your parents or primary caregivers), then who do you think your child is learning from now? And how do you think he or she is learning how to handle life's challenges?

Why is it difficult to change your thoughts?

Sometimes we are aware that our thoughts are causing us to feel angry, sad or stressed, but we have difficulty changing these thoughts.

You may have found that you have already tried to change your thoughts in the past and that you have been successful for a short while, but eventually you end up going back to your old ways. Often this also happens when trying to change other habits (for example, quitting smoking, losing weight, saving money, and so on). Before I understood how the brain works, I would often experience changing my thoughts for a while, then reverting back to my old ways. Logic told me that getting angry and yelling at my kids, or falling apart, wasn't serving me and definitely wasn't serving my kids either, so I would try to change. Each time I tried this I would be calm and patient for a while, but after a few days, my habits in terms of reacting to challenges would return and, of course, so would the cycle of hating myself and feeling like a failure.

Let me explain why this occurs. You are probably already aware that the brain is split into the conscious and the non-conscious.

The conscious brain controls only 2 to 4 per cent of what we do and is like the captain of the ship. It sets goals and judges results. It is responsible for focus, concentration, learning and the power of observation, as well as thinking skills such as will, short-term memory, perception, reasoning, intuition and imagination. It is made up of only about 17 per cent of the brain. We tend to identify with our conscious mind and identify these thoughts as 'me'.

The non-conscious brain makes up 83 per cent and is like the engine powering the ship. The captain (conscious brain) tells the ship where to go, but the engine (non-conscious brain) is actually responsible for how the ship gets there.

The non-conscious is where your beliefs and habits and the memories you store forever reside. Habits are 1000 times stronger than desires – which answers the question, 'Why do I keep doing that?' The non-conscious mind acts like a satellite navigation system. It always keeps the ship on the course that aligns with your beliefs and habits of thought and habitual behaviour.

You might consciously know that yelling at your kids is 'wrong' and you may try to set goals to change this and be calmer and more loving, but all of this is done in the conscious mind.

Non-consciously there is a whole process going on that you aren't aware of which is analysing what this event means by accessing your habits of thought and your memories of what has happened in the past. It then determines what the appropriate response should be, which in this case is anger, even though logically you know you 'should' be calm.

Your conscious mind is trying to steer your ship (by setting the goal to be calm) and this works for only so long before the non-conscious brain (the satellite navigation system) engages, identifies that you are off track and re-navigates the ship back on course, perceiving events back in alignment with what you usually believe and creating how you usually respond.

This is why it can be so difficult to change and this is why you often do things you don't want to do, even though logically you know not to do them. However, there is hope.

How to change your thoughts

Scientists have made some phenomenal discoveries about how the brain develops and thinks, and although they once believed that the wiring of the brain was finalised in early childhood years and was permanent from then on, they have now discovered that this wiring of the brain is *not* permanent. In fact, beyond adolescence the brain keeps changing and adjusting and responding to new experiences, to a certain degree.

We can rewire our brains to think differently by deliberately sending it new information over a period of time, strengthening the synapses (connections between neurons) and effectively creating new habits of thought. And by doing this, we can also weaken the connections between other neurons, allowing old beliefs and habits to die off as the new ones are strengthened.

This must be done at a conscious level first, deliberately repeating this information over and over until it becomes long-term memory – a new habit of thought.

So, if your habitual response to parenting challenges is to become angry, then to become calm, you must rewire your brain to making calmness your habitual response.

This is why I have created the Mind TRACK to Happiness process. This process is designed so that you can begin to identify the thoughts that are causing you to feel stressed or emotional by becoming aware of them (Step 1) and then using the rest of the process to create new wiring in the brain by thinking in a different way.

By using this Mind TRACK to Happiness process repetitively and on many areas of your life, you are helping to rewire your brain to think about challenges in a different way too.

The Fountainhead Method™

So far I have explained that the emotions you feel as a mum are connected with how you perceive the experiences of being a parent and life in general. I have also explained that how you perceive the events in your life and how you respond to them have been mostly set up from your own childhood, through your observations, experiences and environment.

It would be an enormously lengthy and somewhat impossible task to randomly try and sift through all of the beliefs and habits you have gathered over the years in order to begin identifying which ones are causing you to feel stressed and emotional. This is why the first step of the Mind TRACK to Happiness process is to start becoming aware of the thoughts in your mind as challenges arise, so that you can begin to identify some of them.

To assist you in making sense of the thoughts that you identify, I have incorporated The Fountainhead Method™ into the Mind TRACK to Happiness process in Step 1 (Thoughts) and Step 2 (Reality).

The Fountainhead Method™ was designed by the Anti-Depression Association of Australia (ADAA) as a tool to help people suffering from stress, depression or anxiety. It is a simple method that is broken down into two parts: the Get Your Life Right Model – which identifies the thinking that causes stress – and the Personal Development Model – which gives you the tools to upgrade this thinking and view your life differently when faced with life's challenges. This method is becoming increasingly popular in the mental-health field as one of the most effective tools for treating stress-related disorders.

The Get Your Life Right (GYLR) Model is the first half of the Fountainhead Method™ used in Step 1 and is a model of incorrect thinking that lies at the core of all stress. The GYLR Model teaches that due to our conditioning and our experiences of life so far we have developed a specific view of the world around us, of other people and particularly of ourselves.

Although psychology fields have determined that there are many beliefs we hold that can cause stress, the Fountainhead Method™ teaches that all stressful beliefs can be categorised into just three major assumptions that we make about our lives and that these lead to just one core belief. Here are the three assumptions.

1 My life is on the wrong path.

My life didn't go to plan and now I have somehow jumped off the right path and landed on the wrong one. Because I couldn't achieve my goals and expectations, my life has gone wrong.

Example

I can't get my baby to sleep. I can't breastfeed. My child is sick. I'm not who I used to be anymore. So many things have gone wrong. Motherhood was not meant to be this way. Because I'm doing everything wrong, now my child's life is going wrong.

2 I am missing out.

Now that I'm on the wrong path I feel like I'm missing out on what my life needs. I'm missing out on what I would have been experiencing had I been on the right path and achieving my goals, or – as is often the case – I feel like my child is missing out on what he or she needs in life.

Example

I'm missing out on my time out. My child is missing out on a calm mum. My baby is missing out on proper nutrients from breast milk. I'm missing out on who I really am. I'm missing out on the enjoyable experience of motherhood.

3 I/they should/could have known better.

I am, or someone else is, to blame: Now the process of reasoning kicks in and I start to think about the events that led me to the wrong path and to now missing out. I conclude that I or someone else should have done something differently or known better. It shouldn't be this way. Feelings of blame, anger, shame or regret reside in thinking that an event 'should' be different.

Example

I should be able to get my baby to sleep. My child shouldn't be having tantrums. My child is old enough to know better. My life should be different. I should be enjoying motherhood. I should have made a different decision. It's my fault (or it's somebody else's fault).

These three assumptions all lead us to the core belief of all stress, which is:

4 I am worth-less.

Because my life is now on the wrong path, I'm missing out and it should have been different. I determine that I am/my life is now worth-less; that is, of less value because of what has happened. Often we feel as though our child's life has lost some value too.

Example

I am useless. I'm a bad mother. I just can't do this. I'm hopeless. I'm incompetent. My life feels like it doesn't mean anything anymore. I don't feel valued by society. My child's life has been compromised. I'm not good enough.

There are many influences that we are continually exposed to which reinforce this GYLR Model of thinking. Parents who were brought up with certain values about how to live and what defines success teach us to hold this view of life and success. Schools reinforce this thinking, with their emphasis on achievement and the stigma attached to passing or failing. The media reinforce this GYLR Model of thinking with cleverly organised advertisements telling you what you need for your life to be successful or enjoyable (otherwise you are missing out on something in your life). The media also create stories and programs that expose those who haven't got life right, reinforcing what is socially acceptable and what is not. Finally, friends and peers brought up with the same model of thinking reinforce our focus on getting life 'right'.

Let me explain this GYLR Model further using the following diagram.

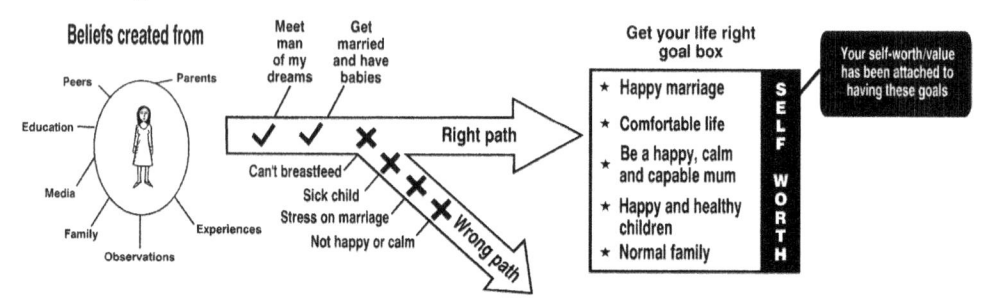

Beliefs created from: Peers, Parents, Education, Media, Family, Observations, Experiences

Right path: Meet man of my dreams ✓, Get married and have babies ✓, Can't breastfeed ✗, Sick child, Stress on marriage, Not happy or calm → Wrong path

Get your life right goal box:
- Happy marriage
- Comfortable life
- Be a happy, calm and capable mum
- Happy and healthy children
- Normal family

SELF WORTH — Your self-worth/value has been attached to having these goals

Through your experiences, observations, and environment so far, you have created your belief system. Incorrectly you may have learnt that there are certain things you must achieve in life in order for it to be successful (or to deem you valuable or worthy). As you go along your journey, life may seem to be going to plan and you are able to tick off some items on your list of goals. Perhaps you found the partner of your dreams, you got married, you became pregnant and seemed to be creating life the way that it 'should' go (according to your beliefs).

Then, unexpectedly you begin to experience challenges that appear as threats to the achievement of your goals. Maybe you have breastfeeding challenges, or your child becomes sick, or you are struggling with the demands of parenting. Maybe this has resulted in troubles within your marriage and you are suddenly feeling very unhappy and highly reactive. All of the goals that you had your self-worth attached to are not coming to fruition and it is becoming increasingly obvious that you are moving further and further away from the way life 'should' be going. You begin to feel stressed.

You start to feel like life is going down the wrong path (point 1) – that somehow you have veered off the right path and onto the wrong path. Then point 2 on the GYLR model kicks in and you begin to feel like you are missing out on what your life needs to be successful (the happy marriage, being a calm mum, having healthy children, and so on). You start to reason that you should be doing something different, or that you could've changed something or done something different in the past or someone else should have done something different.

All of these assumptions lead you to a core belief you have about you and your life – that these events have made your life of less value, or made you worth-less (point 4).

This line of thinking (which is *learnt*) then becomes reflective of the way we view our roles of motherhood – pass or fail; right or wrong – and is the source of stress in parenting.

In order to be successful parents, we think, 'I must get parenting right, otherwise I won't be a very good mother and my child's life will suffer (be worth-less). We attach our parenting goals to our self-worth, believing that only when we can meet these expectations can we be valuable parents to our children.

These goals can be tangible, such as having a husband, a certain number of children, a career, a specific house, financial security, and so on. Alternatively, these goals can be less tangible, such as being happy, being normal, being calm or responsible, being organised or competent, or any other 'idea' we have of what parenting should be like.

For example, I had quite a difficult time breastfeeding both of my children. I had plenty of milk and my body was physically able to feed, however learning the skill of breastfeeding didn't quite go as quickly as I would have liked.

My beliefs about this were:

> I should be able to do this (Point 3: should/could).
> I said I would always breastfeed (Point 1: right/wrong path). If I don't breastfeed, then my baby will not get the best start he needs (Point 2: missing out) and I will not be a good mother (Core belief 4: worth-less). There's no reason why I can't breastfeed. I'm just not good at it. I'm useless and I can't do it! (Core belief 4: worth-less).

This self-talk was causing me a great deal of upset because I had such high expectations of my capabilities as a mother and struggling with breastfeeding, to me, meant that I was failing at providing what I believed to be the best start for my baby. I had attached my self-worth to what I could achieve as a parent, so when I wasn't able to get it right, in my mind, this must have meant something about me – I must be doing a bad job – which was making me feel worth-less.

Self-worth is at the core of all stress because we have been taught by our parents, influences and society to rate our lives based on our achievements and only when we can achieve what we want (that is, get our lives right) can we be 100-per-cent worthy.

Here are some commonly heard statements made by mums who are aligned with the Get Your Life Right Model:

- My toddler just won't listen to me (Point 1: wrong path)
- I never get any time to myself (Point 2: missing out)
- I have to do everything (Point 2: missing out)
- I had drugs during my labour and I didn't want it to be that way (Point 1: wrong path)
- My baby doesn't sleep well and he (or she) should be in a routine by now (Point 3: should/could)
- I get so angry at my toddler and then I feel bad afterwards because I know I shouldn't behave that way (Core belief 4: worth-less; Point 3: should/could)
- My house is a mess all the time (Point 1: wrong path)
- I can't keep up with all these demands (Core belief 4: worth-less)
- I don't know who I am anymore (Core belief 4: worth-less)
- 'x' has happened to my child and now he (or she) won't get 'y' in his or her life (Point 2: missing out; and Core belief 4: child's life is worth-less) ...

The list could go on for pages.

By becoming aware of your thoughts you will be able to identify where on the GYLR Model you are with regard to your thinking and clearly see what it is that is causing your stress. In Step 2 you will learn how you can replace these thoughts with the Personal Development Model – the second half of the Fountainhead Method™.

Using Step 1

Ask yourself: What am I thinking?

We constantly have internal conversations, but we rarely notice them. You need to note this mindless chatter and become conscious of what it's saying in order to identify – and then change – your thoughts.

Once you have become aware of these thoughts, you can identify where they fit on the Get Your Life Right Model and how you have attached your goals to your self-worth.

Write these thoughts down if you need to. Keep a diary of some of the thoughts that you pick up on so that you can start to see patterns of thought emerging. See where these thoughts align with the Get Your Life Right Model: Do I feel like my life is on the wrong path, or that I'm missing out, or that things should be different or someone else should be different? And finally, what have I decided this event means about me (my self-worth)?

Start practising becoming aware of your thoughts every minute you can as this will teach you so much about what is actually causing your stress. Listen to yourself and discover exactly how you perceive the experiences of motherhood and just how much these conversations are causing you to feel lost, consumed or overwhelmed.

Chapter 3

Step 2 – Reality

How are my thoughts in conflict with reality?

Step 2 is all about bringing your thoughts into alignment with reality. It's impossible to think about a solution for a problem if your mind is still stuck on the problem and you're unable to accept the situation you are currently experiencing.

> All stress is a conflict between belief and reality, meaning that our thinking is not agreeing with what is actually happening in front of us (reality). By acknowledging and accepting our current reality and upgrading our beliefs from the GYLR Model by using the Personal Development Model (which we will discuss shortly), you will reduce your stress and be able to start thinking about the solutions to your problem. This leads you up the ladder to Step 3: What do you want?

Case study 1: Brenda

Brenda's daughter is having a loud and violent tantrum. The reality of the moment is that Brenda's child is having a tantrum.

There is absolutely no mistaking it. She is lying on the floor of the shopping centre kicking and screaming, so she's having a tantrum!

However, Brenda is thinking: 'She shouldn't be doing this.' (should/could); 'What are people going to think of me?' (self-worth); 'She's always doing this to me.' (wrong path); 'I'm sick of her behaviour.' (worth-less)

Where is Brenda's attention? Brenda's thoughts are in conflict with the reality that her daughter is having a tantrum because Brenda holds the belief that this behaviour is in some way affecting her self-worth. Her self-talk is in alignment with the GYLR Model and *that* is what is causing her stress – not the tantrum itself.

At this point, Brenda is unable to accept this situation because (based on her GYLR beliefs) she perceives it to be a direct threat to her self-worth: 'What are people going to think of me?'

In order to overcome this stress and move up the ladder towards finding the solution, Brenda must first identify her thoughts about the tantrum, accept the situation before her and move on to thinking about the solution to handling the tantrum.

Chapter 3: Step 2 – Reality

Case study 2: Tracy

Tracy is feeling frustrated by her lack of time out and the lack of help she gets from her husband. Tracy's thoughts are: 'I've had enough of doing everything around here.' (wrong path); 'My husband never helps me.' (missing out); 'He's always off playing golf, or having a good old time with his mates. Meanwhile I'm stuck here slaving away, looking after kids, and never getting any time out for myself.' (missing out); 'The housework never gets done unless I do it.' (wrong path); 'This is not what I had planned for my life.' (wrong path); 'I don't do anything for myself anymore.' (missing out); 'I should be able to have some time for me too.' (should/could); 'I don't even know who I am any more.' (worth-less); 'All I ever do is look after kids all day.' (worth-less); 'I don't even know what I want anymore.'

Firstly, by becoming aware of her thoughts, Tracy would notice that this whole conversation is aligned with the Get Your Life Right Model. Her self-talk is riddled with missing out and thinking that her life is on the wrong path, resulting in the conclusion that her life is worth-less.

These thoughts are in conflict with the reality of the situation, which is that Tracy is currently the primary person looking after her children, resulting in her not getting much time out. This is due partially to the reality of parenting and partially because of the events that unfolded in her past, leading up to this moment in time.

Somehow, over the time that has passed, Tracy and her husband have set up this dynamic, which at some point was accepted by both of them. Somehow, it has been accepted that Tracy was designated as the person who is responsible for most of the running of the house and to be the primary carer for the children, which has now resulted in Tracy feeling like she has little time for herself. This is the reality of what has been set up – but this dynamic is no longer working for Tracy.

Now, of course, she doesn't like it – and that's okay. This step is not about liking the reality; it is just about acknowledging reality by saying, 'Okay, this is where I'm at based on everything that has already happened up until this point. Now what do I want?' (Step 3: Aim)

The Personal Development Model

The other half of the Fountainhead Method™ is the Personal Development Model. This is the model of thinking that is used to upgrade your beliefs from the Get Your Life Right (GYLR) Model to thinking in alignment with reality. It has been designed so that any point on the GYLR Model that your thoughts might be at can be replaced with a point from the Personal Development Model to align you with the reality of life and your true self-worth.

The four points are as follows:
1. My life is a journey.
2. I am always learning and receiving.
3. I/We can only know what we know at any given moment.
4. No matter how my life unfolds, I am always worthwhile.

Let's look at each point in detail:

1 My life is a journey.

This point is the upgrade of the GYLR belief 'My life is on the wrong path'. 'My life is a journey' is the understanding that there is no right or wrong path. There is only one path and that is your life, your journey.

Life is full of ups and downs and all of the experiences you have in your life are what make up your unique life, your story, your one path. Part of your story is now parenting and that too has its ups and downs.

Whenever you experience down times, they are just as much a part of you and your life as your up times. In this GYLR world we are taught to expect only highs in life and that if there are any lows then there's something wrong with our lives or we've done something wrongly. But the reality is that sometimes life just doesn't go to plan because we can't always control life. It doesn't mean you're on the wrong path; it just means that this is another experience in your unique journey through life.

Being a parent, you don't always achieve what you want to. Sometimes your children are uncooperative. Sometimes you don't get the housework done. Some nights you don't get sleep. This is all part of the journey of motherhood. Sometimes you have no idea what you're doing either.

This is where our inaccurate concept of happiness comes from. 'Only when I feel happy do I feel that I have a successful life, a worthy life.' Well, sleepless, uncooperative children don't make you feel happy, but that's all part of the ride and the reality of parenting.

You haven't jumped off the right path and onto the wrong one; you are still on your path – it has simply hit a bump in the road. Sometimes it might feel as if you're hitting lots of bumps in the road and all that means is that there is something to learn and perhaps it's time to find that learning, and use this knowledge to change tactics and try something different.

All of your experiences along the road travelled so far have added to the knowledge that you now have about life and created who you are as a person today. Where you are in your journey right now is because of all of your previous ups and downs and how these events have unfolded in the past up to now. This is your story so far.

2 I am always learning and receiving.

Point 2 of the Personal Development Model is the upgrade to the GYLR belief 'I am missing out'. Often we believe that we have missed out on an opportunity or an experience that we would have liked to have had. Because of our beliefs we expect our lives to go a certain way in order to be successful. If it hasn't happened that way, we feel as though we are missing out and now this new, unwanted experience is impacting on our quality of life.

For example: 'I am missing out on having my time out.' 'I am missing out on "my" life.' The upgrade to this belief is the understanding that we are always learning and receiving something in every situation. Our mind has been taught to search for what we don't have. This point teaches us to search for what we did get from each event.

There are two types of learning that can come from all events: event learning and life learning.

Event learning is where you learn from the event: what worked, what didn't work or what you might do next time.

Life learning is seeing this event in the bigger picture. There is value in every challenge that you experience because of what it adds to your knowledge of life and who you are as a person. You don't just learn about the event: you acquire more lessons about life. In situations where life isn't going your way, you can change your view of the situation (which is what is actually causing you stress) to gain an accurate view of your self-worth (which I will teach you more about in later chapters). Life learning – whenever you experience an event that is not going to plan – is asking yourself, 'What is this experience adding to my knowledge about life and how is it helping me to grow as a person?'

Let's go back to case study 2 on Tracy (page 42). Tracy's beliefs are stuck in 'missing out' and feeling as though she is missing out on her life: 'I'm missing out on time out. I'm missing out on help from my husband.'

But let's look at what she's learning and receiving. The reality is that Tracy is actually gaining a lot from this situation and adding value to her life.

First of all, let's look at the event learning that Tracy is getting. She is learning that certain dynamics have been set up with her husband that no longer suit her needs and she is learning how to renegotiate this with her husband. She is learning more about herself, about how to be a mum and about how to juggle all of the demands that come with that role. She is learning that being a mother takes up a lot of time and that she needs to take a break occasionally in order to be the mother she'd like to be. She is receiving the experience of motherhood with all of its ups and downs. And by not getting help from her husband, Tracy is learning more organisational skills and time-management skills because she is having to 'do it all'.

Sometimes you might feel as if you're not really learning these things as well as you would like to, or you might not feel like you are learning these things at all. For example, you might feel that as a parent you are failing when it comes to having good organisational or time-management skills. Please know that this is you learning! If you knew how to do something 100-per-cent correctly, then it wouldn't be called 'learning', would it? As a parent, it takes time to get our heads around some of the tasks required to organise ourselves, especially with all the curve-balls continually thrown at us. Sometimes we don't do something well because we have to keep trying different ways of doing it in order to learn how to do it. Even after we've become good at a new skill we still continue to improve on these skills as different challenges are met. There's no such thing as failing – only learning what hasn't worked.

What makes you feel hopeless is only your perception of how it 'should' look (Point 3) and the fact that you have attached your self-worth to getting it right when the reality is that you are still learning – and that's okay. Learning takes time and practice and cannot be rushed.

Now that we've looked at Tracy's event learning, let's have a look at the life learning she is receiving. Life learning is looking at the bigger picture and looking at this situation in the context of her whole life. What is this situation teaching Tracy about life and how is it helping her to grow as a person? Rather than thinking that she is missing out on her husband's help, Tracy could view this situation as bringing some much-needed alignment in her relationship, which could benefit the dynamics of her relationship as a whole. Instead of Tracy feeling that she is missing out on time to herself and therefore feeling as though her life is less valuable, she could view this as just one small event in her whole life – one that gives her an opportunity to add to her knowledge of motherhood, relationships and life in general. Finally, by using this method Tracy learns that her self-worth is not determined by how often she gets time out. She can learn to view her self-worth in a different way.

It's only natural to feel disappointed or upset when you've missed out on something that you wanted or that you feel you need. Using this upgrade may not shift the disappointment, but it gives you an accurate view of the situation and disconnects your self-worth from not getting what you want, which will reduce your stress over it. Although you didn't get what you wanted (time out; help from a husband/partner), you still received something of value from this experience and therefore your life is not of less value. When you can really see the value in what you are getting instead of seeing the loss of what you're not getting you will find that you feel very differently about the challenges you face.

No event is pointless or useless. There is always value to be found through something you learnt, or some other way the event has contributed to your life.

3 I can only know what I know at any given moment.

Point 3 on the Personal Development Model is the upgrade to 'should/could' on the GYLR Model. The belief that 'I or someone else' is to blame is upgraded by the understanding that you can only know what you know at any given moment.

What governs the decisions you make and the actions you take is the information and knowledge you have at that time.

Here's what happens when we make a decision or react to something. We perceive the event with one or more of our senses. Then our brains connect this perception to our current beliefs about the circumstance of this event. Our brains sort through which beliefs are the strongest, and then link to the appropriate response associated with those beliefs. This happens very quickly and quite subconsciously sometimes too. The decisions we make and the actions we take are governed by whatever belief is the priority at that time based on the information and knowledge that our brains can access at that time.

In Tracy's case, Tracy is indirectly implying that her husband 'should' be helping her. However, her husband's behaviour is governed by his beliefs, which dictate his priorities. Perhaps he believes that his wife is okay about 'doing it all': '... after all, she hasn't said anything, or when she does I just think she's having a vent and we all do that sometimes'.

Maybe he believes that it's his right to go and play golf and hang out with his buddies – because he works and this is his time out – without even considering what's going on for her.

This doesn't make him a bad person. It just means he has different beliefs from her, and therefore different priorities. Does that mean that Tracy has to just accept this and get over it? No – it just means that she needs to communicate to her husband that there needs to be a new alignment between them that works for them both because clearly they are thinking two different things right now.

If Tracy first determines which beliefs are governing her husband's behaviour, she will see that his behaviour has nothing to do with her value or even how he values her, but more about what's in his belief system, because his beliefs are what is driving his priority to go and play golf.

Let's look at Tracy's beliefs. She feels that she 'should' be having more time out. However, she is at this point largely because of what has been set up in the past with her husband.

Perhaps she was initially okay with this role. Perhaps she wanted to do it all, not realising how taxing this would be on her personally. Maybe due to the beliefs she holds, she somehow feels that she *should* be doing most of the housework and the rearing of the children – perhaps that's why this dynamic was set up in the first place – only now she is starting to see things a bit differently.

The dynamic between Tracy and her husband was set up because they only had the information that they held at that time to call upon, and this governed the way it all played out.

Our beliefs have been formed from everything that has unfolded from our past leading up to this moment because all our prior experiences contribute to our current knowledge about life.

So, let's play around with this some more.

Example

You're beating yourself up over yelling at your 4-year-old daughter because she put red paint on your new cream carpet. She became really upset by it and it made you feel really guilty. You tell yourself, 'I shouldn't have yelled at her and I should have stayed calm – after all, she's only learning and she just made a mistake'.

You were able to think this way only by observing her reaction and using your reasoning skills after the event and after you saw her reaction to your yelling. You had been given new information. Prior to that you had no knowledge of her reaction and could only react according to the current beliefs that you could access at the time of the event.

However, you still torment yourself thinking that if you could only go back in time, then you would take back your reaction and things would be different. So let's pretend to do that ... only you can't go back with the new information you now have about the reaction or the new reasoning, because you didn't have those back then. You can only go back to that moment with the knowledge you had at that time.

So here we go, turning back the clock so that we can stop you from yelling at your 4 year old. When we arrive at that moment we find that you yelled at her because of the story you told yourself about how the carpet was dirty, which meant that there was now going to be a big stain on the brand new carpet that you and your husband worked so hard to pay for only 6 months ago – and now it's ruined. We also find that the underlying belief behind this story is that when you work hard for something it should last. So, in order to change the angry reaction, we need to change this belief – and to do this we need to go back further in time.

Where did you learn that belief? Well, your dad used to work very hard for everything that he earned and used to always say that we need to make our things last and not to ruin them. As a kid, if we did ruin them, then he would get really angry. Alas, you learnt this angry response from him, so if you want to change the yelling you need to turn back the clock even further and change his beliefs. How did he learn this belief? Well, we would have to turn back time even further ... and so on.

When you saw the stain on the carpet, all you had to draw upon in that moment was the current knowledge and beliefs that you held, and these determined the chosen response – the yelling. You couldn't have behaved any other way because that was the habitual response which was created back when you were a child and that was what your mind accessed as the appropriate response at that moment when you saw the red paint on the carpet.

Hindsight is a wonderful thing and it's easy to fall into the trap of feeling that you or someone else should have done things differently, but sometimes you don't have that information at that time. Your behaviour is driven by your brain accessing the current knowledge that you possess to draw upon at the time and determining what the appropriate response is based on your beliefs and habitual responses to past events.

4   No matter how my life unfolds, I am always worthwhile.

This is a big one for many people to accept. It is the upgrade to the GYLR belief that 'I am worth-less'. This statement teaches you that it doesn't matter what unfolds in your life, your worth as a human being never changes. You are always 100-per-cent worthwhile.

Contrary to what we have been taught, our worth is not defined by getting life right or by life going to plan – it is defined because of our very existence. We are 100-per-cent worthy because we are here on this earth doing everything that we do and contributing to the process of life. This is the reality of self-worth.

When you follow the GYLR Model of thinking you feel worth-less. When you follow the Personal Development Model of thinking you are aligned with the true purpose of life and your true self-worth.

Self-worth: why you're worthy just the way you are!

As lack of self-worth is the cause of all major stress, I'm going to go into great detail as to why Point 4 on the Personal Development Model is an accurate way of thinking about ourselves and our lives.

When thinking along the lines of the GYLR Model we conclude that we are worth-less in some way because of something that has happened.

Often when you hear the word 'worth-less' it conjures up thoughts of being completely broken, feeling like a complete loser or having no self-confidence. People often say to me, 'but I don't actually feel worth-less. I feel pretty good about myself most of the time'.

It's important to note here that to feel worth-less you don't necessarily have to completely hate yourself or your life. It's simply feeling worth ... less, meaning that you believe that what has happened in your life has made you less valuable than you were before the event.

Feeling worth-less could mean that you only feel 80-per-cent worthy, when you would usually feel 95-per-cent worthy. Or, for others, it literally means that they feel 10 to 15-per-cent worthy instead of the 85 per cent that they felt before having children.

Looking at my own life, I now recognise that every time something didn't go to plan I would get angry and teary, and feel useless and out of control. When life was going okay, I was upbeat and cheery, but give me a non-sleeping baby or a whingeing, uncooperative child that I couldn't control and off I'd go into a spin, hating life and feeling like an incompetent mother – and hating myself again.

Here's an example of how irrational this worth-less belief is.

When I wasn't getting the technique of breastfeeding, I would get upset and frustrated with myself. I had always said that I would breastfeed my babies. After all, it's the best start you can give your children, right?

In my beliefs, in order to be a good mother I had to give my babies the best start and because I couldn't master a technique that clearly (in my mind) every other mother could grasp, I was useless and wasn't doing a good enough job, all leading to the belief that because of this event (not getting the skill of breastfeeding), I was worth-less.

So – let me see now – only when I can breastfeed my baby can I be 100-per-cent worthwhile. Breastfeeding my baby determines my worth, does it? Hmmm, that doesn't sound rational at all does it?

Let's look at another example.

Again, my beliefs dictated that to be a good mother I should be able to get my child into a sleep routine without hassle.

So now my worth is determined by whether my babies sleep or not (which is not even within my control, but – okay – let's keep digging ...)

A good, stay-at-home mum also has a clean house, plays with her kids and exercises often to get back to her pre-baby figure.

Clean house. Happy kids. Lots of exercise. Check. Check. Check.

So, in conclusion, a breastfed, regularly sleeping baby in a clean house with a skinny mum all determine self-worth, right? Anything less than that and – sorry – you're just not as valuable to this world.

> But, hang on a minute, what about my best friend Mary down the road? The poor thing couldn't breastfeed because her baby wouldn't latch on and she's having all sorts of trouble getting that baby to go to sleep. As a result, I told her the other day that she should just forget about the housework and sleep whenever she could. When I spoke to her she was also worried about her weight (because she had put on 25 kilograms during her pregnancy). I scolded her for worrying about this and said, 'Honey, you've just had a baby. Don't worry about the weight. Your priority is just to let yourself get to know your baby and settle into a routine. Think about the weight later when you have more time. It's not important right now'.

Mary doesn't breastfeed. Mary's baby doesn't sleep well. Mary hasn't gotten back to her pre-baby figure and I bet that her house isn't spotless either. Is Mary worth-less? According to my calculations she should be. But do I see Mary that way?

No, I don't. Why not? These are the standards that I set myself, so why is Mary worthy, yet I'm not?

The answer is that I have attached my self-worth to the list of things I believe I need to live up to and when I don't achieve these things I feel worth-less. I don't see Mary that way because I haven't attached *my* self-worth to *Mary* achieving those goals, only to *me* achieving those goals.

Somewhere along the line, I formed beliefs about motherhood dictating that the only way to be a good mother was to get all these things right. This thinking is all on the Get Your Life Right Model.

But let's look at it from the viewpoint of the Personal Development Model. This model states that no matter how my life unfolds I am always worthwhile. So, if I don't breastfeed my baby, have a clean house and have a sleeping baby, then I am still worthwhile. Why?

Because everything about you and your life is valuable (worthy). All of the events in your life's journey contribute to your personal development through the learning and growing that you do. Furthermore, all of these events also contribute to the development of those around you. Your interactions with others, whether they are strangers or people you are close to, leave an imprint of you that promotes learning, growing and experience in someone else's life, which they wouldn't get if you weren't here.

The world exists because each one of us is here living in it and contributing our little bit to those around us. All of the knowledge that you have today influences how you experience your life, which in turn contributes to how you interact with others. Your interaction with others influences their life in some way. Their current knowledge also influences and contributes to your life in some way.

Your whole journey and other people's journeys contribute to the circle of life. The world is the way it is because we all contribute to one another's development and experience of life.

You are valuable as a mum because you were here on this earth to give life to this child. Everything that you do is contributing to your child's learning and their life's development.

Without your existence the dynamics change. Take you out of the equation and the world changes in a small but significant way. There is a void left if you're not there. You being alive is what determines your worth.

Whether you breastfeed or not, whether your baby sleeps or not, whether you are overweight or skinny, your worth does not change because you are always either gaining from or contributing something of value to every single situation you encounter.

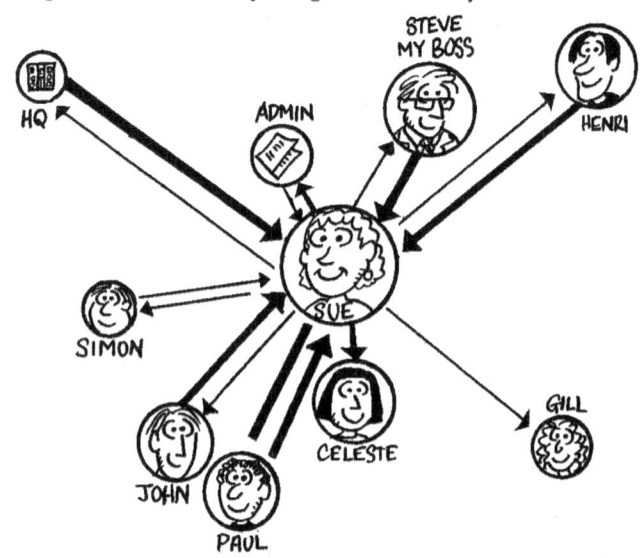

In order to stop feeling worth-less, you must learn to look for the value in each moment, look at *what* you are learning and look for *how* you are still contributing to your and other people's development and life experiences.

Look back at the example of the toddler having a tantrum in the shops (page 14). There is value in this experience because of what it's teaching you, your child and the people around you. If you take yourself and your child out of the equation, then the lessons are not learnt and you have not made that contribution to yourself, your child and those around you.

If everything ran perfectly and nothing ever went 'wrong', no one would learn anything.

Imagine if you had a mother who was walking down the aisle when the tantrum mentioned above occurred and she looked at your child being angry and watched you being very calm and compassionate towards your daughter. She might think to herself:

'Oh, my gosh. I never react that way. That mother is being so nice to her child and I usually get ridiculously angry. What she's doing is working. I'll try that next time.'

This woman goes home to her child and treats her more compassionately when she has a tantrum – and it works. You've just contributed to another human being learning and growing and thus behaving a different way.

You can get an accurate view of your self-worth by seeing each event in the bigger picture. All events have value in them because of their contribution to everyone in contact with the events and the learning and contribution they have made to your and their development. This is the life learning that can come from each and every event.

Self-worth versus self-esteem

Sometimes we find that we don't behave the way we'd like to. What happens if you don't behave calmly to a tantrum and completely lose the plot, smacking and yelling at your child instead? If you've ever reacted like this you would know that it's common to feel guilty for having behaved this way.

Now that you know the GYLR Model of thinking and the Personal Development Model of thinking, you could probably look back at what was happening for you at the time and identify your beliefs being in conflict with the reality that your child was having a tantrum. You might be able to identify that you had decided your child's behaviour somehow meant something bad about you. Perhaps you felt that you were an incompetent mother because your child had a tantrum in public, for example.

Guilt over your reaction can be overcome by recognising that you couldn't have behaved any differently at the time because you only knew what you knew at that time and this was the response that your mind accessed at that moment.

This is not to condone behaving in this way, but to understand why you might behave this way because the beauty of experience is that after we experience something like this we get the opportunity to reflect on it and learn from it, thus adding to our knowledge of life and potentially changing it for future events. This is called hindsight.

Logically, from hindsight and using the Personal Development Model, you could see that your self-worth has not changed just because you got angry and reacted this way because you could find some value in this situation and because it has contributed in some way to your and your child's development.

So here you are, with this new information from The Fountainhead Method™, understanding that even though you did not react calmly to this tantrum at the shops, you are still 100-per-cent worthy. However, you still feel really bad for doing it, right?

What you're feeling is not a drop in self-worth. It is a drop in self-esteem. Your self-esteem is your rating system – that is, how you rate yourself. This rating of your self has also been taught. As a child you would have received information and experiences that taught you how to rate yourself, just as you were taught how to rate your life, your experiences and other people.

Think about someone we hold in high regard – let's say the Dalai Lama, for example. What do we admire about the Dalai Lama? What is it that he does that puts him up there in high regard? Well, he's calm, gentle, peaceful and a happy man. How did he get that way? When he was 3 years old he was chosen to be taught the wisdom of the Buddhism philosophy. He was trained to be a leader who represented the essence of the Buddhism philosophy. His behaviour is a result of his beliefs. He behaves that way because he was taught to behave that way (remember from page 27 how our brains form our personalities in response to our environments?).

Does this make him a more worthy person? No. His worth has not changed. Only our rating of him based on our learnt beliefs that his calm, gentle, peaceful and happy traits are ideals to have in a person, and therefore we rate him as more worthy. Also, it's easy to see the value in his existence because we perceive his influence as being 'positive'.

What about the other end of the spectrum: someone we hold in low regard – let's say a heroin addict, for example. What don't we like about this person? You might describe a heroin addict as weak, dirty, scum or a loser. How does a heroin addict get that way? He or she started out as an innocent baby with barely any connections between neurons and was taught what to believe in response to his or her environment. People's behaviour is governed by what they believe about themselves and their life.

Does this make the drug addict less worthy? No. It just means that he or she has been taught to rate himself or herself differently from the Dalai Lama. Your rating of the drug addict comes from what you have learnt about the traits that are ideal about a person (how to get life right). We think that this person's existence is worth less than the Dalai Lama's because he or she is not displaying 'positive' behaviour or influencing others as valuably as the Dalai Lama does.

MY RATING SYSTEM
How I Rate People

Chapter 3: Step 2 – Reality **57**

However, how much do we learn from drug addicts? A drug addict teaches us how our life might turn out if we were to take drugs. A drug addict influences the medical and psychological career fields to continue researching behaviour and reactions to drugs in order to help other people and to find more medical treatments to help others who take drugs, either on purpose or accidentally. That drug addict contributes to the process of life just as valuably as the Dalai Lama.

We learn from other people's adversities just as much as we learn from other people's successes, and other people learn from our adversities and successes. Everyone is valuable by their mere existence and how they contribute to the world, regardless of their behaviour.

I realise that talking about criminals can be a delicate subject in terms of their worth to society, however it's important to realise that this method is not about condoning behaviour. *It is about helping you to understand it.* The reality is that criminals began as little babies, just as we did, with a clean slate in their minds. Something happened between then and now that made them believe certain things about their lives in order to behave the way that they do. Their behaviour is a priority because of those beliefs. Their self-worth is attached to certain goals they are trying to achieve because they have incorrect beliefs about their self-worth.

Now look at yourself. Are you any less worthy when your children behave differently from how you would like them too? Are you less worthy when you haven't quite mastered the art of being calm every time your 3 year old gives you attitude and backchat, or when your baby isn't in a sleep routine, or the house isn't clean? No, you are not. Your worth never changes. You are always 100-per-cent worthy.

What has changed is your self-esteem – your rating of yourself. How you rate yourself has been taught by observing and experiencing life and consequently building what is now your current belief system. Your self-esteem fluctuates all the time because you rate events differently according to what you believe about them.

If you are still feeling bad after getting angry, even now that you know logically that your worth is still intact, it's because your rating of this behaviour is low, based on your beliefs (for example, holding the belief that if good mothers yell at their children they aren't really being good mothers at all).

You must continue to become aware of your self-talk about what is happening in your life (Step 1 of the Mind TRACK to Happiness process) and continue reminding yourself that your value as a human being never changes.

Using Step 2

Ask yourself: How are my thoughts in conflict with reality?

Step 2 (Reality) is about taking the thoughts that are causing you stress and aligning them with reality. By becoming aware of your thoughts and finding out where you're sitting on the GYLR Model, then comparing these thoughts to what is actually happening (Reality) and the more accurate way to view life (Personal Development Model) you begin to shift your mind into a position where you can begin making some real changes to your life.

Without doing these first two steps of the process you will simply stay at the bottom of the ladder. If you have a problem and you go straight to Step 3 – 'Aim: What do I want?' – then every time you start to notice that you're not getting what you want, you'll feel like something is wrong, something is missing, something is not working or that you have failed, which just puts you right back at the bottom of the ladder again.

Step 1 (Thoughts) and Step 2 (Reality) are the most important steps in the climb up the ladder and out of the hole where anger, stress, frustration, loss of identity, depression and anxiety all live.

Sometimes this Mind TRACK to Happiness process is a quick process in your mind. But other times you might find that it takes a lot longer for more complex issues, such as marital/partner relationships, depression, anxiety – and so on – because you have to sort through many different beliefs and conflicts with reality at the same time.

You're retraining your brain to think differently from how you've been taught to think and, as we've learnt, this retraining takes time, repetition and experience.

Just as in motherhood you are learning new skills that take practice (which is often done through trial and error), so you need to be patient with yourself and just continue to practise embracing this wonderful journey of learning, receiving and contributing.

Chapter 4

Step 3 – Aim

What do I want?

So, you've identified the thoughts that are causing you to feel stressed and categorised them into the GYLR Model. And you've recognised how they are in conflict with reality and you've upgraded these thoughts with what's actually happening and the Personal Development Model.

Now it's time to shift gears and move your attention up the ladder by thinking about what you want.

Completing Steps 1 and 2 detaches you from the 'problem' so that you can see the value in it and are no longer completely consumed by it. However, it doesn't mean that you still won't want to change the situation or experience something different, so this is where Step 3 comes in: What do I want?

Once you've decided what you want, there are a couple of questions that you need to ask yourself in relation to what you want.

Is what I want in conflict with reality?

Brenda is the mum whose daughter is having a tantrum. She has followed the first two steps of the process and is now aligned with the reality of the tantrum playing out in front of her and the fact that this tantrum has value and does not reflect her self-worth.

Her next step is to decide what her aim is and her first thought is to stop the tantrum. The only problem is that, in reality, stopping the tantrum isn't actually within Brenda's control.

Brenda isn't the one actually having the tantrum so she can't be the one to stop it. Sure, there are things that she could do to try and stop the tantrum – for example, distracting or ignoring her daughter – but ultimately it is her daughter's decision to stop, not Brenda's. So, having the aim of stopping the tantrum is in conflict with reality.

Brenda needs to set a goal that relies on her own actions to achieve what she wants, not the behaviour of others to achieve it, otherwise it becomes more by chance that Brenda reaches her aim. She can't control the behaviour of another person.

A more suitable aim that would be within Brenda's power might be to stay calm, just get through it and then find out how to handle such tantrums in the future.

Tracy (from case study 2) might have the immediate aim of getting her husband to pull his finger out and help some more. That would be a natural thing to want. But that's not within her control either. He has control over his behaviour and while she can try and negotiate the terms of her relationship (which might be an aim of hers), ultimately he gets to decide whether he's going to change or not.

Getting more time out might be a more appropriate aim to go for as it is more within her control. In the next step she can look at the 'how' and this may involve her husband, or it may involve taking other measures to achieve this.

So, you can see that the initial aim that you want may not be in line with reality. You can't control someone else's behaviour, so you must take that into consideration when establishing your aim.

Be specific

When thinking about your aim, you need to be specific about what it is that you want.

Tracy's aim is to get more time out. What exactly does this look like? How much time out does Tracy specifically want? Is it daily, weekly, monthly? For how long would she like to have time out? Would she like to join an activity that requires commitment and reliability, such as joining a sports team? Does she just want to be able to plan events and have the support in place to be able to go to these events? Is it just going for a walk when her husband gets home from work, or having the liberty to have a sleep or read a book or have a bath now and again?

When considering what your aim is, you need to imagine having what you want and the exact details of how that looks. It's no good Tracy saying that she wants time out and then not knowing what that looks like because she then can't begin to communicate what she wants to her husband or to her support network. In order to organise getting time out, she must consider exactly what sort of time out she wants.

Why do I want it?

The next thing to test your aim against is why you want what you want. This is really important because you want to check that your aim is not putting you right back onto the GYLR Model.

Something to keep in mind is that we often set goals in order to make our lives 'better' or make us feel 'better' or become 'better' people. This aim to make things 'better' would indicate that things are worse or less without that goal.

Thinking this way puts you back on the GYLR Model as you feel that what is happening right now is on the 'wrong path' or currently making you miss out.

As we have learnt, there is value in all events because they help us to learn and grow and all events contribute to the learning and growing of those around us, and consequently the way the world is. So be mindful of this when setting your aims.

You will always set goals in order to experience something you would like to, but be careful that you are not setting these goals from a place that has not yet accepted the value in the now, because if you don't end up achieving the aim (which is reality –

sometimes life doesn't always go to plan) then you'll be back on the GYLR Model, feeling that you've somehow failed because you haven't achieved your goal and you feel worth-less again.

Understanding that goals don't make your life 'better' doesn't mean that you won't still set the same goal.

For example, let's say that you want to be a calm mum and *that* is your aim. Why do you want to be a calm mum? Because you want to be a better mum and you want your kids to experience kindness and compassion from you. There is value in all events, so even when you aren't being a calm mum, you and your children are still learning and growing from your experiences, so this doesn't make the current situation less valuable.

However, that doesn't mean you still won't strive for the aim of being a calm mother. We always want to grow as people and learn better ways of behaving, so if this is an area you'd like to work on then set this goal for sure. Just be mindful that your life or your child's life will not be more valuable when you are calm compared to when you are not – more enjoyable, for sure, but *not* more valuable. You are still just as worthy when you aren't being a calm mother as when you are – a valuable thing to remember when you're striving to be that calm mother and slip back into old habits.

The important thing is to learn and grow from these experiences and use them as opportunities to teach your kids about the times when you don't feel calm.

Incidentally, when you aren't being a calm mother, your kids are learning about anger and dealing with other people's behaviour. It's a reality of life that they will have to learn to deal with anger eventually. If there was never anger in your household and you protected your children from it, they would go out into the world and not know how to experience anger. Again, this doesn't condone angry behaviour; it just highlights that there is value in all events because of the lessons they bring to us all.

In order to set your aim in this step, you must first understand the real purpose of goals. Logically we know that the purpose of setting goals is to achieve them and to get what we want in life. However, achieving the goal is not the only purpose of setting a goal. By setting a goal we are also learning new things and growing as people. Furthermore, we are experiencing life and contributing to the cycle of life just by creating the goal and taking each step towards this goal.

So, in summary, whether we are on our journey towards the goal, or we achieve the goal, or we don't achieve the goal, we are always learning, growing and contributing to life.

Of course, we will always aim to reach our goals, but in reality, we know that life doesn't always go to plan and sometimes, for various reasons, we just can't achieve our goals.

When testing our aim by asking ourselves 'Why do I want this goal?', we need to check that we are not attaching our self-worth to the achievement of this goal. We need to remind ourselves that there is value in all of our experiences and if we cannot achieve what we want, then we need to look for how this has benefited us and others.

In motherhood we set goals all the time. We set goals to keep on top of the housework, to get our kids to cooperate and behave, to be calm, to be happy, to work on a sleep routine for our babies, to help our children reach their milestones, to return to work, and so on. However, there are many times when we encounter unexpected interruptions (usually caused by our kids changing our plans) where our goals can't be met or where they need to be revisited. This is simply the reality of parenting. We need to accept that this happens and continually seek to find the learning in these events.

Sometimes you will figure out how to manage your time effectively and other times things will come up and you'll get nothing done.

Knowing this doesn't mean that you will stop striving for what you want; however, it will help you to find the value in life when you don't get what you want. When this happens, take the learning from this and re-establish another way to get what you want.

Using Step 3

Ask yourself: What do I want?

When you have accepted that where you are at now is a result of all the things that have happened in your past leading up to now, you are in a position to shift your mindset to establishing what you would like to experience – that is, your aim.

Take some time to deliberately consider what you actually want and what the specifics are that make up this aim. Also, question why you want to achieve this goal, and whether this goal is in conflict with reality. How would I feel if I didn't achieve the goal? Is that feeling due to beliefs in line with the GYLR Model or the Personal Development Model? Are you relying on your actions to achieve this goal or are you relying on the behaviour of someone else to achieve it? Are you attaching your self-worth to this goal and do you believe that your life will be more valuable when you achieve it?

Chapter 5

Step 4 – Choices

What options/solutions do I have?

Step 4, now that an aim is established, is about weighing up the options and potential solutions that are available in order to work towards your aim, and choosing which options and solutions will be the most effective.

Brenda's daughter (case study 1) is in the shopping centre wriggling around on the floor making a lot of noise, and people are looking at her (reality). Brenda wants to stay calm and handle the tantrum gracefully (aim). What are her choices?

After accepting the reality of the tantrum and deciding that she would like to handle it calmly, Brenda now has to figure out what her options are. She could walk away and ignore her. She could make some room in the trolley and put her in there so that she can continue shopping while ignoring her. She could try reasoning with her. She could distract her. She could just stand and wait patiently until she has finished. She could give her what she wants to keep her quiet, then research ways to handle public tantrums in the future. Yes, she's given in this time, but only because she needs to buy some time, to establish a plan of action for next time, so she can teach her daughter that this behaviour is not appropriate.

By considering all of these options Brenda now has her attention on the solution and on ways in which she can approach this situation, rather than her attention being stuck on the problem.

This particular situation is one where you have a small amount of time to decide what to do, so the Mind TRACK to Happiness process happens quite quickly, but it still needs to be a deliberate consideration.

Tracy's situation (case study 2) is a bit different. She has more time for consideration and research. It's not a situation that needs an instant response or decision, so more thought can be put into how she is going to achieve her aim.

Let's say that she has decided that her aim is to get more time out. She has decided that she would like to be able to go out once a week with her girlfriends for a coffee or for dinner and she would like to join the gym and go a couple of days a week. Now she needs to figure out what her options are that will enable her to achieve those aims.

One option may be talking to her husband about what she wants. She could explain how stressed out she is feeling as a mum and that she has decided that it would be helpful for her to take a little more time out than she has been taking. Did you notice that no mention was made of him not helping? This would be a pointless conversation to have at this time, as she would then be back in conflict with reality.

The reality is that you are where you are because of all of the events leading up to the present, and your attention is now on changing that to being what you want. There is no point dwelling on the past. It's over. You have decided what you want; now you are trying to set up a new dynamic so that it happens, so talking with your husband about how you are feeling now and what you want to do about it is one option to explore.

It's important to understand though that in this step you are figuring out the choices that you have and how you can create a plan to get what you want. Tracy's husband is logically the first person to consider when trying to get time out, but approaching him is not the only option to consider.

Does she have family or friends whom she could approach to help her out? Are there crèche facilities at the venues she wishes to attend (for example, at the gym)? Is day care an option for getting time out? If she doesn't know many people in the area, can she join a playgroup and after getting to know some of the people, organise play dates for her children?

Sometimes other mums in the same situation need some time out too, so taking it in turns to look after each other's children once in a while can be extremely beneficial to both mums.

What governs our choices?

With some issues, such as Brenda's example of her daughter's tantrum, the options and the solutions are obvious and easy to consider; however, there is another aspect to making choices that we must consider.

We have already discussed how the choices we make and the actions we take are governed by our beliefs about what we consider important (our priorities), and it's important to reflect on this when looking at the options we have.

You will always make decisions in alignment with what you believe. If what you believe is in conflict with the solutions to achieving your aim, then this will influence the decision you make or make it difficult to achieve the aim.

Tracy (case study 2) has limited time out because of the dynamic that has been set up with her husband, but also because she has made her children a priority over herself. That could just be because her children were at an age where they were babies and needing more of her attention. Now they may be a little older and she is at a point where she can make herself more of a priority.

This is quite common in the early stages of parenting; however, it could also be because Tracy believes that she doesn't deserve this time out.

Her choices (not to give herself time out) have been governed by her beliefs, which could be, 'If I have time out, then I'm a bad mum', or 'My children are more important than I am', or 'Mothers have to be there for their children and husband 24/7'.

There are many different beliefs that Tracy may have that have been stopping her from making time out a priority and these beliefs need to be identified, measured against the GYLR Model and upgraded using the Personal Development Model in order for her to meet her aim.

If a mum wants time out and she believes that a good mum is always available to her children, then she must also believe that she is deserving of her own space too – otherwise she will never follow through with her plans to achieve this aim.

Sometimes you might find that you have wanted something for a while, however you continually find that you don't end up getting it, or following through with what is required to get it.

Remember how your non-conscious is like a satellite navigation system? If you have a belief that is ingrained – a habit of thought – and you do something that is in conflict with this belief, it's like your mind considers that you are off course with what you normally think and will redirect your thinking back to what it knows – the habit of thought.

So even though there is a conscious part of you that doesn't want to make that choice, your behaviour is governed by your beliefs and your mind will unconsciously set your course back in alignment with what you believe.

This often happens with things such as losing weight or quitting smoking too. You know what you need to do in order to obtain these goals, but you don't do it. This is because there is another belief that is more important than the desire to lose weight or quit smoking.

Remember that your mind is self-fulfilling, meaning it is always behaving in the best interests of you and your beliefs. You're not an idiot if you're doing something that you logically don't want to do. Your mind is doing exactly what it has been designed to do and that is to think the way it has been taught to think. Your behaviour is always aligned with what you believe.

Chapter 5: Step 4 – Choices

Case study 3: Liz

This actually happened to a client of mine who had an issue with weight loss (name has been changed).

This mum felt that she had an unhealthy relationship with her weight but could never follow through with being able to change this. Her aim was to lose weight, however she never did what she logically needed to do in order to shed the weight because she never made herself a priority.

She was already aware that she believed she didn't deserve to be a priority, however she was still unable to make herself a priority and put the effort into losing weight.

She described this pattern as self-sabotage. However, the mind is always working in your best interests and in alignment with held beliefs, so there had to be another underlying belief that was causing her to behave this way.

There was a payoff for repeating this behaviour, which was automatically in alignment with something she believed, even though logically she knew what she needed to do to lose weight.

Upon further investigation into her family background, we found that Liz's father had a very strong personality with strong beliefs about the role of a wife.

Consequently her mother was quite subservient to her dad, doing everything he said, and went out of her way to keep her dad happy. Liz actually resented her mum for this more than her dad, as she felt her mum was weak for not standing up for herself.

I asked Liz to consider what she thought her mum's priority was for not standing up for herself. Why didn't she do this? What would happen to her mother if she stood up for what she wanted? Her response was that she would be ridiculed by her dad. Her mother's payoff for staying subservient was the fear of being ridiculed and therefore feeling less worthwhile.

So why was Liz not making herself a priority in order to lose weight? For starters, even though she didn't have an overpowering husband or roles set up such as those of her childhood family, she had learnt from her mother to make everyone a priority except herself, so she played this out in her life when she got married and had children of her own. But the ultimate reason for not making herself a priority was self-protection – the fear of being ridiculed.

She had learnt from her childhood, primarily from her mother, that when you make yourself a priority and stand out you run the risk of being ridiculed.

Losing weight holds the potential for being ridiculed as weight loss can get you noticed more, which could lead to ridicule. It was much safer to stay the way she was, doing everything for everyone else and not doing anything that might draw attention to her and run the risk of being set up for ridicule.

There was absolutely no self-sabotage there. Liz's mind had her best interests at heart 100 per cent of the time, based on what she had been taught to believe as a child, and these beliefs were what was stopping her from losing weight.

Because our choices and behaviour are governed by what we already believe, even if you consider what the options are that are available to you, you will always choose the option that aligns with your beliefs.

You can be mindful of this if you are struggling to make the changes that you want to make. If you have an aim for something that you'd like but have never been able to achieve when you have attempted it in the past, listen to the story you tell yourself about not achieving it and think about your own childhood and what beliefs you might be holding that are governing you to behave this way.

When you discover the belief and upgrade it using the Personal Development Model and work towards reinforcing your new belief and view of this situation over time, this will become your new habit of thought.

Using Step 4

Ask yourself: What are the options/solutions that I have?

The point of this step is to exhaust every possibility, no matter how crazy it is, and analyse whether this might be the action to take to arrive at what you want to achieve.

You can do this through conscious consideration and with research. How do other people achieve what you want to achieve? What are their methods for achieving this?

With some issues, this step might take some time to figure out – for example, a complex issue with your partner, or a behavioural issue with your child or there has been some repetitive pattern that needs investigating and has stopped you achieving this in the past.

There are many different ways to achieve what you want. This step is about exploring those options in order to come up with the plan to overcome your problem.

Chapter 6

Step 5 – Know your plan and action it

This is the final step in the Mind TRACK to Happiness process. It's all about action. You know what your choices are. The only thing left to do is decide on your course of action and go for it!

Knowing your plan is important in keeping you on target towards what you want. For example, having a plan that you have consciously decided on to handle your children's developmental stages (such as tantrums) often diffuses anger and frustration as being the reaction to the behaviour.

It's because you're prepared and you know what you need to do. Being prepared is what this step is about.

Rather than continuing to feel bad about what is actually happening in front of you, this process gets you to deliberately and consciously think about what you want to experience and how to get it.

Even though this is the final step, the process doesn't stop here. It keeps going. You don't get to this point and suddenly your life is fixed. If you are thinking this then you are right back on the GYLR Model.

The Mind TRACK to Happiness process is a way of thinking, not a process to use so that you can get your life going the way you want, which is why it's called the *Mind TRACK* to Happiness.

Remember that there is only one track and that that is your unique journey in life. Everything that you encounter is part of your one path, being your life. It's never the events that cause stress; *it's how you view these events and what you think they mean about you and your life that causes stress.*

Even though you have got to this point on the ladder there may be times when you will encounter other challenges along the way to achieving your aim that send you right back down to the bottom of the ladder. That's okay. This is part of the reality of life that I am now teaching you to embrace. It just means there is more to learn so that you have the knowledge to climb back up the ladder again.

We never stop learning and growing as human beings, and being at the bottom of the ladder is not a bad place to be; it's just that you have come across another experience to learn and grow from and it's all part of life's journey of different experiences.

You might feel that just as you master the art of handling tantrums, your child begins a new stage, such as backchatting and showing attitude, and you need to start all over again.

These challenges can seem never ending, especially when it comes to parenting. This is why you need to change your mindset towards the challenges of parenting by finding the value in them. Otherwise you are constantly waiting for all your problems to be fixed before you can be happy, making happiness very elusive.

Think of it as a game of 'Snakes and Ladders'. Sometimes you roll the dice, make your move and go up the ladder towards your aim and other times you come across a snake where you slide back down again. Sometimes you make it to the end of the game and win and other times you don't get to the end of the game as quickly as you would like, or not at all.

All along the way you are learning life strategies and lessons that contribute to who you are and to those around you and this is what defines the value of life.

When you find yourself climbing the ladder, congratulate yourself for utilising what you've learnt and enjoy your time there, but when you reach a snake and slide back down, remind yourself of what you have learnt from this experience and what else you will learn as you recommence your climb up the ladder.

Incidentally, when you play the game of 'Snakes and Ladders', you don't play the game just to get to the end. You play the game because it's fun to play. Take the same approach with life and the achievement of goals and you will find yourself happier.

Using Step 5

Ask yourself: Do I know my plan?

Decide on the options you will use and create an action plan that you will follow in order to get to your goal. Know that this action plan is not set in stone and will not guarantee that you will achieve your goal because the reality of life is that sometimes we don't achieve our goals, but we always learn and grow through experiencing all the ups *and* downs of life.

Going through this process has, however, shifted your mindset away from viewing this challenge as a problem, and instead seeing it as valuable and important to learning about its potential solution. Achieving the goal is enjoyable and a bonus, but it is not proof of a successful life, or a good mother.

Summary: The Mind TRACK to Happiness process

If you want to be a Happy Mum, then you need to change the way you currently think about life and happiness. The value of your life and why it is always worthwhile is because you are always learning, growing and contributing to the life process.

Being happy comes from being aligned with this reality and understanding the true purpose of setting goals.

In motherhood, and even in our lives in general, we experience many different events. Some of these events are joyous and some are not. Regardless of our opinions on these events we always take something of value from them.

Setting goals is essential in life. Goals keep us interested and give us drive and motivation to try new things and as a result learn new things.

The Mind TRACK to Happiness process can be applied to every single issue that you encounter, whether it be a challenging developmental stage with your child, a complex problem with your partner, or any other aspect of your life.

Simply recognise which **t**houghts are causing you stress, change them to be in alignment with the present **r**eality, shift your attention to your **a**im – what you want – establish your **c**hoices and **k**now what your plan is. These five steps will keep your mind on TRACK to being happy.

Sometimes this process can be applied quite quickly, allowing you to change almost immediately how you feel about a situation.

Other times you need to give yourself the time to work through the thoughts and beliefs you have about the situation and how they are in conflict with reality. Listening to the internal self-talk that you have running on a day-to-day basis can be an enlightening exercise that will help you to understand what the limiting beliefs are that are keeping you stuck in the problem.

If your life seems quite complex at the moment and it feels as though you need to apply this process to so many areas of your life you don't know where to start, it's important to break it down into what's do-able for you.

Start by using the process on easy challenges so that you become confident in thinking this way about issues that are not too emotional; then start working your way up to more complex issues.

You can't change everything overnight, but over time and with commitment you'll be able to completely transform your life. These thought patterns didn't appear overnight and they won't change overnight.

Understand that you are perfect just the way you are and that you're learning about life just like everyone else. You are great at some things and not at others. Other people might not be so good at what you are good at, yet they might be great in areas that you are struggling with. No individual person is better than any other person. We're all different and we're all just a product of our experiences and the belief systems that have been created because of these experiences.

> We live in an achievement-based world where we are repeatedly told how these achievements will add to our worth so when we don't reach the achievements that we have been taught to value, we begin to feel worth-less.

However, you now know that your self-worth is intrinsic – it cannot be changed.

We're all here just experiencing life and contributing to one another's development. *So begin loving yourself today and recognising that you're allowed to learn, you're allowed to make mistakes and you're allowed to succeed.* Incidentally, so are your children.

This is what being alive is about. Enjoy the process while practising this new mindset so that you can be an example for your kids and teach them to enjoy life throughout all their ups and downs too.

Chapter 7

Three common stress disorders

Before applying the Mind TRACK to Happiness process it's important for me to go over a few common disorders associated with stress that might explain how you're feeling about motherhood. They are psychological stress, clinical depression and generalised anxiety disorder (GAD).

Psychological stress

According to the Fountainhead Method™, when talking about any type of stress, the Get Your Life Right Model of thinking is constantly affecting how you are feeling.

It's never the events that cause your stress; it's the beliefs you have about these events and what you believe these events mean about you (your self-worth).

Psychological stress is not simply about running late for work or something small that doesn't go as planned. While we can still feel stressed about these events and the GYLR Model of thinking is still kicking in, the psychological stress referred to in the Fountainhead Method™ applies to long-term stress or stress that has begun having an effect on other areas of your life. This kind of stress makes you feel as though you have come up against a block in your life that you can't get around.

With stress we assume that because an event has occurred, our life is on the wrong path (Point 1). 'Because my life is on the wrong path I am now missing out on something that my life needed'. (Point 2) Now the reasoning part of the brain kicks in and starts to rationalise that we should have done something differently (Point 3) and because of this we are worth-less, meaning our value has decreased. With psychological stress there is a core belief that the Anti-Depression Association of Australia (ADAA) has discovered and it is present in every case of psychological stress. It is:

Core belief = My Life has not gone to plan

Due to the events that have played out, the underlying belief that is causing your stress is: 'What I had hoped or what I had expected for my life is not going to plan and because of that I am worth-less'.

Case study 4: Melissa

Melissa was going into labour for the first time. It was in her birthing plan that she would have a completely natural birth and would deliver her baby in the company of her husband. She wanted them to share their first moments together with their new baby, bonding and breastfeeding as suggested in the books she had read on the best start for her baby.

Melissa had spent most of her pregnancy learning pain-management techniques using yoga, hypnotherapy and breathing – all to assist her with the labour and help her to avoid drugs. She had eaten very well and gone to a naturopath throughout the pregnancy to make sure that everything was set for a healthy pregnancy and labour.

At the end of the pregnancy, with only two days to go until the due date, Melissa went into labour. At the time her husband was at work and for some reason, he was unable to be contacted.

Her labour began quite quickly and intensely and after only about two hours, Melissa's contractions were getting quicker. She had managed to contact her husband, but he was three hours away on the other side of the city in peak-hour traffic.

During one of her routine checks, one of the midwives struggled to find the baby's heartbeat and began to get worried. She called the obstetrician in to take a look and he discovered that Melissa's baby had gone into distress and needed to be taken out by c-section immediately.

Not only was Melissa going to have drugs during her labour, which she did not want, she was now going to have an operation to get her baby out, and not have it the natural way, as she had hoped. Furthermore, her husband would not make it in time for the delivery. Due to further complications, Melissa had to be completely sedated, so she was not even awake for the birth of her son and her husband had still not arrived. Her labour was not going at all to plan.

Melissa felt she had let her baby down and that her little boy had missed out on the love and bonding and special quiet moments that were meant to happen after the birth (wrong path). He had been alone without her and without her husband to greet him into the world (missing out). She began to feel that she should have done something differently – perhaps she could have relaxed more because she was stressed that her husband hadn't yet arrived. She started to blame herself for not being able to do something to prevent the situation from happening like it did. Because her labour went so 'badly', Melissa felt that already she was a bad mother (worth-less), feeling that she couldn't even get the labour right.

All of this caused Melissa psychological stress because of her major belief: 'My life didn't go to plan'.

This situation would cause most people stress at the time and for many people, after a few days, they would come to terms with what had happened and be able to move forward with their lives.

Psychological stress

Beliefs created from: Peers, Education, Media, Family, Experiences, Observations, Parents — Learnt pain management techniques, Seeing naturopath and eating healthy, Completely prepared for natural birth and bonding ✓ ✓ ✓ ✗

Right path

Psych Stress — Early labour, Husband not here, C-section and drugs, Child was alone at birth ✗✗✗✗ Wrong path

Melissa's get your life right goal box for being a mum
* To be responsible for my child
* To protect and nurture my child
* To provide everything my child needs to have a happy and healthy life

SELF WORTH

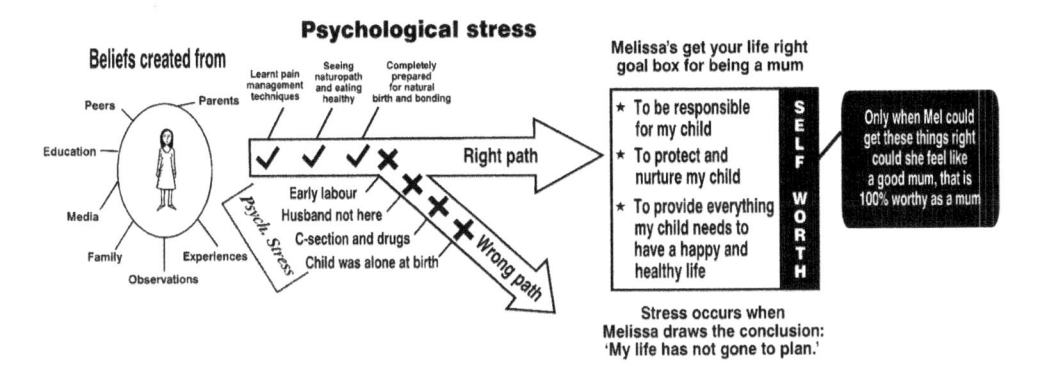

Only when Mel could get these things right could she feel like a good mum, that is 100% worthy as a mum

Stress occurs when Melissa draws the conclusion: 'My life has not gone to plan.'

However, what made this a major stress for Melissa was not being able to get past the fact that her plan did not go the way she had envisaged it would because of what she believed it meant about her as a mother (self-worth). Her stress was also caused by her belief about her baby's life – his life was now worthless because of how he entered the world. These beliefs became a block to being able to enjoy motherhood.

Melissa could not accept the fact that her little boy should have had a peaceful and loving entry into this world and now he was worse off because she couldn't get it right.

It began to affect other areas of her life because she now felt that it was difficult to bond with her son. She was already feeling like a bad mother, and felt that she had little to offer her son at this point, believing that she had failed him already.

Furthermore, it was also having its effects on her husband who couldn't understand why she was so upset when she had a perfectly healthy baby in her arms who had survived it all regardless of how different the labour was from her expectations.

However, what actually caused Melissa's psychological stress was not the labour itself. It was because Melissa already held certain beliefs that her birthing plan was the best way of bringing a baby into this world and that it was her responsibility to protect her son, nurture him and provide everything he needed to have a healthy and happy life. Because she couldn't give her son this beautiful start to life, she felt worth-less.

Melissa's psychological stress was all a result of the core belief that 'Life didn't go to plan, therefore I am worth-less (not a good enough mum)'.

In order to upgrade this belief, Melissa needs to apply the Personal Development Model:

1   Life is a journey.
2   I am always learning and receiving.
3   I can only know what I know at any given moment.
4   No matter how my life unfolds, I am always worthwhile.

The first upgrade – 'Life is a journey' – is the understanding that our lives are full of ups and downs and sometimes things don't go the way we had planned for them to go. This new belief is the major upgrade for people with psychological stress.

The reality is that Melissa was never going to be able to dictate how her labour would go. You can prepare for things and plan as much as you want; however, sometimes you can't predict how events will unfold.

The second upgrade – 'I am always learning and receiving' – is a reminder that from all events there is event learning and life learning.

For Melissa, the event learning was learning what actually happens during labour and the unpredictable possibilities that can occur during labour. Also, she might have learnt that there are things she could do differently when she has her next child.

The life learning for Melissa is the understanding and acceptance of the reality that life doesn't always go to plan and that this event does not determine her self-worth – that is, her value as a mum. It's simply an event within the journey of her life.

The third upgrade – 'I can only know what I know at any given moment' – teaches Melissa that the information that she knew at that time governed the choice that she made at that time.

She could not have done things any differently. All of the events leading up to the labour and how the labour played out could not have happened any other way due to all of the events that occurred leading up to the labour.

Finally, in the fourth upgrade – 'No matter how my life unfolds, I am always worthwhile' – we learn that Melissa's self-worth is not defined by the outcome of her labour and the beginning of her son's life. She is valuable because of the contribution she makes to life and the world around her. Her worth comes from the very fact that she is the mother who produced this child, and now she will be a huge contributor to that child's learning and development.

In addition, Melissa's son's life is no less worthwhile because of the way he entered the world. This was just one experience in his little journey so far and it has contributed to his development. He is still on his path, not the wrong one.

Clinical depression

Clinical depression and the effect that this has on a person's life can mean different things to different people. For some people it's quite severe so that they feel they can't function in life and can barely get out of bed. For others it can be that they have the ability to function on a day-to-day basis; however, in one or more areas they feel hopeless, useless and worth-less.

Current medicine describes depression as a chemical imbalance in the brain and while the ADAA does not dispute this physical change, it believes that in order for the chemical change to be present there must have been a particular kind of belief system or view of life that contributed to the eventual outcome of depression.

To understand how they could make a statement such as this you need to consider the mind–body connection and how the brain works.

Your brain is constantly receiving messages from its environment and responding accordingly. Consider what happens when you see a big, hairy spider crawling on the wall right next to you and what your reaction would be to that.

After viewing the spider with your senses your brain searches for the information it knows about spiders and the appropriate response according to what you believe about spiders. This response might mean that you run a mile, scream, maybe even cry; or it might be to get a container and take it outside, feeling only mildly freaked out.

This reaction was caused by the beliefs that you have about spiders, which were probably set up long before you ever came into contact with this spider, or maybe it was as a result of an experience with spiders in the past.

If your reaction was to freak out and feel afraid you would feel a very physical reaction to that spider which caused you to run, scream or cry. This physical response was caused not by the spider, but by what you believed about the spider. What you believed about the spider caused the physical sensation of fear in your body.

We already know that your belief systems have been developed through your experiences in life, your observations and what you have been taught to believe.

Your response to experiencing life events comes from your beliefs and creates a physical response somewhere in the body too. Close your eyes and think about another recent stressful event and feel where in your body you feel stress and you will literally feel the mind–body connection between what you are thinking and the physical sensation it creates.

It is often believed that depression is the result of something being wrong with a person – that something is broken because of this chemical imbalance in the brain. But what the ADAA has discovered and teaches by applying the Fountainhead Method™ is that a particular belief system is the underlying cause of this physical chemical change in the body.

The core belief behind depression sufferers is:

I am a failure. Why bother having any goals.

The Get Your Life Right Model of thinking still applies; that is, the feeling of being on the wrong path and therefore missing out on what we need in life and believing that things should have gone differently. All of this leads to the conclusion that we are worth-less. However, with depression the major belief is that 'because I am worth-less, I am a failure. I am failing at life. If I feel like a failure because I'm failing at life, then what does that do to me? It causes me pain. I don't want to feel pain. It hurts too much to live like a failure. So what do I do? I stop setting goals.

I stop setting goals in that area of my life because I am a failure in that area and it's too painful to keep failing and being worth-less'.

This can happen in one area of life or it can happen in all areas of life depending on the severity of the depression and what the sufferer has his or her self-worth attached to.

Let's go back to Melissa's situation.

Now that Melissa has experienced her life not going to plan and feels stressed, it's starting to affect her relationship with her son.

She has already begun to view her abilities as a mother as being less than what they should be.

> As Melissa continues along her journey and her new role of motherhood, she starts to learn how to breastfeed her son and at least try to give him the best start she can (since her labour plan couldn't provide that) by breastfeeding and giving him the nutrients that he needs for a healthy start to life (her beliefs).
>
> However, she finds that her son is not latching on, she is not quite getting the skill of breastfeeding and he is not gaining enough weight. Because she is producing a lot of milk and not able to feed, Melissa gets sick and discovers that she has mastitis.
>
> Due to sickness and not being able to feed despite countless efforts to get help and improve the situation, Melissa has no alternative but to give her son formula milk.
>
> None of this is making Melissa feel any better about her abilities as a mum and it is making her feel more and more worth-less.
>
> To top it all off, Melissa is coming across sleep challenges with her baby too. The feeding problems mean that he has not been sleeping well and she has not been able to get him into any sort of sleep routine whatsoever. Melissa is feeling tired and stressed and thinks that she is not being a very good mother (worth-less).
>
> She had so many ideas about parenting. Her beliefs that it is her responsibility to protect her son, nurture him and provide everything he needs to have a healthy and happy life

> are all attached to her self-worth. She now sees that life is not going to plan, that she is missing out on providing enough for her son, and that he is missing out on what he needs to be happy and healthy and she feels that she should be doing things differently.
>
> After this repetitive Get Your Life Right thinking, Melissa comes to the conclusion that she is a failure as a mother and for Melissa this is really painful. All she ever wanted was to be a good mum and provide the best for her child and now that has all gone out the window so she feels like a complete failure and has begun to feel severely depressed.
>
> She begins to think, 'Well, if I can't be a good mother, then my son is better off if I don't have much to do with him. She begins to detach as much as she can from her relationship with her son and her husband is forced to take time off work to look after him because she just can't bring herself to be the primary caretaker.
>
> The underlying belief causing Melissa's depression is 'why bother' setting goals in the area of motherhood. Melissa had her self-worth attached to her beliefs about how to be a good mother and now she feels that because her life has not gone as expected, she is a failure. Wanting to avoid pain is a primal instinct. In order to avoid the pain of failing as a mum Melissa stops trying to be a good mother. In fact, wherever possible she tries to avoid being a mother at all. In her mind her continual efforts to achieve this 'good mother' goal are a direct threat to her self-worth, so she gives up on setting goals to avoid the pain of feeling like a failure.

While Melissa's case is a severe case of depression it is common for mothers to feel like this to varying degrees, especially in the new days of motherhood.

Even as I write this I can see how events played out in my own life after the birth of my second son, which led me into a minor depression. I have literally experienced the feeling of being a failure as a mum because a series of events in the early stages of giving birth to my son did not go to plan.

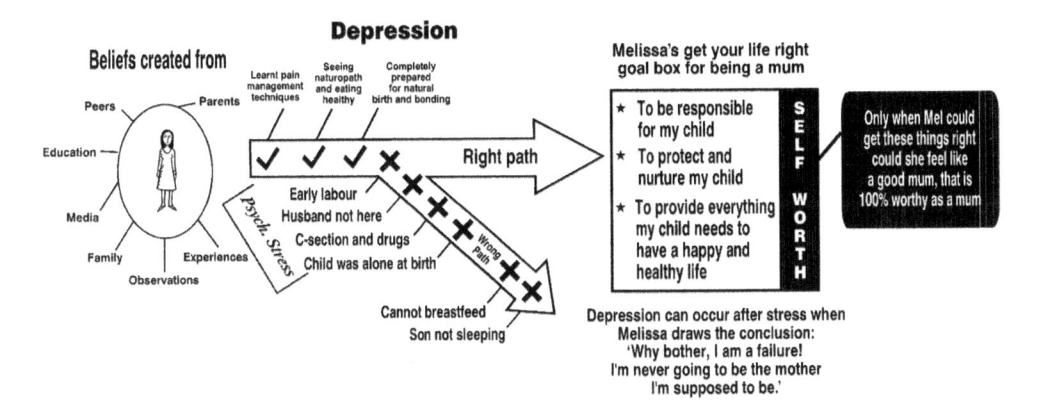

Depression

Beliefs created from

Peers, Parents, Education, Media, Family, Experiences, Observations

Learnt pain management techniques ✓
Seeing naturopath and eating healthy ✓
Completely prepared for natural birth and bonding ✓

Right path

Wrong Path — Psych Stress:
- Early labour
- Husband not here
- C-section and drugs
- Child was alone at birth
- Cannot breastfeed
- Son not sleeping

Melissa's get your life right goal box for being a mum

★ To be responsible for my child
★ To protect and nurture my child
★ To provide everything my child needs to have a happy and healthy life

SELF WORTH

Only when Mel could get these things right could she feel like a good mum, that is 100% worthy as a mum

Depression can occur after stress when Melissa draws the conclusion: 'Why bother, I am a failure! I'm never going to be the mother I'm supposed to be.'

Depression is caused not by events, but by the beliefs that we hold about the goals that we have and expect to achieve and because we believe that these expectations and goals determine our self-worth.

> We can upgrade the beliefs that cause depression by understanding the true purpose of setting goals, which we discussed in Chapter 3 where we discussed our aims.
>
> We will always want to set goals and achieve them, but we must be conscious of the reality that sometimes our goals don't come to fruition. However, there is value to be found in all experiences, and whether we achieve our goals or not, our self-worth does not change. What changes is our rating of ourselves, because we believe that what we are doing rates us as being less valuable than if we were doing it 'right'.

The experiences we have as mums, whether they are part of the picture we have in our minds or not, are a part of our journey through motherhood and it is the reality of motherhood that we don't always get it right. We are always learning new skills and abilities that are contributing to our knowledge of parenting. That's why the second child can often be easier – because we have learnt these skills.

Sometimes we don't learn these skills as quickly as we would like to, but that's okay. Sometimes it takes us longer than others to get a routine happening with our babies, or it takes longer for our children to learn appropriate behaviour than other children.

This is all part of the journey of parenting and is not reflective of being a good or bad parent.

It is important for depression sufferers to start setting goals again with the understanding that whether they achieve the goals or not, they are having life experiences that contribute to the knowledge and experience of life. The true purpose of having goals is to experience different events and to learn more about life.

The achievement of goals does not make you a good mum. Just being your child's mum makes you worthy and valuable to your child as you are always contributing the knowledge that you currently have and influencing your child's development in everything you do, not just when you get it right.

Generalised anxiety disorder (GAD)

Often when we think of someone with anxiety we relate this to having panic attacks. While this is certainly a form of anxiety, it is actually an extreme form of anxiety.

GAD is becoming more and more common in today's society and can easily be misdiagnosed as depression. However, depression and anxiety in terms of the Fountainhead Method™ are two separate disorders and are easily distinguishable.

As with psychological stress and depression, sufferers of GAD must have attained a particular way of thinking or perceiving life in order to become affected by it.

Again, just like the reaction with the spider, in GAD the brain is still working exactly the way that it is meant to be working – in accordance with the messages it is receiving about the environment around it, except a specific belief is dictating the physical reaction and the same belief will be prevalent in the anxiety sufferer all the time.

This core belief is:

**I must control and prevent –
I must control life so that it goes right and prevent so that it doesn't go wrong.**

With anxiety sufferers there is always Get Your Life Right thinking at play – thinking that life has the potential to go down the wrong path and if it does then they will be missing out and life will be less valuable. They believe that things should be done a certain way in order for life to go 'right'.

Due to their experiences and learning (usually already set up in childhood) the GAD sufferer has learnt that life can be controlled so that it goes to plan and so that their self-worth remains intact. Consequently, GAD sufferers are constantly on the lookout for anything that poses a threat to life going to plan and potentially threatening their self-worth, so that they can control events and ensure they go the way they want them to go.

Let's take a look at Melissa again. Let's say that after experiencing psychological stress, Melissa goes into anxiety instead of depression. Here's how Melissa might perceive these events if she were suffering from anxiety.

> So far we have heard that after the traumatic labour that Melissa endured, she came home to face even more challenges. Breastfeeding problems, having to give her baby formula milk, sleeping problems and getting mastitis have all made Melissa feel worth-less.
>
> She begins to view these events as a threat to motherhood going to plan. Her beliefs dictate that in order to be a 'good mum' (that is, worthy) it is her responsibility to protect her son, nurture him and provide everything he needs to have a healthy and happy life.
>
> Because Melissa views these events as a threat to life going to plan (that is, doing all the things that she needs to do to be a 'good mum'), she starts to feel out of control.
>
> Before having children Melissa was always able to control things to a certain degree and these few events have made her start to feel that things are going very badly and she is struggling to regain control of the situation. As a result she begins to feel panicky and worried all the time.
>
> She starts worrying that her son is not getting enough of what he needs or that she's not doing things well enough to provide what her son needs. She starts feeling that because of her, her little boy is missing out on what he needs and that she should be doing a better job for his benefit.

> Melissa starts to focus most of her attention on observing her son's behaviour for signs of sickness or for things that she needs to improve on so that his life will be better, and she puts extreme measures in place so that he is getting everything that he needs.
>
> She is making sure the house is completely quiet every time he goes to sleep and is irritable and anxious if anyone makes a noise or the phone rings. Melissa begins taking him to the child-health nurse more regularly or ringing child-health information lines to see whether there is something that she is doing wrongly and should be doing differently, and scouring the internet for ways to improve her son's development.
>
> Melissa's behaviour becomes consumed by her attempts to control her son's health and happiness and prevent anything 'bad' from happening to him.
>
> It's not the events that are causing Melissa's anxiety – it is the beliefs she has about those events and what they mean about her.
>
> She believes if she can just control her son's happiness and prevent anything from going 'wrong', then she will somehow become the good mother she's trying to be and her son will have the life he should be getting.

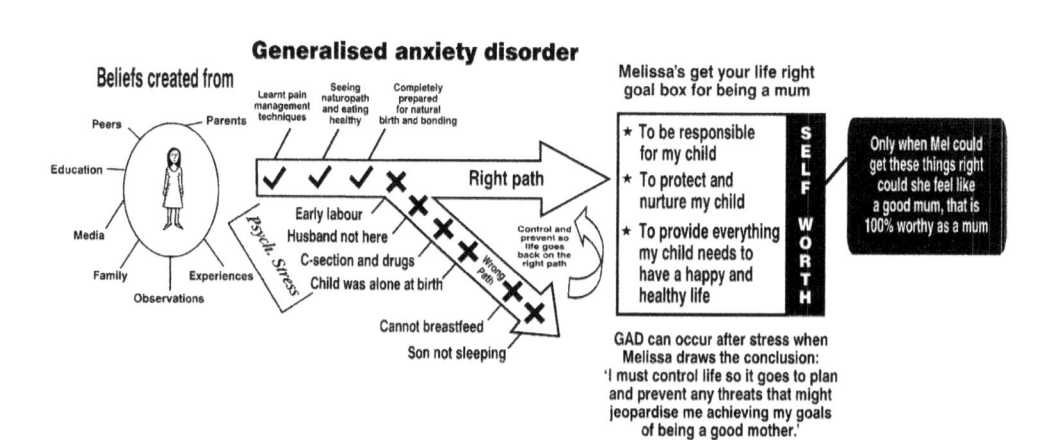

Generalised anxiety disorder

Beliefs created from: Peers, Education, Media, Family, Parents, Experiences, Observations

Learnt pain management techniques ✓
Seeing naturopath and eating healthy ✓
Completely prepared for natural birth and bonding ✓

Right path ✗

Psych. Stress — Early labour, Husband not here, C-section and drugs, Child was alone at birth, Cannot breastfeed, Son not sleeping — *Wrong Path*

Control and prevent so life goes back on the right path

Melissa's get your life right goal box for being a mum
* To be responsible for my child
* To protect and nurture my child
* To provide everything my child needs to have a happy and healthy life

→ SELF WORTH

Only when Mel could get these things right could she feel like a good mum, that is 100% worthy as a mum

GAD can occur after stress when Melissa draws the conclusion: 'I must control life so it goes to plan and prevent any threats that might jeopardise me achieving my goals of being a good mother.'

Anxiety can be quite a common disorder and it's little wonder why.

Look around at society and we are surrounded with evidence to support the theory that control and prevention works in our lives. Media campaigns are built on this undertone: 'Buy this product so you'll never be unhappy with your life again!'

What clearly distinguishes anxiety sufferers is that they are constantly on the lookout for any threats that could jeopardise their goals. They create many goals to control life so that things go 'right' and to prevent them from going 'wrong'.

The upgrade to the beliefs that cause anxiety is the understanding that life can't always be controlled and that when life doesn't go to plan it doesn't change how valuable your life is – it's just another experience in your life's journey.

Melissa needs to understand that she can't control her son's health and happiness every single moment. She can do what she knows how to do in terms of providing him with the care and nutrition that she believes will support his health, but she can't control how his body operates and how he lives his life. She can't control his emotions, his temperament or his behaviour and her self-worth is not defined by the outcome of his life.

> Melissa's self-worth is defined by her existence and her son's self-worth is defined by his existence. Both of them are in this world learning and growing as human beings, experiencing their lives and interacting with those around them, thereby contributing to their lives.
>
> It is instinctive for mums to want to protect their children from harm or from experiencing pain, but what we must be conscious of is that they are on their own journeys to. Within that journey they will experience ups and downs in life, just as we do and we cannot control how their life unfolds. They have to learn and grow too and they will do this through their own adventures and adversities. Of course, we need to protect them in certain ways, but we must also learn to let go sometimes. Their lives are no less valuable or worthy when they experience hardships and we must help them to search for the value in these moments too so that they can learn to handle the ups and downs of their lives.

The reality of life is that it is full of both enjoyable and unenjoyable experiences and none of these experiences make us more worthy, nor do they make us less worthy. They are simply experiences that we have in life and are opportunities to learn and grow from.

We need to understand that we can't always control the outcome of events and we can't always control life so that it goes the way we want it to. The point of creating goals is to achieve them – of course – or we wouldn't make them in the first place, but sometimes they don't come to fruition, and that's just the reality of life.

Clinical depression and generalised anxiety disorder (GAD)

Some medical specialists are diagnosing that depression and anxiety are the same. However, the ADAA has identified that these are two separate disorders with two very distinguishable belief systems underlying them.

Depression sufferers usually have their attention in the past. They believe that something went wrong that led to them missing out, and that they should have done better and therefore are worth-less and failures because of it. They believe they are failing at life. With depression there is an absence of goals in one or more areas of life.

Anxiety sufferers usually have their attention in the future: controlling life so that it goes right and preventing life from going wrong so that they don't miss out; feeling that they should be able to do this or that to prevent and control things. They are constantly on the lookout for any potential threats that could jeopardise their goals and consequently their self-worth. With GAD there are lots of goals – many goals and back-up plans are created to make life go to plan.

Often people can move in and out of depression and anxiety from moment to moment. Depression sufferers can move out of depression by setting a new goal and then becoming anxious about that goal coming to fruition. If the goal doesn't come to fruition, they can go straight back into depression again.

Some people begin with anxiety – trying to control and prevent circumstances so that life stays on the 'right' path. However, when life goes 'wrong' because they haven't been able to control it, they can spiral into depression. They feel that their lives have become less valuable (worth-less) and that they are failures, so they stop setting goals. This can become a vicious cycle.

However, the fundamentals of anxiety and depression are the same. All of the GYLR Model of thinking will be prevalent and all of the upgrades need to be applied, with a specific focus on the beliefs about self-worth and why their worth is still intact, regardless of how life unfolds.

The Anti-Depression Association of Australia (ADAA)

The Mind TRACK to Happiness process was created to give you a process to follow that will help you handle the challenges that mums face in their day-to-day life with a healthy mindset and a solution-focussed approach – all with the intention of reducing stress among mums.

I have used the Fountainhead Method™ within the Mind TRACK to Happiness process in Steps 1 and 2 in order to help you to identify the conflict between thoughts (GYLR thinking) and reality (Personal Development Model) and to illustrate how the conflict between the two – not the actual events – is the cause of all stress (such as a child not sleeping, or tantrums).

I must re-clarify that while the GYLR model is always being played out in any form of stress or stress-related disorder, there are specific belief structures, as I've just discussed briefly, that are responsible for major stress, clinical depression and generalised anxiety disorder.

In order to understand your own life and how these disorders may have become predominant in your life, further in-depth exploration and investigation about your life and your experiences is required. This will help you to understand how your beliefs have contributed to these disorders.

It would take more than one book to explore The Fountainhead Method™ more deeply so I have included only the basics in this book.

The Anti-Depression Association of Australia (ADAA) runs courses and retreat programs that give the in-depth help that you may need in order to thoroughly apply this method to your life; change how you view your life and your self-worth; and cure yourself of major stress, depression and anxiety.

With this in mind, I recommend that if you do suffer from any of these stress-related disorders you should contact the ADAA and discuss your options for getting this training so that you can apply this method more specifically to your condition and stop having to live with feeling severely stressed, depressed or anxious.

The ADAA's contact details can be found at www.adaa.org.au.

PART B

Applying the Mind TRACK to Happiness process to your life

Chapter 8

Introduction to Part B

From here the approach of this book changes to the application of the Mind TRACK to Happiness process. It's time to hand this process over to you and start applying it to your life.

As we saw on page 18, TRACK is a five-step acronym that stands for:

Thoughts:	What am I thinking about this situation?
Reality:	What is the reality that my thoughts are in conflict with?
Aim:	What do I want to achieve?
Choices:	What are my choices, options and solutions?
Know your plan and action it:	How am I going to get what I want?

You can read this part of the book in consecutive order if you like, or you can just turn to the area that is an issue for you right now and start there. Each area stands alone and applies to an area of motherhood that you might be struggling with or need a little help with. I have designed it this way so that you can get the help you need without having to read the entire book, as I know time is limited for mums.

The areas covered are:
- Behavioural and developmental challenges (Chapter 9)
- Anger and guilt (Chapter 10)
- Loss of identity (Chapter 11)
- Time out (Chapter 12)
- Relationships: You and your partner (Chapter 13).

All five steps of the Mind TRACK to Happiness process are applied to each of the above areas.

There are interactive exercises that you can do to promote thinking and questioning in order to apply the process to your own life. You will also find many different examples of how each part of the process can be applied, so it might be useful to dedicate a notebook to use specifically for this process.

It's time to start making the changes to your life and to begin retraining your brain to approach life with acceptance, embracing all life's challenges and becoming the Happy Mum you want to be.

Chapter 9

Behavioural and developmental challenges

Dealing with the forever-changing developmental stages of a child is possibly one of the hardest challenges that we face in our lives, and certainly in parenthood.

Looking after your own needs can be hard enough, but looking after the needs of a child and having the responsibility of raising and influencing another human being is a momentous undertaking.

What I have learnt about myself over the past five years of being a mum has been more than I've learnt over the past ten years put together. As I said in the opening chapter, I discovered that I was not one of those mothers who was naturally patient when it came to the challenges of parenting. I have had to learn and retrain myself to continually observe my thinking and consciously change my thoughts and actions in order to accept the reality of my new role and work my way out of mild depression and anxiety. This new way of thinking is currently an ongoing undertaking for me.

The challenging behaviours of our little ones bring out the best in us, but they can also bring out the worst in us. Our intentions are pure, but sometimes our behaviour goes astray among the confronting personal issues that can arise from becoming a parent.

We desperately want to do a great job with our kids so that they can grow up to be healthy, moral, polite, happy adults, but sometimes our parenting is a far cry from how we'd like it to be.

For me, this roller coaster of wanting to do the 'right' thing and then having to deal with my reactions and behaviour – which I felt were the 'wrong' thing – caused me a lot of stress and disappointment. The feeling of ruining my children's lives was always looming over my head and I felt under constant pressure to do things correctly, so that they would be raised the 'right' way.

This pressure is exactly what needs to change in order for you to raise happy children and be a Happy Mum. This pressure to get it right will actually lead you to teaching your kids a lot more of what you *don't* want them to believe than you may realise.

The theme of this book has been to change your viewpoint from trying to get life right, to seeing the reality of life; that is, there are always ups and downs and we are always learning and growing from our experiences and adding to our current knowledge of life. Sometimes – yes – we make mistakes, but that's the beauty of learning. How do we learn how to do something if we don't learn how *not* to do something? Whether that means learning from someone else or through your own trial and error, this is how you learn.

Before we look into some specific examples of how to use the Mind TRACK to Happiness process in regard to the behavioural and developmental challenges we come across, there are a few points I'd like to make.

It's okay to be human

If you want to raise happy and healthy-minded kids, you must first be happy and healthy-minded yourself. To become this, you must first understand that life isn't about getting it right. It's about learning and growing as a person and experiencing a variety of life events.

It's okay that you aren't perfect in your journey through life and you have to show your kids that you aren't perfect so that they know that they don't have to be either. The truth is that we don't know everything and we are always learning new things, so be honest about that with your kids and admit when you're wrong. Apologise for losing the plot and explain what made you react the way you did. Tell them how your thoughts were in conflict with reality (in children's terms, of course). Tell them that it's okay to learn from your mistakes and that sometimes these are the best lessons that you can get. You'll be surprised how much they 'get it', and even more surprised when they start repeating this stuff back to you as my five year old is starting to.

If your child is only a baby, then learn to become accepting of your humanism, and when you do lose the plot use the methods taught in this book to understand the beliefs that drove you to lose the plot – and then move past it.

Learn to accept the reality of what happened in past situations and to not dwell on the past. Every moment that you don't get what you want is a teachable moment – a time to learn from – not a time to regret, self-criticise or judge others.

When you accept the reality that life is full of ups and downs and really appreciate the downs in life as valuable learning you will be better able to pass that knowledge on to your children. They will see this in your behaviour, your attitudes and your emotions. They will learn this from their experience of you.

You are only human and they are only human too and we all have days when we feel uncooperative and want to be left alone. Think about how you sometimes feel. Don't you sometimes feel tired, cranky, like not wanting to conform to the rules, like wanting to slacken off, lazy, like not following procedures, like getting angry, like a failure, like acting irrationally, like not bothering, or do you have similar feelings to these?

It's important to allow room for you and your children to feel this way sometimes too, recognising that it's the perceptions and view of events that cause us to feel this way. We all experience events that are enjoyable and ones that are not so enjoyable. We all experience events that motivate us or make us feel that we couldn't really be bothered dealing with them. This is the reality in everyone's life, including yours and your child's.

Even if your child is a baby, he or she is still behaving the way he or she does because of his or her perception of the situation. 'I am hungry. I am tired. I have pains in my tummy (reflux). I want to crawl and I can't. I want to walk and I can't. I'm frustrated because I want your attention.'

Even though children can't always articulate why they feel the way they do, it is something very real for them and they feel no differently from how you sometimes feel.

By looking at your children's behaviour in this way it's easier to feel more compassionate about what's happening for them. They are not behaving this way because of anything you are doing correctly or incorrectly. They are behaving this way because there is something going on within them – because they think and feel just as you do and it's normal to feel discontent at times. Their brains are functioning the exact same way that yours does and it's not a reflection of your capabilities.

It's okay for you to be human and make mistakes. This is how you learn and grow and when you make it okay for you, then you make it okay for your children. Life's not about getting everything right, and this is an important message to get through to your children, both through your words and through your behaviour and reactions to their behaviour.

You are their teacher of life

The mindset to take on as the mother of your children is that of a teacher of life. You are teaching them how to function in life, become individuals and learn reasoning and decision-making skills so that they can use them independently as they grow up. The very best way to do this is by example.

Remember, we are born with limited brain function and our beliefs, thoughts, habits, personality (and so on) are formed in response to our surroundings. You are literally writing on the slate of who your children will be. Of course, they will have other influences in their lives, but you are a primary one and you can be a major contributor to the healthy mindset of your children just by learning to understand and accept the reality of life and passing it onto them.

More so when children reach one year of age and onwards and start becoming more independent, wilful and aware of their surroundings, the behavioural challenges increase and it is easy to feel as though you are on a battle ground with your children. It can feel as though you are fighting a lost battle and that you are not respected, not appreciated and forever repeating yourself.

You can change this mindset by reminding yourself that whatever this behaviour is, it is not naughty behaviour; it's learning behaviour.

Their brains come into this world with only structure and limited function, and no knowledge of how to behave or function past their abilities to eat, sleep, breathe and stay alive.

They are learning the rest through experience. Whatever behaviour they are displaying is all part of the learning process. How do children learn? Through repetition and consistent exposure to their environments.

If you are having to repeat yourself and witness the same behaviour from your child over and over (even though you've told him or her a million times not to do something), it's because this is how your child is learning how to behave. He or she is literally growing and strengthening connections between neurons, which are creating his or her behavioural patterns, habits and personality.

Over time children learn what's required and respond appropriately according to how they've learnt to respond. It slowly becomes their habit. This is why experts and friends always say that however you discipline your children, you need to be consistent. Show them the same consequences for their behaviours over and over again and you will be teaching them how to behave. Show them the same reactions to their behaviours (desirable or not) and they are likely to learn that this is the appropriate response to have to similar events.

If children are getting mixed messages about how to behave then you will get a variety of results. If you want your children to behave in a certain way, you must teach them a certain way, over and over again. This happens whether you are teaching them how to sleep, how to use a spoon, how to play by themselves, how to treat you and others, how to be gentle or how to be respectful. Look at everything they already know and ask yourself how they learnt that (through consistency and repetition).

We need to stop viewing these behavioural and developmental stages as battles and start seeing them as the natural process of learning. All of their undesirable behaviours are teachable moments – opportunities to reinforce lessons in life in order to cement this information into their long-term memory.

Their behaviour doesn't determine your self-worth

Sometimes it can be easy to think that your children's behaviours or developmental stages mean something bad about you ('I'm a bad mum') or that they negatively affect your life in some way (that is, make your life worth-less). For example: 'I feel like they are doing this to me'. We often attach our self-worth to the behaviour of our children: 'When my child does "x", then I am a good mum'.

Apart from the inaccurate belief about self-worth there are two other valid points to consider about your children's behaviour.
- It's not within your control. If you have your self-worth (being a good mum) attached to their behaviour then it becomes random that you will feel like a worthy mum because you are relying on your children 'getting it right',

but the reality is that they aren't always going to. No one ever does. They are learning and growing too.
- Their behaviours are a natural process of learning how to live in this world and during this learning process they won't always behave the way you want them to.

Whatever your children's behaviour is at any developmental stage of their lives, it's not a reflection of your self-worth.

Here are some examples of assumptions that we sometimes make and how we attach our children's behaviour to our self-worth.

1. 'My child is always whingeing at me.'
2. 'Those tantrums are making me so angry.'
3. 'I can't believe he speaks to me this way. He has no respect for me after all that I do for him.'
4. 'I can't breastfeed; therefore I'm not a good mother.'
5. 'She's constantly clinging to me, so I never get any time out.'

These statements all revolve around the same undertone that because my children are doing 'x' this means 'y' about me or my life.

Your children are simply learning to exist in the world. Whatever they are doing, they are not doing *to* you; they are simply trialling ways to experience life and are waiting to be taught what is appropriate, moral, respectful, polite – or whatever other qualities you might like to teach them. If you have babies who can't speak yet, they are simply trying to find ways to communicate their wants and needs to you.

Any thoughts in conflict with this reality are bound to cause you stress. Children are learning and growing and *any* behavioural or developmental challenges that you face are the reality of the experiences you will encounter as a parent and are always opportunities for you to implement your teaching role and help them to learn about life.

One more thing to remember is what actually drives behaviour. Children's priorities in each moment are governed by their beliefs. Look at why your children are behaving the way they are and what beliefs are driving their behaviour. What you will find is that it's *not* about you – it's all about them.

Let's look at each of the five statements in terms of reality and why they don't mean anything about you.
1. 'My child is always whingeing at me.' Whingeing happens because children feel they have a reason to whinge. There is something going on that they want addressed. That is their priority in that moment. They aren't doing it to annoy you or hurt you; they are doing it purely for reasons that are important to them and it doesn't mean anything about your self-worth. The stress you feel over the whingeing comes from the story you tell yourself about the whingeing and how that is affecting you or your life right now – *not* from the behaviour itself.
2. 'Those tantrums are making me so angry.' Tantrums are a natural way for children to trial getting what they want and sometimes it works for them if they are not taught otherwise. It is not their tantrums that are causing you to feel angry. Your thoughts and what you believe the tantrums mean *about you* or your life are what's causing your anger. The beliefs behind the emotion of anger are also aligned with Point 3 on the GYLR Model ('should/could'; see page 190). You believe that something should be happening differently: either you should be doing something or your children should be doing something differently. At this time, we need to remember the upgrade that 'we only know what we know at any given moment', and an understanding of what drives our behaviour.
Once again, tantrums are yet another teachable moment for you to reinforce appropriate behaviour.
3. 'I can't believe he speaks to me this way. He has no respect for me after all that I do for him.' Again, the way your child speaks to you is because a) he is testing the waters to see if he can get away with it, or b) he's already learnt from prior experiences that he can get away with it. It's learning behaviour, not naughty behaviour, and it's not a reflection of what he thinks about you.
It is true, however, that you teach people how to treat you. Respect is taught to those around you and you need to have

self-respect in order to teach it, otherwise you inadvertently teach your children to disrespect you. You need to expect a level of treatment and consistently reinforce consequences for them if they treat you in a disrespectful way so that they can learn to respect you.

Incidentally, their behaviour has nothing to do with 'all that you've done for them': they would rarely even give that a consideration, if at all. Don't expect them to respect you for anything that you do. They will show respect when they have learnt how to behave in a respectful way.

4. 'I can't breastfeed; therefore I'm not a good mother.' Being able to breastfeed has nothing to do with you being a good or bad mother. It's either a choice, or circumstantial whether you do or you don't. You either decide that you don't want to, or you find that you can't for whatever reason. That's it. It doesn't mean anything about you or how good a mother you are. It's just another event that is part of your whole life and is only a small portion of what you will contribute to your child's life.

5. 'She's constantly clinging to me, so I never get any time out.' Although this might be a reality in terms of her behaviour limiting your ability to take time out, it doesn't mean that your life is of less value. Another viewpoint to consider is that this is simply another teachable moment and you are in the role of that teacher. Her behaviour is working for her for reasons that are valid to her, and here is another opportunity for you to identify these reasons and learn ways to teach her independence.

Teaching your children to be independent and happy – by themselves, away from you – can be a tremendous life lesson for them.

It is easy to take your children's behaviour personally, but by viewing their behaviour as a teachable moment where you and they are learning, your perspective changes and the stress you feel is lessened. You are no longer in conflict with reality because you can recognise that their behaviour is developmental, not a deliberate implication of you or your life's worth. You, in these moments, are the teacher of these children. This is part of who you are and the current contribution you are making to their lives.

Another important point to understand is that sometimes our children learn lessons straight away, but sometimes learning takes place over an immeasurable length of time – and not only because you've said something one time, or 100 times. It happens when the connections between neurons have been strengthened enough for the information to become a habitual response. All we can do is continue to find opportunities to keep reinforcing these lessons until they become their habitual responses as a result of repetition and maturity. To make it easier, remind yourself that with each attempt to reinforce these lessons, you are one step closer to making this their habit. Until then, lots of mummy breaks are needed when you notice that your self-talk is going downhill fast!

We can't control how quickly children develop, retain information or even whether they are going to take on what we are trying to teach them because the reality is that we are not the only ones influencing and teaching them about life. Sometimes they get mixed messages from other sources that contribute to their behaviour too, and it might take longer for our message to be their primary belief or perhaps our message won't get through at all.

We can only ever assist our children by observing their behaviour and by checking their choice of words for incorrect perceptions that might be driving their behaviour, and keep repeating and showing them appropriate behaviours and responses until they 'get it'.

Just keep reminding yourself that your self-worth is not tied up in their behaviour and their achievements and that all of their behaviour is developmental and they will soon pass through this developmental phase.

The first five years of challenges

Developmental challenges start from the second your children are born and you are completely thrown into unknown territory where new skills have to be learnt.

From zero to six months the challenges are usually sleeping and feeding routines; handling the transition into your demanding new role; getting to know your new baby; organising your life; and adjusting to the physical, emotional and mental changes that are occurring within you.

From 7 to 12 months, things are usually starting to settle down in the sleep department or are hitting a point where finding the solution to sleep problems becomes a top priority.

Teething, solids and 'is my baby doing everything he (or she) should be doing'-type challenges are met.

At 12 to 24 months behavioural challenges start to present themselves. Walking, talking, independent-minded children emerge and you begin to teach them how to live in the world and what is appropriate and not appropriate behaviour.

From two to five years of age, behavioural challenges are at their peak, with tantrums, backchat, attitude, emotional confusion and the battle of wills at the forefront, which can sometimes be just as stressful as the early days of having your baby.

Regardless of how diverse these challenges are, one thing will get you through this time with your sanity and your happiness intact, and that's a healthy mindset. Applying the Mind TRACK to Happiness process will ensure that you have a healthy mindset during this time.

On the following pages I have broken the process down into the five steps (TRACK) using two examples of mums applying this process.

If a particular area is causing you stress at the moment, you can work through the process by using the exercises given at the end of the step that relates to your area of stress to help you learn how to create a healthy mindset.

Just to refresh your memory, the five steps of the Mind TRACK to Happiness process are:
1. **T**houghts
2. **R**eality
3. **A**im
4. **C**hoices
5. **K**now your plan and action it.

Steps 1 (Thoughts) and 2 (Reality)

Steps 1 and 2 go hand in hand. Firstly, there are the *thoughts* (which create stress) and secondly there is the *reality* (which your thoughts are in conflict with).

Step 1 is actually identifying the cause of your stress and Step 2 is the alignment with reality that will take you to a place of acceptance where you are then able to move towards planning what you want.

Sometimes Steps 1 and 2 are the only steps that you need to complete in order to change how you feel about a situation. Once you can recognise the conflict between your beliefs and reality then you might feel that you can continue on without necessarily having to set goals. This understanding between Step 1 and Step 2 might be the simple answer needed to release your stress. For this very reason, I have joined Steps 1 and 2 together.

If you are feeling stressed by a situation, you now know that your thinking is on the Get Your Life Right Model and your beliefs and perceptions about the situation are what is causing you the stress – *not* the events themselves.

Just like the example I gave you of when I was 'just trying to get the dishes done', thoughts and the story that you have in your mind about the event can spiral out of control, causing you to feel useless, like a failure and incompetent – that is, worth-less.

Our thoughts can get stuck in what we are doing 'wrong' – that because I'm not doing it the 'right' way, my children are 'missing out' on something that they need or I'm 'missing out' on what I need. We reason that we 'should' be doing something differently – that somehow, we 'should' know the 'right' way to go about things in order to get the results we 'should' be getting, and all this must mean that 'I'm not doing the best thing by my children and that makes me a bad mother', or 'My life is now less worthwhile because I'm experiencing this event in this way'.

Thoughts to this effect can easily lead you down the path towards stress, depression and anxiety, as these events are not aligned with your desire to be a good mother and fulfil all of the expectations you had as a parent.

The reality of being a new parent is that you are simply learning new skills. You've never been a parent of this particular child before and we can't always know what you need to do. This is something that you will figure out and learn over time.

Understand that this parenting stage of life is a new thing that we have to learn. It's common for mums to think that they should instinctively know how to handle some of the challenges of parenting. However, this information is *not* just sitting inside us waiting to be accessed. If you don't know how to do something then you don't know how to do something (reality) and the only way that you will know is to learn how.

This goes for every single aspect of parenting and your life. Sometimes we don't have the answers and have to go searching for them.

Let's look at an example of how to use Steps 1 and 2 for behavioural and developmental challenges.

Case study 5: Rebecca

Rebecca has a five-month-old baby girl, Alanah, and she is having a lot of trouble getting her into a sleep routine. She gets up to her every two hours during the night, and during the day Alanah's sleep is erratic and unpredictable.

Rebecca is tired and feeling like a failure. All her friends' babies seem to be sleeping okay and all the different advice Rebecca has been getting has the same undertone that she is doing something wrongly and her baby should be in a sleep routine by now. Rebecca has been trying to notice her own thoughts about this situation and this is the self-talk that she has observed:

'There must be something wrong with me. I just can't get Alanah to go to sleep. Everyone else has got it right, but not me. I must be doing something wrong. I know that all babies are different, but I should be able to instinctively know what's happening with my baby and help her. She needs to sleep so that she can be a happier baby. I need to sleep so that I can be a better mum. How can I ever be a good mum if I'm tired and cranky from lack of sleep? I thought I was doing so well up to now, but maybe I'm just not a very good mother.'

Chapter 9: Behavioural and developmental challenges **113**

Now go back over Rebecca's self-talk and see if you can point out the Get Your Life Right points in it, which are:
1. Wrong path/right path
2. Missing out (on what my life needs)
3. Should/could
4. Worth-less

Practise identifying these points yourself before you read on so that you can get better at recognising them in your own self-talk.

The first point that stands out to me in Rebecca's self-talk is 'wrong path/right path'. Rebecca feels as though she is doing something the wrong way because she is comparing herself to her friends, whose babies are all in a sleep routine.

Because Rebecca now thinks she's doing it 'wrong' she also thinks that her baby is now missing out (on a good mother and on sleep). Furthermore, Rebecca feels that she is missing out on the opportunity to be a good mother because she feels tired and cranky all the time and, of course, is missing out on sleep.

Now that she is doing it 'wrong' and therefore she and her baby are 'missing out', her reasoning kicks in and she starts to think about her own decisions and behaviour. She starts to reason that she should be doing something differently – that instinctively she should know what to do. These first three points have all led her to the conclusion that she has come to; that is, that she is not a very good mum (Point 4: worth-less).

Rebecca's self-talk can be categorised into the following GYLR points:

Wrong path/right path

'There must be something wrong with me. I just can't get Alanah to go to sleep. Everyone else has got it right, but not me. I must be doing something wrong.'

Missing out

'She needs to sleep so that she can be a happier baby. I need to sleep so that I can be a better mum. How can I ever be a good mum if I'm tired and cranky from lack of sleep?'

Should/could

'I know that all babies are different, but I should be able to instinctively know what's happening with my baby and help her.'

I am worth-less

'I thought I was doing so well up to now, but maybe I'm just not a very good mother.'

Now, let's have a look at Step 2: the reality of the situation. Now that Rebecca has identified the thoughts that were creating her stress and how she had perceived the lack of a sleep routine to mean that she is not a good mother, she now needs to accept the reality of the situation and then upgrade the beliefs that are causing her stress by aligning them with the Personal Development Model.

Regardless of how she got to this point, her current situation is that Rebecca is in need of some sleep and her baby is not getting enough sleep, which is affecting her and her baby's temperaments. This is the reality of Rebecca's current situation and thinking that it shouldn't be this way and that she should be experiencing it differently, are thoughts that are in conflict with this reality, and this is what is causing her stress.

Rebecca's thoughts, which are in conflict with reality and making her feel worth-less, can be upgraded using the Personal Development Model.

The four points on the Personal Development Model are each upgrades to the four points on the Get Your Life Right Model. These points are:
1. Life is a journey. (The reality of life is that it is full of ups and downs.)
2. You are always learning and receiving.
3. You can only know what you know at any given moment.
4. No matter how your life unfolds, you are always worthwhile.

Let's look at how Rebecca can use this model to upgrade her beliefs about the Alanah's sleep routine.

Life is a journey

The reality of life is that it is full of ups and downs. This also applies to the journey of parenting. Sometimes raising children doesn't go according to our plans and sometimes things are more challenging then we expected them to be.

The reality of having a new baby is that there are going to be times when you have got it all figured out relatively quickly (ups) and there are going to be times where you have no idea what to do (downs).

There is nothing wrong with Rebecca; she is simply experiencing an event that she has never experienced before – a new experience – and she is simply learning how to handle this experience. We are talking about raising another human being who has his or her own behavioural response. We can't expect that we will always know what's happening for him or her or that we straight away know how to deal with it. You have to expect that there are going to be challenges in parenting that require time and learning to get through. These challenges don't make something wrong; they are simply the reality of being a parent.

You are always learning and receiving

Throughout life, you are always receiving new information and experiencing events that you can learn from, and you are always learning about your children, about yourself and about how to be a parent.

While the reality is that Rebecca is missing out on some sleep, there is value in every moment she experiences and this is because of the learning and receiving in every moment. Rebecca is learning what doesn't work for Alanah by trying different things to get her baby to sleep, and she is receiving more information about her baby's unique personality, which she is still getting to know.

Rebecca needs to shift her viewpoint from missing out on sleep to seeing that she is already learning and receiving what she needs in order to get more sleep: she is learning about her baby's needs and cries and using the process of elimination to work out what's happening and what needs to change.

There is always value in every moment, and in order to shift Rebecca's mindset from thinking that this sleep challenge is 'wrong' and that she is 'missing out', she needs to find the value of the situation by seeing all of its benefits. If she never experienced this situation, she would never gain the information that is now adding to her knowledge about parenting.

You can only know what you know at any given moment

What drives our decisions, behaviours and how we handle life is our beliefs. In any given situation our senses observe a situation and the brain processes an event based on what we already know and then determines what the appropriate response is (our behaviour).

How Rebecca is currently handling this situation is governed by what she currently knows, which has come from all of the experiences in her life leading up to this one.

She has never had this particular child in her life before and does not always know what is needed in every situation. She can only ever draw on the information that she has learnt up until this point in time, so she can't know any differently until she learns differently; therefore she can't know to behave differently.

Rebecca thinks that she should instinctively be able to get Alanah to sleep. However, Rebecca can't miraculously access information on how to do this because it's simply not in her brain to access. She hasn't learnt this yet.

Hindsight is a wonderful thing, but what gives us hindsight? Having learnt new information from our experiences. That's why there is value in this event, as it is giving Rebecca more information about parenting and about her baby's needs, which adds to her knowledge of parenting and which she might use in the future with subsequent children or by passing the knowledge onto someone else with a new baby.

By the time Alanah is five months old, Rebecca will have already tried many different ways of getting her to sleep and now she knows what doesn't work. What she does next time will be with that knowledge in mind as she tries something else.

No matter how your life unfolds, you are always worthwhile

The fact that Alanah does not have a sleep routine does not make Rebecca a bad mother – it simply means that her child is not sleeping well, and that's it. Rebecca's worth doesn't change. Her worth always stays 100-per-cent intact.

What changes is her self-esteem, her rating of herself, and this is learnt. Rebecca has beliefs about getting parenting right and about what constitutes being a good mother. In her mind her self-worth has dropped, but actually her rating of herself is what is making her feel bad. If she behaves differently from what she believes is the right way, her rating of herself decreases. Her worth hasn't changed – her rating of herself has.

Rebecca's self-worth is still 100 per cent because it comes from her very existence. The mere fact that she has shown up in life to be this child's parent, to be learning what she's learning and to be giving to her child the experiences she is giving her is what makes her worthwhile.

The learning that Rebecca is receiving right now is contributing to the eventual outcome of getting her baby into a sleep routine, or will lead her to seek outside help in this area, meet other people and learn a different way of dealing with the situation.

Through meeting other people or just figuring out how to do it herself, her experience and interactions will go on to contribute to the lives of others and their learning and experiences. She will talk about her experiences with other people and thereby add to their knowledge, which will influence the people around them, and so on.

Every experience that Rebecca has leads to the next one and they all contribute to the interactions, learning and experiences of other people. Whatever is happening in Rebecca's life, the very fact that she is existing in this world and contributing to both her and other people's lives is what makes her worthy.

Although this example was primarily about getting a baby to sleep, the reality remains the same for every experience you come across.

Life will not always go to plan. There will be days when you have got it all figured out and there will be days when you are clueless as to what is happening. There has to be an acceptance of this reality in order to have a healthy mindset.

All of life's experiences are teachable moments, particularly those times when life isn't going the way we would like. In our achievement-based world we have been taught that we need to be achieving and getting it all right in order for our life to be travelling well, but what we haven't been taught, or what hasn't been widely acknowledged, is that throughout the times when we aren't achieving and life isn't going the 'right' way, we are always learning valuable lessons about our lives from those very 'wrong' experiences.

In parenting, it's too easy to view challenges as being wrong or believing that they shouldn't be happening. However, these are the very times when we are adding to our knowledge of parenting and of life, which makes up who we currently are.

When we can learn to look at challenges as being just as valuable as life going right, we can pass this viewpoint on to our children. With this kind of mindset being taught to our children we are changing the next generation and the way a society thinks. It's that important!

Let's look at one more example of a mum feeling stressed by a situation involving her child.

Case study 6: Karen

Karen is the mum of a spirited boy named Jeremy. Jeremy is nearly four years old and is constantly on the go and constantly challenging Karen's sanity. Here is Karen's current perception of this situation.

'I can't handle this boy anymore. Sometimes he's such a good boy, doing everything that I ask him to, listening to me, is affectionate, loving and considerate, but most of the time he is rude, obnoxious and out of control. If we don't do things "his" way, he will yell, scream, kick, slam doors and generally make life very difficult. We are always butting heads and I have tried so many different discipline techniques, but they don't work. I don't know where I'm going so wrong. I feel like I've tried everything and nothing works. I'm just not enjoying him at the moment either. I love him dearly, but I can't help but feel like I want to be away from him as much as I can to get a break and that makes me feel so guilty. He's nearly four now and he knows the rules. He should be starting to come out of this now, right? He should be starting to know the difference between right and wrong, shouldn't he. All I ever seem to do is yell at him and smack him when I've finally lost the plot. I feel like such a bad mum when I do this and I feel helpless, like I don't know what else to do. He's wearing me down and I just want to stop him from behaving this way and making me feel like this.'

First of all, see whether you can highlight the Get Your Life Right points in Karen's story before you look below.

Again, they are:
1. Wrong path/right path
2. Missing out
3. Should/could
4. Worth-less

Step 1 (Thoughts)

Wrong path/right path

'Sometimes he's such a good boy, doing everything that I ask him to, listening to me, is affectionate, loving and considerate (right path), but most of the time he is rude, obnoxious and out of control (wrong path). If we don't do things "his" way (right path), he will yell, scream, kick, slam doors and generally make life very difficult (wrong path). We are always butting heads and I have tried so many different discipline techniques, but they don't work (conflict between you being right and him being wrong). I don't know where I'm going so wrong (wrong path).'

Missing out

'I feel like I've tried everything and nothing works. I'm just not enjoying him at the moment either. I love him dearly, but I can't help but feel like I want to be away from him as much as I can to get a break.'

Karen feels that she is missing out on 'getting it right' and 'missing out' on being able to enjoy her son. It also sounds as though Karen is feeling that her son is missing out on a mum who is enjoying him.

Should/could

'I love him dearly, but I can't help but feel like I want to be away from him as much as I can to get a break and that makes me feel so guilty. He's nearly four now and he knows the rules. He should be starting to come out of this now, right? He should be starting to know the difference between right and wrong, shouldn't he?'

Worth-less

'All I ever seem to do is yell at him and smack him when I've finally lost the plot. I feel like such a bad mum when I do this and I feel helpless, like I don't know what else to do. He's wearing me down and I just want to stop him from behaving this way and making me feel like this.'

Karen is starting to feel that she is a bad mum and is helpless; that she is worth-less to her son and as a mum.

It is common to feel this way when encountering ongoing behavioural challenges with a child. If this behaviour is the norm rather than the exception, it can be quite exhausting too.

It's easy to feel overwhelmed, and the reality is that it's challenging. I'm certainly not debating this. However, it's important to recognise what you're thinking about this behaviour too. Remember: it's your thoughts about the situation that cause stress and Karen needs to align her thoughts with reality and true self-worth.

Step 2 (Reality)

The first thing to do is to take stock of the reality of this situation: what is actually happening? Karen needs to accept that his current behaviour is the reality. This is where Jeremy is at in his development. Whatever the reason is behind the behaviour, everything that has unfolded has been learnt and experienced by him before now and has contributed to his current behaviour.

Understanding this doesn't mean that Karen will suddenly enjoy this reality, but she needs to accept that this is where her son is at right now and that this is how he is behaving right now. This is the only way she can shift her mindset towards finding a solution, or being able to accept this reality until it changes or he grows out of it.

Let's also see how we can take Karen's thoughts through the Personal Development Model to try and change her mindset towards her son's behaviour.

Life is a journey (upgrade of 'wrong path/right path')

In all our lives there are moments where things are great and moments where life isn't so great. The reality of this situation for Karen is that her life is just hitting one of those challenging times and this is all part of the process of parenting.

This is also true for Jeremy's path. Along the journey of being a child, he is learning how to behave in the world, get results, reason, negotiate, deal with emotions, understand morals and process how life works.

In Karen's story, she spoke a lot about what Jeremy was doing 'right' and what he was doing 'wrong'. However, Jeremy's behaviour is not right, wrong or naughty. He is learning and this behaviour is just a part of his journey through childhood towards maturity. He's not deliberately trying to offend her.

Describing Jeremy as a good boy when he's being affectionate, listening, loving and considerate implies that when he's not behaving this way he is not being a good boy. This is how we inadvertently teach our children an incorrect view of self-worth. Only when we are doing the 'right' thing (in this case behaving) are we being good and therefore accepted and worthy.

Of course, the reality is that we want to teach our children morals, respect and appropriate ways of behaving, but our choice of language needs to be considered to avoid describing one behaviour as good (the right path) and another behaviour as bad or naughty (the wrong way). All behaviour is learning behaviour and we need to look at it from this perspective instead of labelling the behaviour as good or bad.

You are always learning and receiving (upgrade of 'missing out')

Some of our least enjoyable moments are times when we learn and receive our most valuable life lessons. Jeremy is not missing out on anything because he is getting some valuable information on how to function in the world. Regardless of Karen's reactions and behaviour, he is getting information that will influence the development of his life.

Karen is getting some valuable lessons about her own reactions as well as how to deal with the behaviour of her son. She also receives an opportunity to use this behaviour as continual reinforcement of the lessons that she would like to teach her son and the morals that she wants to instil in him.

Remember that kids will learn in their own time and we cannot rush someone's development. There is not one event that goes by where Jeremy is not getting valuable lessons that contribute to who he is. Just because you can't immediately see the effects of your teachings does not mean these lessons are not having their effect. They certainly are and only time will show you that.

Sometimes parents have to wait years to see the product of all their hard work, sometimes well into adulthood and sometimes they never get to see it or get appreciated for the morals that they taught their kids. But all the time, your children are receiving lessons about life and they learn these lessons just as much, and probably more so, when they display undesirable behaviour as when they are being 'good'. How do we learn if we don't know what *not* to do?

We can only know what we know at any given moment (upgrade of 'should/could')

What governs our behaviours is our priority at the time, which is driven by our beliefs. Jeremy's behaviour is driven by what he believes at the time of his behaviour. He accesses his beliefs to perceive the situation and then he accesses his beliefs to identify the appropriate response to the situation. Based on where he is at in his development, his brain can only draw on the current knowledge it has in that moment to determine the appropriate response to the situation he is experiencing.

At this stage of a child's development he or she is still forming beliefs and continually trying out new behaviour based on mimicking his or her surroundings and doing what has worked in the past. This is mostly what governs a child's behaviour.

When you look at your children's behaviour from this perspective, you can begin to look for what their priority is at the time, based on their beliefs at that time. What are they trying to achieve though this behaviour? What do they get from it? What is the payoff? That payoff is their priority over doing what you consider is the 'right' thing.

For example, I once spoke to a day-care teacher about language in relation to the 'right' thing and the 'right' choices. She used the example of a child who had taken his shoes off and thrown them in the corner instead of putting them in his bag. She asked him whether he thought he had made the 'right' choice.

With her permission I explained to her that rather than looking at it as a 'right' choice – which would imply that there was a wrong one – I would be looking at the priority that he had in that moment and what he might have been thinking in that moment. Now, I'm guessing his priority was something along the lines of 'quickly take my shoes off so I can get back to playing'. It wasn't that the boy was trying to be disobedient; he just had different priorities from hers based on his beliefs (possibly that he didn't want to miss out on having fun with his friends) compared to her priority of keeping the room tidy.

Furthermore, I suggested that instead of using the term 'right' choice, I would be explaining how the room works, why we need to respect our room and put things away, and teaching him the rules of the room. The reality of day care is that children do need to cooperate in a team environment and it's part of a teacher's job (just as it is a parent's job) to help kids learn how to function in the world.

In this situation, it would be much more empowering for the child to teach him to understand specific values such as cooperation, consideration and respect rather than the difference between 'right' and 'wrong'. This tendency to teach right and wrong when talking about behaviour can set children up to feel disapproved of and worth-less whenever they don't get something right, when in fact it might have only been a difference in priorities that needed addressing.

In applying this point to Jeremy's life, Karen can begin to look for the priority that Jeremy has for behaving this way and the beliefs behind this priority. What is he trying to achieve by behaving this way and how can Karen align his needs with appropriate behaviour?

It may also be relevant to look at Karen's role in Jeremy's behaviour because how they have reached this point in time is the result of how everything has unfolded up until this point, and Karen is part of how this has played out. Her behaviours and actions are governed by her priorities and what's important to her.

Karen's approach (meaning her behaviours, reactions and decisions) is also governed by her priorities, which are – perhaps – to teach Jeremy the 'right way'. Or, her reactions could be the result of considering his 'wrong' behaviour to mean something about her or her life.

If Karen looks at her own beliefs about this situation and upgrades them to align with the Personal Development Model, she might find that her behaviour, reactions and decisions start coming from a different mindset, which might just make a considerable difference to Jeremy's behaviour.

For example, in Karen's story she mentioned that she felt guilty because she was not enjoying Jeremy at the moment. It's important to note that any feelings of guilt, shame, anger, resentment or blame are associated with Point 3 (should/could) on the GYLR Model. Guilt or shame implies that we should have done something differently, so whenever we have these feelings, we need to apply the relevant upgrade: we only know what we know at any given moment.

In this case Karen obviously feels that she should be enjoying Jeremy and might feel that she is a bad mum for not enjoying him and not wanting to be around him.

Because we are upgrading our beliefs, it is valuable to understand, again, what governs our priorities. Our most basic human instinct is to avoid pain. If Karen has her self-worth attached to Jeremy's behaviour, believing that when he is behaving the 'wrong' way she is a bad mum, then every time she experiences him behaving this way she feels even more worth-less and this causes pain for her. It is painful to feel worth-less.

No one ever wants to feel worth-less, so it becomes an instinctive priority to avoid feeling this way, which would explain Karen not wanting to spend time with her son. She can only know what she knows at any given moment and what she knows in that moment (that is, what she believes) is that her self-worth is defined by his behaviour and is driving her desire to be away from him, thus avoiding the pain. Until Karen aligns her beliefs with the reality that her self-worth is not attached to his behaviour, it will continue to be her priority to avoid the pain of being around his behaviour.

Changing her views to be in alignment with the value in all events and the learning that comes from this challenging event will also change Karen's priorities and consequently her behaviours and reactions, which could possibly change the way she approaches the whole situation.

What I am proposing to you is that we stop seeing children's challenging behaviour as being bad, naughty or wrong and consequently creating a rating system for whether we are being good parents or not and start seeing that there is a reason for this behaviour and an opportunity to correct the beliefs behind this behaviour.

This approach is much deeper than teaching children the difference between right and wrong. It is still right and wrong in terms of morals and appropriate behaviour. However, the emphasis has been taken away from success and failure and placed on learning and growing instead – a much more empowering approach for children.

This needs to be done, again, through repetition and consistency. Furthermore, aside from just looking at our child's behaviour, we need to recognise that we are also playing a part in our child's behaviour through our reactions, decisions and behaviour. Be honest and realistic about your expectations and what really drives your own behaviours.

There is every possibility that when we look at things from this angle, we might just discover that what we came up against were some beliefs of our own from the Get Your Life Right Model and that this could make all the difference to the behaviour of our children and how we perceive this challenge.

> **No matter how my life unfolds, I am always worthwhile (upgrade of 'I am worth-less')**

In order for Karen to start seeing her son's behaviour differently, she must start to see the value in his challenging behaviour and by doing that she will see that her life and Jeremy's life are not of less value because of his behaviour.

When upgrading the GYLR belief 'I am worth-less' you need to start looking at what this event means in the bigger picture. When we feel worth-less it is only because we have rated ourselves as worth-less because of how we have perceived an event. Our perception of the event is due to the beliefs that we hold. Therefore, it is our beliefs that make us feel worth-less, not that we actually are worth-less.

Our 100-per-cent worth comes from our existence and because we exist in this world and play our role in the process of life. Consequently, by existing we are always contributing to the learning and development of ourselves and others around us.

The trick to applying this understanding of true self-worth to challenging circumstances where we feel worth-less is to identify exactly *how* we are contributing to the learning and development of ourselves and others.

Karen feels like a bad mum (worth-less) because she rates her worth based on two perceptions: 1) her reactions to Jeremy's behaviours, and 2) because of how Jeremy's behaviours are affecting her life.

Firstly, her reactions are in the past and cannot be changed. All she can do now is understand her reactions by identifying the beliefs that triggered them and by upgrading them, hopefully avoiding these reactions in the future. Furthermore, Karen's reactions still contributed to Jeremy's development and her development. He is learning more about what happens when he behaves this way and Karen is learning more about herself. All of this learning happens because of the events and because of Karen's reactions, thus making them valuable.

Secondly, once Karen understands that Jeremy's behaviour means nothing about her self-worth, she can detach herself from the behaviour. Jeremy's behaviour is developmental and is a normal process of maturing and growing and when Karen can accept this reality, her reaction to yell, smack or lose the plot will change too.

Karen says, 'He's wearing me down and I just want to stop him from behaving this way and making me feel like this'. This statement implies that Karen's desire to 'stop his behaviour' is driven by her desire to stop 'feel[ing] like this' (worth-less). However, it is Karen's beliefs about Jeremy's behaviour that are causing her to 'feel like this' (worth-less), not Jeremy's behaviour. Karen will stop feeling worth-less when she understands that his behaviour means nothing about her as a mum or as a person. His behaviour is not devaluing her life in anyway – in fact it is adding to her life because she is receiving lessons for her own development from Jeremy and Jeremy is receiving learning for his development from Karen.

By looking at how events contribute to the bigger picture of your life you will begin to see how valuable each event is and how you are worthy through all of the experiences you have – whether they are enjoyable or unenjoyable.

Applying Steps 1 and 2 to your life

Now that we've looked at a couple of examples it's time to begin applying Steps 1 and 2 of the Mind TRACK to Happiness process to your own life. I have spent quite a bit of time on these two steps as they are the absolute foundation for changing your mindset, enjoying your life and enjoying your children.

So grab a notebook and pen and let's get started.

Exercise 1

To begin with, you need to identify an area of parenting in relation to developmental or behavioural challenges that you are currently experiencing as stressful or challenging and answer the following questions.

1. Give a detailed description of the situation that is causing you stress with your child.
2. What are you saying to yourself about this situation?
3. How should this situation be different? What should be happening in order for it to be going 'right'?
4. What do you feel like you are missing out on because this situation is happening this way?
5. How does this situation impact on you or your life?

Using a highlighter, go through your answers and identify and highlight all of the GYLR thinking you find that aligns with these four points:

1. Wrong path/right path
2. Missing out
3. Should/could
4. I am worth-less

Beside each highlighted word write which point you think you are on.

Asking yourself these questions is going to help you identify the thoughts that are aligned with trying to get life right. These thoughts are the ones that are in conflict with reality and causing your stress, so this is quite an important exercise.

Exercise 2

1. What is the reality of the event? What is actually happening? Keep to the facts (for example, 'My daughter is sleeping irregularly', or 'My son is having lots of tantrums'). Write your answer in your notebook.
2. Create a table on your page with the GYLR Model on one side and the Personal Development Model on the other side and a line down the middle, like the following example.

Example

The upgrade

Get Your Life Right Model thinking	Personal Development Model thinking
1. Wrong path/right path	1. Life is a journey (full of ups and downs)
2. Missing out	2. I am always learning and receiving
3. Should/could	3. I can only know what I know at any given moment
4. I am worth-less	4. No matter how my life unfolds, I am always worthwhile

Under each of the GYLR points, write the actual thoughts that you identified from the questions in Exercise 1. On the other side upgrade the GYLR Model thoughts to align with the Personal Development Model. Be as detailed as you can and try to think of as many different ways of viewing the situation in alignment with reality and your new understanding of goals and self-worth as you can.

This exercise might take some time and it's important not to rush these two steps because they are the foundation for changing your mindset.

Step 3 (Aim)

After identifying your thoughts about a situation and how they are in conflict with reality and then re-aligning your thoughts with reality, you will undoubtedly be feeling a whole lot better about the situation that has been a problem for you.

However, knowing that there is value in all events and that they don't alter your self-worth in any way doesn't automatically imply that you still won't want to do something about changing these circumstances.

It does, however, give you an acceptance of the *now* so that you are no longer in resistance to what is happening. Only when you have no resistance to what is happening now are you ready to begin planning where to go from here.

So, let's begin identifying your aims by using the case study of Rebecca and five-month-old Alanah, who isn't sleeping well (see page 113).

There are four things that Rebecca must consider in order to establish her aim.
1. What do I want?
2. Be specific.
3. Is what I want in conflict with reality?
4. Why do I want it?

What do I want?

First and foremost, Rebecca's most obvious aim is that she wants to get more sleep, both for herself and her baby.

Be specific

What exactly does Rebecca want? Does she want Alanah to sleep through the night, every night? Is she okay with her being awake during the day as long as she sleeps at night? Is she aiming for both routines to be established?

Personally, how much sleep is Rebecca aiming for? Does she just want to catch up on her sleep so she feels better about tackling Alanah's sleep issue? If so, how much time will she need?

Answering all these questions will help Rebecca to establish a plan and a rough time line that she can follow in order to meet her goals, which are discussed in Step 5 (see 'Know your plan and action it' on page 144).

Is what I want in conflict with reality?

Before she starts looking at sleep being her aim, Rebecca must first consider whether this is in conflict with reality.

While there are things that Rebecca can do in order to establish some extra rest without relying on Alanah to sleep (such as getting her husband to help out, or finding other support systems), the aim of getting Alanah to sleep more is really in the hands of Alanah responding to the techniques that Rebecca tries.

It's okay that Rebecca's aim is to get Alanah in a sleep routine, but she has to be aligned with the reality that achieving this goal is reliant on Alanah. The reality is that we can't control how quickly our children develop, so this aim is not actually something that Rebecca has control of.

With this in mind Rebecca can still make this her aim, but with the understanding that the time frame for achieving this aim is up to Alanah, not Rebecca. Rebecca may accelerate the achievement of this goal by implementing a technique that works for Alanah, or Alanah may just grow into a routine on her own. Either way, the time line for achieving this goal is unknown and Rebecca has to be mindful of this reality in order for this to be her aim, otherwise she is in conflict with reality.

Why do I want it?

The answer is a no-brainer when it comes to sleep. Naturally, Rebecca wants sleep so that she can feel more rational and better able to handle the challenge of Alanah's sleep issues.

While the reality is that Rebecca needs to get some more sleep (as lack of sleep does have a dramatic effect on how you feel about things), it's important for Rebecca to make sure that this aim is not also about 'getting it right' and being like all the other mums. That is, she must not think that by getting Alanah into a sleep routine she automatically becomes a good mum – because this is in conflict with the reality of true self-worth. She's already valuable as a mum simply because she is here existing as a mum.

This is why we test our aims against the GYLR Model of thinking and try to measure what we think we are going to get from achieving our aims with reality.

Rebecca is no less worthy because Alanah isn't in a sleep routine than she is when Alanah is in a sleep routine.

Having a real understanding that a) getting Alanah into a sleep routine is not essentially within Rebecca's control and could happen at any time, and b) this sleep routine will not prove that Rebecca is a good mother when measured against others can have a dramatic effect on how Rebecca approaches this aim and how she feels during the ups and downs of achieving this aim.

This is the road to a healthy mindset – continually assessing where you are at on the GYLR Model and upgrading it to the Personal Development Model.

Let's look at our second case study, that of four-year-old Jeremy and his mother Karen and the behavioural challenges that Karen is facing.

In order for Karen to align with the reality of this situation, she had to change her views on good and bad behaviour by seeing that there is value in Jeremy's current behaviour simply because it is contributing to him learning about life. His behaviour doesn't make him good (worth more) or bad (worth less). His behaviour is simply learning behaviour.

From this perspective, Karen can now start looking at Jeremy's behaviour through a different lens. We established that Jeremy's behaviour was governed by his priorities in each moment, which are dictated by his beliefs – that is, the information he currently has stored in his mind.

Knowing this, Karen can now look at why he is behaving this way instead of viewing his behaviour as meaning something about him (his worth of being good or bad) and also meaning something about how she is or isn't parenting. It's a totally different perspective.

Remember that this process is not about trying to get your life right – it's about accepting reality and developing a healthy mindset towards parenting. There really needs to be an acceptance that sometimes life doesn't go to plan and that there is learning and value at all times and in all situations. Karen really has to be conscious of her mindset towards this situation and towards her son.

There is every possibility that no matter what aim she sets in terms of discipline, routine and consistency, only time and maturity will make a difference to Jeremy's behaviour. This might be the reality for her child. Not every child is the same; some children are more wilful and more challenging than others.

Having a healthy mindset where she understands that his behaviour doesn't mean anything about her and that there is value in this situation will help her to get through this challenging time without experiencing major stress, depression or anxiety. So, let's take Karen's situation through the four things to consider when establishing her aim.

What do I want?

Karen's aim might be to improve Jeremy's behaviour. This aim seems to be the most logical one and one that would make life a whole lot easier.

Be specific

What does Karen want Jeremy's behaviour to look like when it is improved? How high an expectation does she have for Jeremy? Karen has to be very careful here that she is not placing Jeremy on the GYLR Model with her expectations. A reasonable and realistic aim might be to simply start seeing improvement – some results that indicate that he is starting to learn and understand more of what behaviour is appropriate. More about *how to do this* will come in the next step.

Is what I want in conflict with reality?

While it's okay for Karen to have the aim of seeing an improvement in Jeremy's behaviour, she must also accept – just as Rebecca does – that this aim is not within her control.

Ultimately, it must be Jeremy who changes his behaviour and this will come from him shifting his priorities and learning how to behave appropriately.

This is not an aim that can be anticipated in any specific length of time as it could happen at any time. It could happen in response to Karen's disciplinary methods, or it could happen as a result of Jeremy maturing and growing (or, it could happen as a result of both of these actions put together).

All that Karen can do is keep working towards this aim until, over time, it pays off. As labour intensive as this is, it's the reality of raising children. Any thoughts contrary to this reality will only cause stress.

This is why a healthy mindset is crucial – because life doesn't always happen the way we'd like it to.

Why do I want it?

The Fountainhead Method™ teaches that although achieving our goals is initially the reason why we set them, this is not the true purpose of goals. By taking each step towards your goals, you are adding to the wheels of life in motion. The world is how it is because each of us is in it working towards our numerous goals.

During this process of setting and achieving goals there is learning and contributing taking place while getting to the goal; when we have reached that goal; and also when we have not been able to reach our goals. So, whether we reach our goals or not, we are always receiving lessons for our development and contributing to life unfolding. From this perspective, the point of setting goals can become more about our desire to experience something that we'd like to experience, rather than setting goals in order to make life more valuable. This understanding also helps us to avoid thinking that once I get 'x' I will have a better life.

Why does Karen want to improve Jeremy's behaviour? Is this to make her life better? It will certainly make it easier for Karen and if this is her reason, then this is fine, providing she recognises that her life is not worse in its present form – harder, yes, but worse, no. There is value, learning and growing happening as a result of this situation, so it is just as valuable, if not more so, than if Jeremy was behaving appropriately.

If, however, Karen's desire to improve Jeremy's behaviour was so that she wouldn't be embarrassed or so that Jeremy would be a good boy, then she is back on the GYLR Model, thinking that he has to be a certain way, or the 'right' way in order for a) Karen to feel she is a worthwhile or good mother and b) Jeremy to be on the 'right' path.

This kind of thinking will always lead to stress whenever Jeremy's behaviour is not meeting Karen's expectations of what she thinks he 'should' be doing.

It's always important when establishing your aim that you test your goals against the Get Your Life Right Model to ensure that you are not setting yourself up for more stress.

This process is designed to teach you a way of looking at life that will help you to accept and see the value in all of your life experiences, not just the experiences that are going right. The purpose of setting goals is not just to achieve them but to understand that learning is taking place while getting to the goal and if the goal doesn't come to fruition for whatever reason, or takes longer than you'd like it to, there is still learning and growing taking place. This is the true purpose of goals.

Teach your children that there is value in everything and while having and achieving goals is great and motivational, the true purpose of goals is to learn about and experience life and as a result grow as a person. This will set them up to embrace all of life's events, hopefully avoiding depression, anxiety and psychological stress when their life doesn't go to plan.

My day care centre sent home a form asking me what I'd like my eldest son Cody to learn from their Kinder program. My immediate response was to teach him that while it's great to have goals, the achievement of goals is nowhere near as important as what he learns while getting to the goals. Wouldn't that be a fantastic place for schools and educational systems to put their attention?

Applying Step 3 to your life

Now it's time to apply Step 3 to your situation.

Exercise 3

In your notebook, consider and write your responses to these four questions and statements, just as we did for the case studies above.

What is your aim?

What do you want to happen? How would you like this situation to look? What is the experience that you would like to have?

Be specific

How exactly will your life look when you achieve this aim? Can you narrow your aim down to specifics, as we did for the case studies? You need to be as specific as you can.

Is what I want in conflict with reality?

Is this aim realistic? Is it something that you can personally achieve or are you relying on the behaviour of someone else in order to achieve it?

Why do I want it?

How would achieving this aim change or alter your life? What is driving your desire to achieve this aim? How would you feel if you didn't achieve this aim?

After writing your answers in your notebook, go back and review them to see whether any of them are aligned with the Get Your Life Right Model or have the undertone of this model. If you are really honest with yourself you will be able identify it very quickly if they are. You must test your aim against this model in order to see whether it is a reasonable aim to go for.

Remember, even if you are aware that you are trying to make your life 'better', that's okay as long as you acknowledge that there is value in the now and that achieving an aim does not alter your self-worth or how valuable your life is. You are always 100-per-cent worthy.

Keep revising and challenging your aims until you come up with a goal that is aligned with something you'd like to experience and that is not in conflict with reality, or that you think will make your life go the right way.

In conclusion to this step, write in your notebook:

My aim in the area of 'Challenging behaviour and developmental stages' is: _____

Step 4 (Choices)

Step 4 is about assessing all the choices that you have for achieving your aim and finding out the possible options and solutions to your problem.

It is important to remind you here of what drives the choices that we make and the actions that we take in our lives.

Choices are made according to the priority we have at that time. Our priorities are governed by our beliefs. When you are assessing and weighing up all the options that you have in front of you, your choices will always be governed by your priorities – what you believe to be most important – and this can only be derived from the knowledge you have at that time.

This is why The Fountainhead Method™ teaches that we can only know what we know at any given moment. Whenever a situation presents itself, you will access the beliefs you currently hold to determine the appropriate responses to that situation, which will be dictated by the most important beliefs in that moment. This is your priority.

For example, let's look again at Rebecca and her daughter Alanah.

There are two parts to Rebecca's aim. Let's call Part 1 'Getting Rebecca more sleep' and Part 2 'Getting Alanah into a sleep routine'.

In order to get Rebecca more sleep she will need to set up an initial support system so that she can take a little time out to catch up on some much-needed sleep and be in a better frame of mind to approach Alanah's sleep routine. This might need to happen several times before the problem is solved.

So, the first thing that Rebecca has to do is look at her options in relation to support. Can her husband give her some time out? Does she have family or friends she can call on for support? If she has none of this support, can she make it a priority to sleep nearly every single time Alanah goes to sleep with the exception of having to do the 'basic' chores to keep living. What do other mothers do to get more sleep? This is the research that Rebecca needs to do in order to create her list of possible options and solutions.

Now, when assessing these options, this is where Rebecca's beliefs – which govern her decision-making process – will kick in.

If she has a belief that she needs to have it all figured out and she can't be a 'burden' to her friends, family or working husband, then Rebecca is going to try and go with the second option: sleeping every time Alanah does.

However, if she also has a belief that a housewife 'should' have the house clean for her husband when he comes home, she is hardly going to take the opportunity to sleep during the day when Alanah does because this belief makes housework a priority over her sleeping. Beliefs such as these are going to make it very difficult for Rebecca to meet Part 1 of her plan.

In order for Rebecca to meet her aim, she must make her aim a priority over all other beliefs. To do this she has to be aware of the beliefs that are in conflict with her aim, and align them with the Personal Development Model.

It can be useful to list all of your options and the potential solutions available and consider why you would eliminate each one. Find out what your beliefs are about each option and consider whether these beliefs are on the Get Your Life Right Model and need to be upgraded. Doing this will change your perspective on these options and you might just make a different choice than you might have originally made.

Part 2 of Rebecca's plan is to get Alanah into a sleep routine. To do this she must research different ways of achieving this. After five months, she has already tried numerous methods, so she already knows what isn't working and now she needs to research even more ways of trying to get this to happen. Books, DVDs, parenting forums, advice from other mums or even looking into a sleep school are all resources that could help Rebecca to create a list of options for consideration.

Now Rebecca needs to go through each option and consider which choice she is going to make, look at why each one is either 'good' or 'bad' and think about what her beliefs are about them.

For example, Rebecca might have strong beliefs against the control-crying method because she considers this too emotional for her and her baby, so her priority to protect her baby in this way will probably override her desire to get Alanah into a routine using this method. However, after assessing exactly what her beliefs against this method are and aligning them with the Personal Development Model, she might change her viewpoint and give it a try.

No matter which option/s Rebecca chooses, they will always be governed by her beliefs and which belief holds the highest priority at that moment.

Let's look at this step again using the case study of Karen and Jeremy.

Karen's aim is to see some noticeable improvement in Jeremy's behaviour. Already having tried many different techniques, Karen is now at the point where she needs to decide on the next thing she will try, even though she is conscious of the fact that Jeremy's behaviour is not within her control.

Again, books, advice and other resources could present her with options.

By reviewing her own behaviour, decisions and actions in relation to Jeremy's behaviour, Karen might now have a different perspective of her challenge with Jeremy and she might revisit some of the old techniques that she's tried in the past. With her new perspective she might just find that one of these techniques works because she is now reacting and behaving differently.

Whatever choices Karen makes will be governed by which beliefs take priority over others.

Applying Step 4 to your life

Exercise 4

1. The first thing you need to do is research, research, research. Gather all the options and potential solutions that you can from all the information you can find and create a list of things that you could do. If you are in the moment (for example, in the shopping centre with your child who is having a tantrum) then obviously you don't have the time to do this quickly, so you would mentally assess all the different things you might do to just get through the moment. In the moment, you will only have the information that you currently have to access, so it may not be the most desirable or effective choice. However, later on you will be able to assess whether you could do something differently in the future based on what you have learnt and by applying the process of options and solutions at a later time. You don't always have to have the 'right' answer in the moment. Just do what you can to get past the moment and then look back at this event, learn from it and review your options in preparation for this happening next time, particularly if it's starting to become a habitual challenging behaviour.
2. After you have created this list, you need to assess all of your options and document what your thoughts are about each option. What beliefs spring to mind when considering and imagining applying each option? Are any of those thoughts on the Get Your Life Right Model and do they need upgrading?
3. Now that you have looked at all of your options, you can choose which one you are going to try to implement for this problem and how long you will allow to see whether it is successful.

Step 5 (Know your plan and action it)

This final step is where you cement your ideas and formulate them into a plan with the intention of reaching your aim.

Having a plan in place to achieve your aim can be very empowering as the plan becomes a deliberately considered response to a situation, rather than a habitual response.

For example, if you have decided that ignoring the tantrum and using distraction techniques is the way that you are going to handle tantrums, then as soon as the tantrum happens you begin implementing your plan.

You are less likely to become reactive because you have a contingency plan set up for when that behaviour occurs. It's less of a surprise and you simply spring into actioning your planned response, not your automatic one.

Sometimes you also need to enlist the help of people around you in order to implement your plan. For example, if you have decided on a specific disciplinary plan to teach your child the consequences of his or her behaviour you need to let other key carers – such as Dad, a grandparent or a day-care provider – know that you are trying this and would like their help to follow through with it too.

You may also need to communicate your new plan to your child so that they know the new rules that you are implementing and the consequences for breaking the rules.

Applying Step 5 to your life

Exercise 5

On paper or on a poster, write your plan of action and keep it handy to remind you of what your plan is and to keep you aligned with your aim when the challenges are at their peak. A simple layout such as the following one is all that is required.

My aim is _____

_____

What are the details of my plan or what are the specific steps? _____

_____

What support do I need to implement this plan? Do I need to communicate this plan to other carers or to my child in any way?

_____

_____

What are some statements that I would like to remind myself of as I am implementing this plan? _____

_____

_____

> The last question is helpful if you are aware of certain thoughts from the Get Your Life Right Model that keep coming up. Write yourself some statements or affirmations that are aligned with the Personal Development Model which will help you to remember how to think. For example: 'His behaviour is not about me. His behaviour is learning behaviour, not naughty behaviour. I am always 100-per-cent worthy. There is value in all events. I am always learning and receiving. The reality is that life is full of ups and downs'.

Little reminders such as this can make a massive difference to how you approach your child's behaviour. Remember, with this mindset you are literally trying to retrain your brain to think differently about life; that is, to retrain it from thinking according to the Get Your Life Right Model to thinking in alignment with the Personal Development Model.

Repetition and consistency over time is the only way to do this. For adults you are not only trying to grow and strengthen new connections, you also have to stop using the old ones so they can die off. That's why it can be more difficult for adults to change. However, you can change: just keep on practising.

Let's have a look at what the plans of our two case studies might look like.

Mum Rebecca (case study 5) might have a plan that looks like this:

My aim is

to regularly catch up on my sleep in order to be physically prepared to then work on getting Alanah into a sleep routine.

What are the details of my plan or what are the specific steps?

1. Align a time with Joe (my husband) to look after Alanah for a few hours so that I can catch up on my sleep.
2. I'm using a sleep technique from a video that my child health nurse gave me. Its steps are as follows:
   a. Once I notice my baby's sleep signs I place her in the cot on her side facing away from me.
   b. I gently hold her arm down so that she is not wriggling around and I gently pat her while saying 'shhhhhh'.
   c. I keep doing this until she stops crying.
   d. As soon as she stops crying I take my hands off her and let her fall asleep by herself.
   e. If she commences crying again, I do this again.
   f. If she continues to cry for five minutes, I pick her up, give her a little cuddle and talk to her with a soothing tone, and then place her down on her other side, still facing away from me and start again for another five minutes.
   g. If after doing this three times (that is, for 15 minutes in total) she is still not asleep, then perhaps she is not ready for sleep or something else is going on. Stop trying for 15 to 20 minutes before putting her back in the cot and trying again.

   Points to remember:
- She might not be ready for sleep yet.
- She might be hungry.
- She might be too hot or cold.
- She might be uncomfortable.

What support do I need to implement this plan? Do I need to communicate this plan to other carers or to my child in any way?

I will show this sheet to my husband and my mum who also put Alanah to bed sometimes, so that we are all following the same routine.

What are some statements that I would like to remind myself of as I am implementing this plan?

Alanah is simply learning how to sleep in her own time. Alanah's sleeping pattern does not define me as being a good mother. I am learning new skills on how to teach my baby to sleep.

Having a plan such as this in place gives Rebecca a clear idea of how she is going to handle this situation, which should help her feel better immediately.

She avoids becoming reactive when Alanah is not sleeping because she knows what she needs to do in order to approach this behaviour.

You will be amazed at the difference following this entire process does to your mindset, particularly for ongoing or long-term behavioural and developmental challenges.

Mum Karen's plan could look like this:

My aim is to see a noticeable improvement in Jeremy's behaviour.

What are the details of my plan or what are the specific steps?

1. Over the next few days I will begin by observing Jeremy's behaviour when he is being angry, frustrated, disrespectful or rude and I will try to identify what his priority is and what beliefs he might have that are driving this behaviour.
2. I will also observe my own habitual responses to his behaviour over the next few days.
3. I will document any observations that I make about Jeremy or myself to see how they fit in with the GYLR Model of thinking and how they can be upgraded.
4. I'm going to sit down with Jeremy to discuss his recent behaviour and ask him to explain to me what has been going on for him. I will then explain how my thinking has been causing my reaction and explain to him that I am going to try and change my reactions too so that we can work together on changing both of our behaviours and how we relate to one another.

5. During this conversation I am going to ask him to contribute some rules and consequences for behaviour so that we can all learn to cooperate, be respectful, get along and treat each other with love.
6. Together we will create a chart that can be put up in the kitchen with all our rules and consequences and get him to write his name (or his version of his name) at the bottom to show that he agrees with this chart and everything on it.
7. Whenever his behaviour conflicts with our agreement, the consequences are issued.
8. I will continue to observe his view of life and my reactions to give him and me an understanding of the Personal Development Model.

What support do I need to implement this plan? Do I need to communicate this plan to other carers or to my child in any way?

These steps need to be followed with all of my children at the table who are old enough to participate in the making of the rules and I need to get my husband on board with the rules and administering the agreed consequences of these broken rules, where needed.

What are some statements that I would like to remind myself of as I am implementing this plan?

- Jeremy's behaviour is learning behaviour, not naughty behaviour.
- Jeremy's behaviour is not right or wrong and is only a result of the priorities that he has in that moment based on what he knows and believes.
- Jeremy is not doing this *to* me and his behaviour is not about me. I am always 100-per-cent worthwhile and am learning from this experience too.
- Both of us can only know what we know at any given moment and both of us are learning as we go along.

Having completed the five steps of the process, Karen is approaching Jeremy's behaviour from a very different angle. She has changed her viewpoint from being in resistance to his behaviour, to seeing that as a human being his behaviour has a reason and this reason is governed by his beliefs.

In addition, Karen's behaviour, reactions and decisions must come from a healthy mindset in order to deal with the behaviour calmly and also to teach him to think with a healthy mindset, so she has taken that into consideration too.

Summary: Behavioural and developmental challenges

The main message that I'd like to convey in this chapter is for mums to begin viewing the challenges that we are faced with as parents as valuable opportunities for learning and growth.

Be kind to yourself and recognise that new skills are being learnt about how to raise another human being who has his or her own ideas and mindset and who is observing, learning, growing and finding the best ways to function in the world.

This is not an easy job and there has to be an understanding that there will be ups and downs in behaviour, emotions and reactions, both in you, your child and everyone else in your family and these times are not due to anything you are doing wrongly. This is the reality of all families.

Developmental and behavioural challenges can indeed be exhausting and stressful at times and this is all part of the parenting experience. While the GYLR Model of thinking is always playing its part in stress, it's important that you aren't trying to get the Personal Development Model of thinking 'right' and thinking that the GYLR Model of thinking is 'wrong', which, of course, only puts you right back on the GYLR Model of thinking.

There will often be times when our thinking will cause us stress and this is still part of our learning experiences and is not the wrong path. The Mind TRACK to Happiness process is not trying to teach you to get life right by never feeling stressed again. It is trying to help you to understand what causes your stress and help you to detach events from your self-worth. Then it teaches you to set goals and find solutions using the same mindset.

The relationship between you and your children is similar to being in one with your partner or a flatmate. We are all learning how to get along, live with each other's individual traits, support each other, love each other and sometimes deal with behaviour that we don't agree with.

As a parent you do have that added role of being a key contributor to your children's growth and lessons in life, so you want to begin observing what you are teaching your kids and the messages that you send to them through your behaviour, decisions, actions and reactions, because they are likely to be already copying them.

I believe that undesirable behaviour simply tells you that there is something to learn or being learnt and possibly that children's current thinking may already be aligned with the GYLR Model of thinking and needs correcting so that they can learn an accurate way to view life and avoid stress, depression and anxiety in the future.

As parents we are their teachers and you can potentially set your children up with this powerful knowledge, which will hopefully assist them in accepting and finding value in *all* of the events in their lives, not just the ones that they think are fun and successful.

At the same time, you also now have the information that, when practised and applied, will change your mindset to being the Happy Mum and happy woman that you'd like to be. Remember that this has to start as a deliberate and conscious effort before it can be cemented in your brain and become your unconscious habitual mindset.

When applying the Mind TRACK to Happiness process to developmental or challenging behaviours you may find that you can complete the process quite quickly in your mind and don't need to write it down. Especially over time you will find that you will observe and listen to your thoughts and your behaviour as well as your child's and you will automatically begin to use this mindset.

However, sometimes other events may occur that are more emotionally charged or are complex behaviours that require more detailed analysis and research. At these times you will benefit immensely from writing out the process.

Either way, the process can become a valuable tool for creating the mindset aligned with being a Happy Mum.

Chapter 10

Anger and guilt

Applying the Mind TRACK to Happiness process

Anger and guilt are feelings often experienced in motherhood that can severely influence how enjoyable our experience of motherhood is.

The Mind TRACK to Happiness process can be used on both of these feelings.

Step 1 (Thoughts)

As discussed earlier, whenever we experience an angry emotion we have first activated a belief that has caused the physical sensation of that anger.

The beliefs that cause anger and guilt can primarily be categorised as Point 3 of the GYLR Model of thinking (should/could: 'I am or someone else should be or could have behaved differently').

The emotion you feel will depend on which beliefs you access when you observe an event combined with the self-talk that takes place in your mind – as well as your habitual responses to experiencing an event such as this.

Identifying the story that's playing out in your mind will most definitely show you all the 'should' beliefs that you have about the situation. You will find that you will be telling yourself how this situation should be different from how it actually is and how you or someone else should have done something differently, putting you in conflict with reality.

Anger

Anger results when you have an expectation (belief) about how something should go: you have a certain picture in your head of life going to plan and when it doesn't the picture in your mind is in conflict with reality and it causes the sensation in the body that produces anger.

For example, you awaken in the morning and have a picture in your head of getting out of bed, your husband/partner getting the kids their breakfast like he usually does, while you start your day with a nice shower to wake you up, easing you into the day. All of a sudden, your husband walks through the bedroom door and announces that he is going to work in two minutes and you have to get up. There goes the shower, and to top it all off, both kids are cranky and irritable.

Moments after opening your eyes, you are bombarded with two loud and demanding children, there is no husband around for help, and you don't get to have a shower. You are up and into it. The reality is different from what you had expected and your anger comes from the attachment you have to the expected picture you had (your beliefs) and denial of the picture you are actually seeing (conflict with reality).

After accessing your beliefs about this new reality and how it differs from the picture you had, you form a conscious opinion in your mind as to whether the difference is good or bad, and enter into self-talk about how this good or bad event is affecting you (and your self-worth).

That self-talk – those thoughts – create a physical feeling within you. If the conversation/thoughts are negative, then you will start to feel your body tense up and the anger begins to build. If you continue the negative conversation, the thoughts expand in that negative direction and the feeling this creates gets worse and worse until you are physically tense and your blood begins to boil, where anger is now spewing out of you.

General beliefs that cause anger can include how we expect our children to behave, household rules that need to be obeyed (for example, no food on the carpet), the state of our house, who does which chores around the house, how quickly we adjust to motherhood and our new role, and so on.

Guilt

Guilt, on the other hand, occurs when we believe that we should have done something differently or that we should feel differently about something (which is often the case for mums).

Mums sometimes feel endlessly guilty about how they raise their children and this can be a huge source of stress.

Often the biggest guilt factor is balancing work, your life and the quality of care for your children. Over the years, women have been taught that they can 'have it all', but they soon learn that having it all comes at a price.

There are only so many hours in a day and we cannot have an evenly balanced life when we are taking on work, household chores, quality time with our children, time with our partners and still trying to do something for ourselves. It's just not possible to give equal time to each area. Something has to give and this is often a source of guilt in mothers who hold the belief, 'I should be doing something more than I am'.

Even if you don't work, the belief that you should be equally balancing all of the other areas of your life could be in conflict with reality, causing stress.

Again, you will have an entire story playing out in your mind of all the things that you should be doing and how not doing them is affecting your life or your child's life.

Whenever you feel anger or guilt, identify the conversation that you are having in your mind and you will be able to identify all of the GYLR points in this conversation. You will find, primarily, that Point 3 – 'should/could' – will be the dominant one.

Exercise 1

> The next time you feel angry or guilty, take out your notebook and write half a page on what your story is about this event. Then identify the point/s on the GYLR Model of thinking that is causing your stress, or – if you don't have time – just become conscious of your self-talk and see whether you can identify the point/s.

Step 2 (Reality)

Whether you are feeling angry or guilty, you are still in conflict with the reality that is playing out before you.

Anger

Anger is the conflict you have between what you expected and what is actually happening. The reality is that the picture you had in your head is not happening, and you need to accept this.

For example, let's say that you've asked your son to do something, such as putting on his shoes, because you need to go out somewhere. You have a picture in your mind (expectation based on beliefs) that he will put his shoes on, as asked, but it doesn't happen.

He completely ignores you and continues to watch TV. What has just happened is that the picture in your head differed from the actual event that you are witnessing. You begin to have a conversation with yourself in your head about the difference between the event and the expected picture. It might go something like this:

'Gosh he's frustrating me. He's ignoring me again (opinion). He never listens to me when I ask him to do something. It makes me crazy when he does this. (frustration – this is where the negative self-talk progressively gets worse). Every time he does this, I have to argue with him just to do what I want him to. Why can't he just do as he's bloody told for once? ('should/could') I'm going to ask him one more time to put his shoes on, and if he doesn't put his bloody shoes on, then so help me I'm gonna ...' (anger has arrived).

This conversation has created the feeling of rage inside you because your mind's conversation was in conflict with the reality that your son did not put his shoes on and your conversation has progressively strengthened in momentum to reach the stage of physical anger in your body.

The way to stop this is to first accept the reality that he is not doing what he was asked. Secondly, because the anger is related to Point 3 ('should/could') on the GYLR Model, you need to upgrade this belief to Point 3 on the Personal Development Model: 'I can only know what I know at any given moment'.

Your son is ignoring you for a reason that is valid for him. He is accessing his current beliefs and deciding on what his priority is in that moment and this will definitely be different from yours in many cases.

Perhaps he's totally engrossed in what he's doing – watching TV or playing – and this is his priority. Perhaps he's ignoring you to get a rise out of you because it's funny for him to see mummy get all red in the face, or maybe he wants your attention.

There will always be a reason why our children behave the way they do and their priorities being different from ours doesn't make them naughty or wrong – it just makes them different. Your son can only know what he knows at any given moment and he may not yet understand that you need to get out the door on time, or perhaps he does and it's just not that important to him.

It doesn't mean that you don't still need his cooperation to get out the door on time; it just means that if you can understand that his priority is not the same as yours, you can at least start changing your tactics so that you can get out the door without feeling angry.

Think about: 'What is it that is actually making you feel angry? Is it that he's ignoring you and that that makes you believe he's not valuing your authority, or that he's disrespecting you, therefore making you feel worth-less? The reality is, his behaviour is not about you – it's about him, and his priorities are based on his beliefs in that moment.

By identifying the conversation in your mind that is causing the anger and upgrading it using the Personal Development Model, you can diffuse your anger (because you are now in alignment with reality) and move forward with finding another solution to achieving your aim.

Guilt

Guilt is felt because of the belief that we should be doing something differently or that we could have done something differently.

You can upgrade the beliefs that cause guilt by understanding that whatever you are doing that is different from what you think you should be doing, is being done because you have made it a priority. So, if you're feeling guilty that your children aren't getting enough of your quality time, it's because you are making other things a priority over the quality time with your children.

This might be the reality that you are in conflict with because sometimes there are things that have to take priority over some of the quality time you spend with your kids, such as going to work, for example.

Beliefs that commonly cause guilt are:

- I am working instead of being at home with my kids.
- I yelled at my kids and I feel really bad about that.
- I'm always getting angry and smacking my kids.
- I should be able to breastfeed and I feel guilty that my baby isn't getting the best start.
- I just want to get away from them and I feel guilty that I don't enjoy motherhood like I should.
- I should spend more time playing with the kids because I don't work and have the time, but everything else seems to get in the way.
- I feel guilty for sending my child to day care.
- I feel guilty because I let my child watch too much TV.
- I feel guilty because I've felt slack for giving my children take-out twice this week.

Chapter 10: Anger and guilt **159**

- I feel guilty because one child gets more of my attention than another.
- I feel guilty because I can't afford to buy something for my children.

In every moment, you experience a situation, analyse the information and what your beliefs are about the situation and determine how to act in accordance with what your priorities are at that time.

If work is taking your time over the kids, it is because you have made work your priority (which might be the reality of what you need to do based on your current financial position). This is the same with day care: based on the information you had at the time and the priority at the time you decided that day care was the best option.

If you feel guilty about not enjoying motherhood and wanting to take time out, it is because you have beliefs about why you don't enjoy motherhood and they have priority over your desire to enjoy motherhood.

If you've smacked your kids and become angry, it's because the beliefs you had about the situation in that moment led to the physical sensation of being angry.

Whatever it is that you are doing or that you did to cause the guilt, you did it because it was a priority for you at the time based on the information and beliefs you had at that time. It cannot be any different.

When you understand what governs your decisions and actions, and accept that this is the way it is (reality), then you are in a position to decide what it is you want and to move up the ladder towards creating the ideal of what you want.

In the meantime, realise that this guilt feeling comes from the incorrect beliefs that you should be doing something differently. However, you are making it a priority for a reason. If you don't want to make this a priority, you can change it by setting yourself another aim and continuing the Mind TRACK to Happiness process.

Guilt is usually also followed by the feeling of your children missing out because of something that you have done or that their lives are now on the wrong path because you didn't do something. All of the GYLR Model of thinking will be there contributing to the guilt and you need to identify the thoughts that are in conflict with reality and then apply the Personal Development Model to accept the reality of the event and get rid of the guilt, or at least understand it and minimise it.

Exercise 2

> After identifying what you are thinking about a situation that is causing you anger or guilt, identify what the reality of the situation is and how you can upgrade your GYLR beliefs using the Personal Development Model of thinking to help you accept the current reality of the situation.

Step 3 (Aim)

We now move on to the aim that you are trying to achieve and what you want from the situation.

Anger

1. What do I want?

'I have now accepted that my expectations were not met, so what can I do now? What is the new ideal that I will try to achieve?' If anger is a repetitive response for you, you may want to make it an aim to work on changing this habitual response by looking at anger management techniques and continuing to practise recognising your thoughts and upgrading them using the Personal Development Model.

2. Be specific.

'What exactly do I want and what are the specifics of what I want?' For example, now that I've woken up and didn't get my shower, I want to be able to feel differently about my day and increase my energy in another way. Or, I'm still trying to get out the door on time, so I need to find another way to get my child to cooperate – or just do it myself.

3. Is what I want in conflict with reality?

'Does this aim rely on me or on the behaviour of someone else?'

4. Why do I want it?

'What beliefs are driving me to achieve this aim? Am I aiming for this to make my life 'better'? Are my beliefs on the GYLR Model or the Personal Development Model?'

It is quite possible that Steps 3 to 5 of the Mind TRACK to Happiness process do not need to be completed. By identifying the beliefs that caused the anger and then upgrading them you may have already diffused your anger and may not feel like you need to set a new aim. This is quite normal and I personally find that this is often the case with my own anger.

Guilt

1. What do I want?

If you feel like you 'should' be doing something differently, write down what it is you actually want. What do you think you should be doing and what do you want to be doing? You might want to reconsider what it is you do want, because if you are feeling guilty about not spending enough time with your kids, for example, then maybe an aim might be to reduce work hours or to manage your time better to increase the time you spend with them.

2. Be specific.

You need to be specific about what you want that will improve what you are doing. You believed that you should be doing something differently, so this step is your chance to actually aim to do something differently. This might mean being really specific about how much time you want to spend on each area of your life. It might mean that you need to be specific about how you want to treat your child.

3. Is what I want in conflict with reality?

Does this aim rely on me or the behaviour of someone else?

4. Why do I want it?

What beliefs are driving me to achieve this aim? How will I feel if I don't achieve this aim: guilty again? Am I aiming for this to make my life or my child's life 'better'? Are my beliefs on the GYLR Model or the Personal Development Model?

Are you trying to achieve this aim because you feel that your children are missing out on something in their lives and you feel that their lives are less valuable in some way? If this is so, then you need to align your beliefs with the upgrade to 'missing out' – that is, there is always value to be found in every event and we are always learning and receiving something that is valuable to our lives and that is contributing to our development.

Exercise 3

> Using the questions above, establish the aim that is going to help you move away from feeling anger or guilt.

Step 4 (Choices)

Anger

If you have not done so already in Steps 1 and 2, it is important to identify which beliefs have been causing you to feel angry and upgrade them with reality so that you can learn from your past behaviour and keep working towards changing your habitual response.

If anger is a common response for you and you want to change that, then you are going to need to become very conscious and deliberate about what you think in order to retrain your brain to think differently.

Perhaps there is a deeper issue causing your anger that you need to really address, such as regret or blame from a past relationship or past event that you need to accept and move on from. Healing this issue might become one of your aims.

If you have been feeling guilty, then identifying the beliefs that have been governing you to feel this way will help you to identify your aim. At this step, try to find different solutions and options you could explore that will help you become aligned with what you want to achieve.

For example, if you don't want to work as much as you are working, then in this step you could explore what your options are for reducing your hours; or if you need more time to yourself, you could explore possible day-care arrangements.

In this step, you want to research all of the different ways to achieve your aim, so that you can decide on the appropriate course of action to take.

Be mindful that in motherhood we have many things that we need to do, so we are always having to choose which task is a priority over another. This is the reality of parenting and sometimes you have to let something fall by the wayside in order to get something else done. For example, sometimes one child will not get attention where the other one does.

You will need to consciously weigh up your beliefs on each option and decide which one takes priority and why. Once you do, then know that this is the best decision you can make based on the information you currently have and learn to accept this decision so that you don't experience any more guilt.

Exercise 4

> Spend some time researching and brainstorming the possible options and solutions you may have that will help you to work towards your aim and write them in your notebook. Be mindful of the beliefs that are triggered when considering each option and test them against the GYLR Model and the Personal Development Model.

Step 5 (Know your plan and action it)

Depending on what the options were in Step 4, you may need to create a plan of action or steps that you need to take in order to achieve your aim.

If you have prepared an anger management plan, you might need to create a specific plan and keep it somewhere handy so that you can remember the steps that you need to follow to help you, or create a list of affirmations that will remind you of the new way to think.

If, after analysing the beliefs that are causing your guilt, you have rearranged your priorities, this might require some planning including putting together a list of steps that you need to follow in order to rearrange your life in accordance with your new priorities.

Exercise 5

> Create a plan of action that you need to follow in order to achieve your aim of overcoming your feelings of anger or guilt.

Summary: Anger and guilt

Every mother feels angry and guilty sometimes. This is a normal, everyday occurrence for most of us.

The important thing to remember is that we are not doing anything wrongly; we simply feel this way because of how we perceive the various challenges that motherhood brings.

The reality of motherhood is that it is a constant juggle and often things don't go the way we plan them too. This can be frustrating and cause us anger, or it can cause us to feel guilty that we are not doing what we think we should be doing.

The story that plays out in our minds about the demands of parenting is what causes us to feel angry or guilty and if we can identify these thoughts and upgrade them with the reality of the situation and the reality of parenting and self-worth, then we will be able to minimise or totally diffuse these emotions and have a more accurate view of these challenges.

It's not an easy thing to prioritise all of the things we need to do and under the pressure of a society that tells us that we can and should be able to 'do it all', we can sometimes believe that this is yet another way that we need to get life 'right' in order to have a successful life and be a successful mum.

Be mindful that you are not attaching your self-worth to being that super-human mum who has to have life a certain way and be achieving all the things society says you can.

Everyone's situation is different and you have to do what's best for you and your family. Observe what your expectations are of yourself and really take some time to consider if what you are doing is what you really want and what's really best for your family, and use this process to start creating the life that you want, rather than one that is about keeping up with the Joneses or what society is teaching you.

This is your life and your journey and you can make it how you'd like it to be, not what others dictate it should be.

Chapter 11

Loss of identity

Before children I knew myself to be a very confident person. I had no problems meeting new people or making new friends. I got jobs easily. I knew myself to be intelligent, capable and even funny at times.

I generally liked how I looked. Of course, there were physical parts of me I would have liked to change, but I generally felt good about myself. I actually liked who I was.

I was an achiever. If there was something that I wanted to achieve, I created a plan and achieved it. Nothing would stop me from going for what I wanted.

However, when I had my children something changed. Suddenly I lost my confidence and it was quickly replaced with self-criticism and self-hatred.

How did that happen? How did I go from being a confident, easy-going achiever to being useless, bored and miserable in under two years? Was my identity really lost?

B.C.   A.C.

How did I lose my identity?

It's common for mums to feel as though they have lost themselves in their roles as mums. Life becomes consumed by the day-to-day of raising kids, and mums can feel as though their personal lives are a thing of the past. 'Who am I now that I am a mum? Where is the person I used to be? What about what *I* want?'

When I look back at who I was before children and who I became after children, it is clear to me what was going on to cause me such stress and anxiety in the first couple of years of being a mum.

All of those definitions – all of those labels of being confident, carefree, the achiever, liking my look, being capable, meeting people and making friends – all of those things were what defined me, what made up my personal identity.

Little did I know at the time that these 'labels' were also attached to my self-worth. Being able to live out this identity in my mind was what made me valuable and how I was able to fit into society.

And then suddenly my body shape was different; how I was perceived by others was different; how and what I could achieve was often out of my control; and I certainly wasn't confident or capable in a lot of parenting skills when my boys were babies.

My reference point of who I was and what defined me was completely out of whack as I was unable to play the usual roles of who I was, which – incorrectly – had made me feel worthy.

This made me feel like something was wrong. I should have been that person who was carefree; who achieved everything I wanted; who was capable, funny and attractive. If I was unable to live up to this person I thought I 'should' be, then who was I? I felt as though I was 'missing out' on being me and suddenly I felt that I was no longer worth as much as I used to be.

As you may have already guessed, all of my thinking about what this major change had done to my life and my self-worth was all aligned with the Get Your Life Right Model, ultimately causing me major stress and anxiety.

Before children, I thought I liked myself. I thought I had self-confidence and self-love. But in reality I only loved myself when life was going 'right', when I was doing things 'right' and when I behaved in the 'right' way (as per my identity). What I actually loved was the 'idea' I had of myself.

This 'idea' that we have of ourselves is our personal identity, the definition we have in our minds of what makes up our personality.

As well as the ideas we already have of ourselves before becoming a parent, we also adopt more ideas of what sort of mother we want to be and what sort of life we want to provide for our children. We did this prior to ever having experienced being a mother and added them to our new identity as a mother, wife, housewife, and so on.

So, going into motherhood you now have all of these 'ideas' about yourself that you are trying to live up to. Some of them from your pre-mother life and some are how you want to be as a mum. However, some of these ideas are just not compatible with the reality of being a mother. We created some of them when we had absolutely no experiential understanding of being a mother at all.

Sometimes we have all these 'ideas' of ourselves (our identity) attached to our self-worth, meaning we can only feel good about ourselves when adhering to these 'ideas'. So, whenever we experience a major life change such as motherhood where unexpected events make it difficult to play out an 'idea', we can begin to feel lost, unimportant and not as valuable to the world. This is the feeling of lost identity.

Feeling as though you have lost your identity makes you feel that your life is less valuable than it was before, even though at the same time you know that your life is somehow worth more or is more complete than it was before simply because you have this beautiful baby in your life. This conflict between feeling that your life is more and less can be quite confusing. You love motherhood, but you resent leaving parts of your old life behind. At least, that's how it was for me.

However, in reality your life is neither worth more or less – it has simply changed and it has changed you as a person. As a result this 'idea' that you have of yourself must change too. Conscious consideration must be given to how you previously defined yourself and the expectations you have of being a mother, and whether these 'labels' and definitions realistically fit with this new way of life.

In addition, you must also separate your identity from your self-worth and understand that while it's great to have a sense of who you are and what your qualities are (identity), these things don't define your worth.

What defines your worth is simply that you are here and you are contributing to the process of life. You are always 100-percent worthy just by showing up every day as you do – not because you are carefree, calm, good at breastfeeding or good working in a particular job.

So by using the Mind TRACK to Happiness process we can look at what your personal identity is, whether it's in conflict with reality and whether you have attached your self-worth to it. From this point of view we can explore what you want out of your life and how to get it.

Your identity is not lost – it has simply changed. This chapter is about deliberately and consciously redesigning who you are and who you want to be and taking a realistic look at the balance between you as an individual and you as a mum.

Step 1 (Thoughts)

What is identity?

The first thing to identify in this step is how you currently define your identity. In the first step of the Mind TRACK to Happiness process we are always looking at what *you* believe about the current situation, understanding that it is never the event (new life after baby) that is causing you stress, but the way that you view this event (lost identity).

So, let's look at the actual definition of identity:
1. the name or essential character that identifies somebody or something
2. essential self – the set of characteristics that somebody recognizes as belonging uniquely to himself or herself and constituting his or her individual personality for life.

Source: *Encarta Dictionary: English* (UK)

I believe that your identity is made up of the following:
- the labels you place on yourself (wife, sister, daughter, mother, secretary, and so on)
- how you view your personality (smart, funny, adventurous, spontaneous, and so on)
- your beliefs about how you fit into society (business developer, designer, entrepreneur, teacher, the one who has it all together, the supporter, the friend you can depend on)
- your expectations and the qualities that you possess (quick learner, rational, positive, great achiever)
- your interests and hobbies (singing, dancing, camping, painting, going to concerts, coffee with friends, sports, going to the gym, and so on).

All of the events, experiences and knowledge that you have gained up until now have defined a certain viewpoint of yourself and what you consider to be your identity ('... the set of characteristics that somebody recognizes as belonging uniquely to himself or herself').

Essentially, your identity is made up of your belief about yourself. Often, this can be *learnt* beliefs that aren't really serving you and possibly beliefs that you've taken on but have never really deliberately considered.

If you take a look at some of the examples above of what makes up this identity, you will agree that some of those ideas just aren't compatible with being a mum.

For example, if part of your identity before becoming a parent included being spontaneous, this is now probably no longer a possibility – at least not the majority of the time or in the initial stages of having a new baby. This would be a huge change for someone who defined themselves this way. What about the belief that 'I'm the one who "has it all together"'? This is not a realistic label to have when dealing with very little sleep and a child who is constantly crying from colic, is it?

So you can see that the definition of identity that we hold going into parenting definitely needs to be reconsidered and aligned with the reality of motherhood.

We need to deliberately consider how we have been defining ourselves and contemplate whether some of the items on our list are in complete conflict with the reality of parenting, or whether they need to be slightly altered.

Exercise 1

First of all, we are going to look at how you used to define yourself before having children and then take a look at the expectations that you set yourself as a mum and what you consider an ideal mum to be. To do this, in your own notebook answer the following questions:

Past identity before children
1. The labels you had of yourself are …
2. How would you describe your personality?
3. What made you fit into society? What defined your place in the world?
4. What expectations and qualities did you have of yourself?
5. What were your interests and hobbies?

Expected or desired identity as a mum
1. What is your ideal of the perfect mother? (for example, calm, patient, loving, supportive, never yells or smacks, never gets angry, selfless)
2. Before you had children, what were the specific ideas you had of the sort of mother you wanted to be? (for example, care-free, flexible, energetic, fun)
3. Think back to when you were expecting your first child and the feeling of soon becoming a mum. What did you envisage being a mum would be like? (for example, full of love, fulfilling, exciting, can't wait to be at home full-time, lots of time for me when baby is sleeping, would never put children in day care, would enjoy playing with the baby all the time, taking baby on enjoyable day trips, and so on)

Now that you have your list, create a table such as the one in our example below and consider which items from your list are still relevant to the reality of motherhood and which items could be in conflict with this reality and may need to be reconsidered.

Example

From our list above here are some things that I would put in each column.

Past identity

	Items NOT in conflict with the reality of parenting	Items in conflict with the reality of parenting and need to be reconsidered
Labels	Wife, sister, daughter, mother	Secretary
Personality	Smart, funny	Adventurous, spontaneous
How you fit into society		Business developer, designer, entrepreneur, teacher, the one who has it all together, the supporter, the friend you can depend on
Expectations and qualities		Quick learner, rational, positive, great achiever
Your interests and hobbies	Singing, camping, painting, coffee with friends	Dancing, going to concerts, sports, going to the gym

Expected or desired identity as a mum

	Items NOT in conflict with the reality of parenting	Items in conflict with the reality of parenting and need to be reconsidered
Ideal of the Perfect Mother	Loving, supportive	Calm, patient, never yells or smacks, never gets angry, selfless
The mother I wanted to be prior to being a mum		Care-free, energetic, fun, flexible
How I envisaged being a mum		Full of love, fulfilling, exciting, can't wait to be at home full-time, lots of time for me when baby is sleeping, would never put children in day care, enjoy playing with them all the time, enjoyable day trips

The point of this example is to become aware of some of the labels and expectations that you might be trying to live up to and to recognise that these were created at a time when you weren't a mum and at a time when you had no experience of your current situation, hence creating conflict between belief and reality.

Exercise 2

> Now take a highlighter and go through your list again. Highlight any labels that you think you have attached your self-worth to, meaning that if you cannot live up to these labels then you are no longer as valuable, or your life feels diminished in some way.
>
> Be honest when you do this and ask yourself how it makes you feel if you can't live up to this idea you have of yourself. Do you feel like a failure? Do you feel like a bad mum? Do you feel like you've let others or yourself down? Do you feel like you're missing out or your life's on the wrong path?

Step 2 (Reality)

In Exercise 3 you will be using the (self-worth) labels you highlighted in Exercise 2, taking each one and aligning it with the reality of motherhood and your true self-worth. Here are some examples from Exercise 1 of how to do this.

Examples

Past identity

Secretary. Reality: Right now I am no longer a secretary. My job is being a stay-at-home mum. I might go back to it some day in the future.

Adventurous. Reality: I can still take on adventurous projects and hobbies, but these must now be planned in most cases and must take into consideration my responsibilities as a parent (for example, my safety).

Spontaneous. Reality: Sometimes I'm just not going to be able to be spontaneous. A lot of my time is now going to revolve around routine and plans, at least while the kids are young. Sometimes I can be spontaneous, but I can no longer define myself as a spontaneous person all the time.

The one who has it all together. Reality: Motherhood is a massive change for me and I don't really know what I'm doing a lot of the time, especially when my child is changing his (or her) behaviour so often as he (or she) grows. So, it's okay if at times I don't have it all together because I'm just learning.

The friend you can always depend on. Reality: My children take up a lot of my time and sometimes I'm just not going to be able to do things for people like I used to. I will still be a great friend, but sometimes my family will have to come first.

Quick learner. Reality: Some skills are harder to learn than others and sometimes I need more practice than I need in other areas. That's okay.

You can see that in some of these examples, I am not trying to completely change the labels, but simply put them in alignment with reality.

Expected or desired identity as a mum

Patient. Reality: It's unrealistic to expect that I'm going to remain patient at all times. Sometimes I am going to feel under pressure and will not react with patience in mind. That's okay. Parenting is quite demanding and I won't always behave the way that I would like to because my habitual thoughts govern my behaviour and while I'm learning to change them, I will probably get impatient at times. I am always learning from all my experiences, and patience is also an art that I am learning.

Never gets angry. Reality: Everyone feels anger at one point or another, especially parents. Anger is when you are identifying with your mind that something isn't meeting your expectations. You have a conversation in your mind that analyses that this event 'should' be different and therefore means something about you. I have been taught to react this way when life doesn't go to plan and it's going to take some time to change that. I am always learning from experiences such as these.

Exciting. Reality: Being a mum is not always exciting. Sometimes I need to deliberately create other things in my life that inspire and excite me.

Never put the children into day care. Reality: When I made this decision I had never been a mum and was never in the particular situation that I'm now in. It's okay to revisit the decision with the view of real-time events and to reconsider if necessary.

Enjoyable trips out. Reality: Sometimes, even though I'd like things to run smoothly, when I go out with my child it may not be enjoyable. I cannot control how my children behave. I can only control my own behaviour.

Exercise 3

Now it's your turn. Take your two lists and look at the ideas that you particularly had your self-worth attached to. Try to realign these ideas with the reality of being a mum in your current situation.

The reality of being a mum

Your view of the way you used to be before children needs to change. By deliberately reviewing some of the ideas you have of who you are, you quickly become aware that you cannot be that person anymore, at least not for now.

Especially during the first three-to-five years of your child's life, a lot of your time is taken up with raising your children. If you have subsequent children, then the number of years increases. This is the reality of parenting and it is a reality that you have to be aligned with, or it will cause resentment, unhappiness and stress.

Being the primary caregiver to your children means that you are the one who is on call 24/7 for your child and you are the one who needs to sort through the developmental changes that occur and figure out the appropriate way to handle them.

For this period of time when your child is at his or her most demanding, this role will be a large part of who you are. Being a mum is part of who you are. You haven't lost you, this *is* you. Of course, it's not all of you, but especially in those initial years when your child needs you a lot, it makes up most of you and this is the reality that you must come to terms with.

Does it mean that you cannot do anything for yourself? Absolutely not. But it does mean that you cannot expect to have the time to do things for yourself that you used to have. As my girlfriend once said, 'You decide what you want to do and then you plot and scheme around your kids to do it'.

Does it mean that you have to like this reality all the time? No. There will be many days where you still feel overwhelmed and exhausted by this reality, but the difference is that you will know that you have not lost your identity. Motherhood is now part of your identity and days such as this are part of your new reality of being a mum. This does not reduce your quality of life; it just makes it different from the way it used to be.

You need to change the picture in your mind of what your life used to look like to what it is now – otherwise you are in denial with reality. The past is over and you only have the now – and for now you are a mum who has a child taking up a lot of your time. It won't be forever, but it is for now.

When you find yourself feeling overwhelmed and exhausted it is also an indication that some time out for you needs to become a priority. In the next chapter we'll be looking in more detail at time out and time management and how you can make these priorities.

Exercise 4

In your notebook, write a paragraph – or a page, if you want – that describes everything that you feel is contributing to your lost identity. Why do you feel that your identity has been lost? You might like to consider the following questions to help you.

1. How has my life changed now that I'm a mum and how is it different from the way it used to be?
2. What events make me feel guilty as a mum?
3. Do I have any criticisms or judgements of my parenting capabilities?
4. What do I feel I am missing out on since becoming a mum?

These questions are only a guide to prompt you to think about how you feel. You don't have to use them if you don't want to. Just write how you feel about your lost identity.

Exercise 5

When you have finished writing how you feel, go through what you have written and highlight the four Get Your Life Right points. The GYLR points are:
1. Wrong path
2. Missing out
3. Should/could
4. Worth-less

Leave room in your notebook for upgrading these beliefs in the next step.

Case study 7: Jody

I don't know who I am anymore (wrong path) because I just don't do any of the things that I used to do (missing out). It feels like I'm just a stay-at-home mum and all I ever do is stuff to do with my baby (wrong path).

I don't earn any of my 'own money'. I don't get to use my brain like I used to do in my work (missing out). At work I used to be the organiser, the one who people would come to for help, and now I just feel like I barely get to consult with any adults anymore (missing out).

I love being a mum, but I feel like I've lost me (missing out) and that there should be more to me than just being at home with bub (should/could). I also feel like everything is getting on top of me (self-worth).

The house is always messy, I feel consumed by the constant challenges of my forever-changing children (wrong path) and I just don't get any time to do the things that I want to do anymore (missing out). I just don't feel like I'm really doing anything anymore other than being a mum (missing out).

Exercise 6

Now you need to take a look at your paragraph on lost identity and recreate this paragraph in alignment with reality. You can practise using the Personal Development Model as a guide to replacing your Get Your Life Right thinking and recreate this paragraph in alignment with the reality of your life right now.

The Personal Development Model steps are:
1. My life is a journey (of ups and downs).
2. I am always learning and receiving.
3. I can only know what I know at any given moment.
4. No matter how my life unfolds, I am always worthwhile.

Here's how Jody's recreated paragraph might look:

I am a new mum who has just entered a new stage of life that I've never experienced before. At the moment this means that I am rediscovering who I am within this role and realising that things don't happen the way they used to.

My child is taking up a lot of my time right now, but that just goes with the territory of being a mum with a young child. I know that I am not just a mum, but it does make up a large part of who I am right now.

I need to arrange some time out so that I can also do some things that I like to do other than being a mum.

Although I don't earn any of my own money, I am a team player in our family and money is not the only contributor to a family's needs. I contribute to other areas of need too.

I need to make time to use my brain in ways that stimulate me, just like when I was at work because that was important to me. My self-worth is not defined by the person I was at work. It is defined by what I contribute

> to everyone around me: that includes my kids, my husband and my friends because I myself am learning and growing as a person.
>
> Being a mum *is* part of me and I just need to make sure that I make time to include other parts of me too so I don't get overwhelmed and consumed with the demanding role of being a mum.
>
> Even though I'm not doing some of the things that I used to do, being a mum is incredibly valuable too. It's just that it doesn't come with the approval that other things did. I am making an important contribution to the world by being a mum. I just need to make sure that I also get to experience other things.
>
> Now, doesn't that feel completely different from the first paragraph? Now it's your turn to try and rewrite your paragraph on your identity in alignment with your current reality.

Identity and self-worth

A lot of stress can arise in mums who feel that they have lost their identity because they have attached their previous identity or their expectations of their new identity to their self-worth.

'Work defined me. My role as a "teacher" defined me. I used to be known as "x" and now I can't do that anymore. I wanted to be a happy mum. I wanted to be a breastfeeding mother. I wanted to be calm, patient and flexible. If I can't be or do "a" then this means "b" about my life.'

The reality of being a mum is that sometimes it can be tedious and monotonous and feel very much like 'groundhog day' and while most mothers feel this way at one point or another, the difference between a mum who doesn't feel like this for long and one who does, is their attachment to self-worth.

Take a look at your child's developmental stage. Is your child a newborn, baby or toddler? At this stage they require large amounts of time spent on them, which means less time for you. As they grow older, this amount of time decreases and more time is freed up for you. It has nothing to do with your life being worth more or worth less. It is simply the reality of having a young child. It means that your life slows down a little and things that you want to do take longer, can't happen right now or require 'planning and scheming'. This is the new reality of being a mum.

Your life's worth hasn't decreased, nor has it increased. It always remains the same. However, if you feel that it has changed, then it is your rating on your life that only when life goes a certain way can it be valuable. This rating is learnt and comes from your beliefs. How you rate your life before and after becoming a mum contributes to your perception of lost identity. I hope in these two steps you have begun to identify how you have been rating your life as a mum and how these labels, these 'ideas' of who you are, are not an indication of how valuable you are as a person – they are simply how you identify with yourself.

Step 3 (Aim)

In Step 3 we begin to consider what it is that you want.
When talking about lost identity, there seems to be a desire to reclaim some individuality, to feel that there is a sense of self that is separate from being a mum. Without forgetting that the reality of your children being little is that being a mum is part of your self – and right now is a large part of your self – being able to play out other parts of your identity is equally important.

In this step there are four categories to consider when establishing what you want:
1. What do I want?
2. Be specific.
3. Is it in conflict with reality?
4. Why do I want it?

What do I want?

So what is it that you want and aren't getting? It is easy to stay in conflict with what used to happen in your life and what you are not getting now, but what do you actually want?

If you want more time to spend being an individual outside of being a mum, what does that mean? Is it more time out to just chill out? Is it time for a hobby that you have? Is it time to learn something new? Is it just to re-establish what sort of person you want to be and research how to become that person? What exactly are you doing that will meet this desire?

Exercise 7

In your notebook, brainstorm some ideas of what you might want that will give you this sense of independence.

Be specific

Exercise 8

Once you have this list, choose some items from it and try to be more specific about what you want. For example, 'I want to try and get at least two hours a week to paint like I used to', or 'I want to take a relaxing bath once a week'. Be specific about what exactly you want and what amount of time you will need in order to carry out your wish.

Is what I want in conflict with reality?

Remember that it is important to consider what you want in terms of your current situation – for example, what age your child is. If you have a three or four year old who doesn't have a day-time nap anymore, then it is not likely that you will get one-to-two hours during the day to concentrate on painting (they would likely want to join in), so this must be considered as a night-time event when your child is asleep.

Also, if you want to take on a new challenge by studying, you must consider the reality of how much time you are going to be able to spend actually studying at this point in time. This would determine whether you would take on study part-time or full-time. Check whether any of the items on your list are in conflict with reality and need to be adjusted.

Why do I want it?

What benefits does having this aim give you? Why do you want it? Is it to experience something new, or do you feel that it is going to make your life 'better'?

Remember, it's okay to think that your life is going to be 'better' when you achieve this, as long as you aren't thinking that your life is worse now. Your aim in terms of your identity is about being able to make some time to play roles in your life other than just being a mum.

It's not that being 'just a mum' makes your life worse; it's just that you have a desire to do other things too. This is an important point to grasp because you don't want to start placing more value on achieving these desires. Sometimes you might not be able to achieve these desires because your responsibilities as a mum have to take priority over your personal goals. This is simply the reality of being a mum and the ups and downs that come with being a parent.

Exercise 9

> Compare the list of wishes you identified in Exercise 8 against the GYLR Model and upgrade them where necessary.

Step 4 (Choices)

We've all read the books and heard the advice that we need to take time out and do things for ourselves, but why don't we just do that? Why don't we just organise some time out and take it?

Is it really because we have too much housework to do, or that the kids really need us, or that we don't have enough time?

The choices you make and the actions you take are governed by your priorities at that time. Your beliefs dictate what your priorities are.

It's way too common for mums to feel as though they don't have any time for themselves, when in reality their beliefs don't allow for them to make time for themselves.

Examples

1. 'I don't do things for myself because when my husband is home I want to spend time with him, not just leave the baby with him and go out.'
2. 'I never get any time out for me because every time I get a free minute there is housework to be done or groceries to be bought and it's so much easier to do the groceries without the kids.'
3. 'I am a single mum. I never get any time out because I don't have any family or friends to look after the kids and I'd never put them in day care, because that's just not right.'

The mum in Example 1 has made spending time with her husband a priority over her time out.

In Example 2, the mum has made housework and grocery shopping a priority over her time out. In addition, shopping without the kids further supports her making shopping a priority over time out.

In Example 3, the beliefs the mum has about day care override her priority of taking time out.

Incidentally, none of these examples describes right or wrong priorities. They are simply examples of how our choices are governed by our beliefs. Each mother holds certain beliefs about something else being more important than her time out.

If you want more time to explore other parts of your identity, then you must make it a priority to do that. You can only make it a priority when you believe that it is more important than anything else at that time – otherwise you won't allow yourself that time.

Remember the case study in Part A of Liz, who wouldn't make herself a priority? This was because she was taught from childhood that making herself a priority potentially opens herself up for ridicule.

Your brain is always working in alignment with your beliefs, and making yourself a priority will be determined by whether you believe you deserve to be the priority or not.

In the next chapter, we will look at time out and time management more thoroughly, and in the context of the priorities governed by your beliefs. I mention it here to make you aware that in order to action the plan that you create to fulfil other parts of your identity, you are going to have to make the plan a priority over other things.

Options/solutions

Now we get to the 'how' of your aim. How do I create a plan so that I can get what I want?

Well, whether it's time out for hobbies, coffee with friends or taking a relaxing bath once a week you need to search for the solutions and options that you have available in order to make this time.

1. Research

What do I need in order to meet my aims?

If it's time out, you need someone to look after your child. Your partner, babysitters and day care are all options. There might be several ways that you can go about getting what you want. You need to investigate each option and weigh up which one looks the most viable.

2. Preparation

Once I have that sorted, what other preparations do I need to make in order to do what I want? For example, if you were going to paint, you would need to make sure that you had all the materials ready to go.

You will often be on a strict time limit when you're having time out, so it's imperative that you organise whatever you need before your time starts. That way you can make the most of the time you have to yourself.

3. Thoughts

When looking at each option, be aware of the thoughts that spring to mind and what you are thinking when imagining yourself doing whatever you would like to be doing.

Remember that your choices are governed by the beliefs you have, so be conscious of those little conversations that enter your mind about whether you can or can't do something and why. You might just find that a self-limiting belief has crept in there that tells you why you can't achieve this option, and this needs to be addressed.

When you notice these thoughts see where they fit in the Get Your Life Right Model and upgrade them using the Personal Development Model.

Step 5 (Know your plan and action it)

If you go back to the beginning of this chapter, you will see that we began by addressing your feeling of lost identity and what you feel this means about you.

As we explored further, we could see that it was not that our identity was lost; it was merely that some of the things we felt defined our identity were no longer relevant to our new life of being a mum.

We have also established that it was the perception that we have of this identity that caused us to feel unhappy or stressed by this change.

Our worth is not defined by the ideas or labels that we place on ourselves. It's defined by our existence – by way of our contributions to the circle of life – and through our own learning and growth. We are always 100-per-cent worthwhile.

This information sent our search for identity in a new direction. Rather than thinking that our life was worth-less because we could not live it out the way we thought we should, we have now directed our attention to looking more at what we would like to experience – not what we are missing out on and how we can make something happen.

It's a very distinct shift in perspective. *The Mind TRACK to Happiness process is all about shifting your mindset, not trying to find ways of getting your life 'right'.* There are no specific identities you can have that make up the perfect person and there is no right or wrong way for you to live. Neither being a mother, nor not being a mother defines your worth and it's only your rating of your identity that makes you feel like it does.

It was intentional that I shift your mindset away from thinking that your identity is lost and more to recognising that being a mother is a large part of your identity now and that other areas need to take second place to that sometimes, depending on the age and stage of your child.

Furthermore, it doesn't mean that those other areas should be completely neglected either; it just means that they don't form a large part of who you are for now, especially while your children are young. As your children get older, this balance will start to shift and even itself out a little more, but, of course, only in alignment with your priorities and your beliefs.

Your final step in the topic of lost identity is really keeping all this in mind as you go about your daily life. Set yourself plans to take time out and do things for yourself. Enjoy your time away and feel refreshed and grateful for it.

Always have a plan for the next time you're going to do something for yourself – even if it's only something small – so that you can look forward to it, especially in times where you do feel like things are getting overwhelming or monotonous.

Finally, it's important to do things other than being a mum so that you do get to experience those other parts of yourself that are just as fulfilling, rewarding, challenging and enjoyable.

Life is about experience, learning and growing, and just because your children are at ages where they take up a lot of your time and need you right now, it doesn't mean that this has to be the be all and end all of your life. You just have to make it a priority to experience other things too, because this time of being a mother can be consuming, so you need to take care of your needs to.

Boredom and lost identity

Often boredom can be largely attributed to the feeling of lost identity. It is reality that the repetition involved in being a mum, especially when your children are younger, can be a big adjustment to make, particularly if your life was very busy and full of interesting events before having children.

The Mind TRACK to Happiness process can also be used in the case of boredom to change how you feel about the monotonous aspect of parenting, which could make a huge difference to how you feel about being a mum.

Let's see how we can do this.

Step 1 (Thoughts)

Even with boredom, the GYLR Model can be playing out.

1. Wrong path:

You might believe that your old life is the right path and that the mundane things you are doing are on the wrong path.

2. Missing out:

You might feel that you are missing out on all the exciting things that are happening outside of the home, such as back at your old work, in your social life or in relation to your old favourite past times.

3. Should/could:

You might feel that you should be enjoying parenting and that you shouldn't feel bored, or that you should feel grateful that you can stay home with the kids. This is where the guilt kicks in.

4. Worth-less:

All of these thoughts will lead you to the belief that your life is somehow less worthwhile because you are at home with the kids.

Step 2 (Reality)

In this step you need to upgrade the GYLR Model with reality and the Personal Development Model.

The reality is that at this stage of your life this is what you are doing and the tasks involved all form part of what you have to do as a parent. This is the reality of parenting. You will have to do repetitive tasks such as cooking, cleaning, changing nappies, spending lots of time getting your children to sleep, solving arguments and interacting with your children at their level. This is all part of the experience that you signed up for.

The Personal Development Model upgrade would look like this:

1. My life is a journey.

What you are currently experiencing is part of your journey in life. The tasks that you are participating in don't put your life on the wrong path. This is just the path you are currently on at this stage of your life because your children are young. This is where you're at on your journey because you have taken on the role of a parent and because you currently have young children. It doesn't reflect your entire life; it just reflects your life for now.

2. I am always learning and receiving.

Being a mum at home has enormous value for your development because of the vast array of lessons you learn from being a mother and for what you are receiving from your child. Instead of seeing the tasks that you perform as tedious and monotonous it's time to start seeing the value of being at home with your children and what you can appreciate about being able to spend this time with them and doing what you are currently doing.

3. I can only know what I know at any given moment.

You perceive being at home with the kids as being boring because of the beliefs you hold about what makes for an interesting life. You can only work with the beliefs you currently hold and you can't feel differently about this situation until you find a different way to think about it. You can't enjoy motherhood instead of feeling bored until you change your beliefs on how you perceive your role as a mother and change how you rate your life as a mum. Find the value in being a mum and all you do as a mum (even the monotonous tasks) and your rating will increase.

4. No matter how my life unfolds, I am always worthwhile.

Your life is not less valuable because you are staying at home with your children doing what you do. Although society doesn't often publicly acknowledge the work that mothers do, mothers are tremendously valuable to the way the world operates.

You are contributing to the raising of a future adult – installing in them knowledge and teaching them about life. You are learning about your life and adding to your knowledge, which you also pass on to your children and those around you.

This learning and contributing is what dictates your life as worthy and meaningful, not the mundane tasks that you are doing. No matter what you are doing in life, your worth comes from existing as a human being and contributing to life by living it.

Step 3 (Aim)

Even though you have completed Steps 1 and 2 and are now aligned with the reality of your situation and your self-worth (which may have been obvious facts to you anyway), you still might feel that you are not as stimulated as you would like to be.

Being at home with the kids can get boring at times, but it doesn't have to be that way all the time. You just need to decide what it is that you want to do and then make plans to do it.

Think about what you want as opposed to the 'boring' life and begin working out how you can organise things to be this way.

This might be to create more time out for yourself away from the kids; it might be to create more outings with the kids to get away from the house; or it might be to find a support network or make new friends so that you can have someone to answer the 'What do I do now?' questions. Whatever the aim is, make sure you think about the following points too, just to test your aim against reality:

- Why do I want it?
- Be specific.
- Is what I want in conflict with reality?

Step 4 (Choices)

Now it's time to get solution focussed about your 'boring' life. What are the options that you have available to make life more interesting? What are other mothers doing to pass the time and feel more enthusiastic about their role?

Here are a few suggestions of my own relating to how you could approach this area of concern.

- Join a mother's group where you can interact with other mums and get some adult time while your kids play.
- Research games and interesting activities you can do with your kids that are exciting to you and them. You get to spend quality time with them while also enjoying what you're doing.
- Spread your household chores out over the week in between other interesting activities so that you don't feel like you are endlessly doing housework.
- Make sure you give yourself some adult time by yourself and with friends so you get that sense of individuality and separation from your role as a mum.

Be mindful while you are exploring these options of the beliefs that arise when you are considering these for your plan. Are there any thoughts that are in conflict with the possibility of actioning these plans? Do they make you feel guilty or make you think that you 'shouldn't' do these things? Be aware of these thoughts and see whether you can upgrade them using Steps 1 and 2.

Step 5 (Know your plan and action it)

From your list of options and possible solutions, create a list of all the things you are willing to do that will help you feel as though your life is more exciting and eventful.

If you need to, keep a diary or create a schedule of the places where you are going, or maybe even plan your week or your month factoring in all of the things that you need to do and all of the fun things that can be incorporated into it as well.

Make sure, though, that you realise that this doesn't make your life more worthwhile or meaningful. However, it does make it more interesting because the reality is that some of the tasks involved with being a mum can become repetitive and monotonous.

Chapter 12

Time out

'There's never any time for me anymore.'

'I don't have time to do the things that I like to do.'

'The kids always come before me.'

'There are just so many things that I need to do all the time and then there's no time left for me.'

Does this sound familiar? Do you find that at the end of the day there is just not enough time left for you to do what you want to do?

Lack of time out and loss of identity can go hand in hand, causing a lot of stress among mothers. Logically we know that as mums it's important to take some time out from our parenting role. It refreshes us, helps us to gain some perspective and gives us the opportunity to experience things we enjoy other than just being mums.

We already know that motherhood can be a demanding job and you have probably experienced firsthand how important it is to take time out for yourself. You already know the value of time out, so this chapter is not going to rehash all of the reasons why you need to take time out and give you information that you already have.

Lack of time out seems to occur because there are so many things to do, such as caring for the kids, housework, running errands, spending time with your husband/partner and, in many cases, fitting work into the mix. Somehow you are the one who ends up missing out on doing things for yourself, especially when the kids are quite young and need a lot of your attention.

So our time-out issues don't come from not knowing that we need it for the benefit of ourselves and our kids, because we logically know that we need it. Our lack of time out seemingly comes from there just not being enough hours in the day for mums to do the things we love to do as well.

Time out is non-existent or limited because there isn't enough time to do everything. Or is it? Is lack of time really the reason why we don't get time out, or is it something else?

'Prepare to be set free as you learn the watch words of time management. Guess what? Neither of them is time or management. The need-to-know magic words are choice and focus.' (Source: *Time Management for Manic Mums*; Allison Mitchell: 2006)

What Allison expresses brilliantly is that managing your time has very little to do with time. It's all about what you *choose* to do and what you *focus* on.

What have we learnt so far about what drives our choices? That's right: our priorities. And our priorities are governed by what we believe.

If you have not been getting any time out lately, it has little to do with how much time you have available and a lot to do with what you believe has more of a priority than taking time out.

All of those chores mentioned above – such as housekeeping, running errands, looking after the kids, your husband/partner – have been made a priority over your time out and thus you have put yourself last. It's that simple. This has happened because you hold beliefs that these things are more important than your time out.

We're going to approach your time out a little differently in this chapter by exploring the beliefs you currently hold – that is, putting your time out on the backburner and allowing everything else to come first.

We can apply the Mind TRACK to Happiness process to the topic of time out by figuring out how our thoughts are in conflict with reality and then determining what we want and how to get it.

Why isn't 'time out' my priority?

In order to find out why time out is not a top priority for you, you need to first identify what is your priority and what your beliefs are about why everything else is so important to you.

Step 1 (Thoughts)

In the next four exercises, we will look at your beliefs about five different areas of our lives that we juggle our time around and what you believe about each category. This will give you some insight into why you prioritise your activities the way you do.

Exercise 1

1. Think about events in your life over the past month and rearrange the following list in order of how you have been spending your time. Number 1 will be what you have been spending most of your time on.
   1. You
   2. Work
   3. Your marital/partner relationship
   4. Your children
   5. Housework
2. Under each heading, write a short paragraph on why you consider this to be ranked where it is.

Here is an example for one mum (Lucy), showing the order she would put these categories into and why.

Chapter 12: Time out

Case study 8: Lucy

1. My children. My children are only two and four so they require a lot of my time at the moment. Especially my two year old. He is going through the terrible twos at the moment and is a lot of work, so he takes up a lot of my time and of course I have to try and balance that out with the four year old so he doesn't feel left out.
2. Work. Work is really important to me because I need an outlet too and I need to stimulate my mind. Also, I need to help bring money into the home so that we can pay the mortgage, eat and live the lifestyle that we want. I work three days a week.
3. Marital relationship. In order to keep the relationship healthy, I need to juggle my time between my husband and my kids, otherwise he might feel neglected and our relationship might fall apart. Anyway, I really like to spend time with him.
4. Me. I'm trying to fit myself in here where I can. I do consider 'me' important; it's just that right now the other things are important too, so I guess I do put myself down quite low on my list of priorities.
5. Housework. I don't care too much about the housework. I do what I can when I can and if the house is untidy then that's okay by me for now. The kids are at young ages and mess it all up anyway, so as long as it's hygienic then I'm okay with a bit of mess.

Exercise 2

The following questions will give you some insight into what your beliefs are about the above categories and why you prioritise as you do.

Answer these questions related to each category in your notebook.

Parenting

1. In your view, what defines a good mother?
2. Where did you learn that these qualities encompass what a good mother is?
3. How would you feel if you were unable to live up to your expectations of a 'good mother'?

Work

1. Why is work important to you?
2. How would you feel if you couldn't work?

Marital/partner relationship

1. What defines a successful relationship?
2. Where did you learn that this defines a successful relationship?
3. How do you feel when you are not meeting these expectations?

Housework

1. What expectations do you have about the level of cleanliness that your house needs to be kept at?
2. Which events have contributed to you believing it needs to be kept this way?
3. What happens if it isn't kept this way and how do you feel if your house doesn't meet these expectations?

Me

1. What do you think your needs are outside of being a mum?
2. How do you feel if your needs are not met?
3. How do you feel when you take time out for yourself (for example, guilty, free, excited, ashamed, as though you are doing something 'wrong')?

Exercise 3

Go back over your answers in Exercise 2 and highlight/underline any GYLR Model points that you discover.
1. Wrong path/right path
2. Missing out
3. Should/could
4. Worth-less

This is how Lucy might respond to Exercise 3.

Parenting

1. In your view, what defines a good mother?

> A good mother is there for her children. She is supportive, is the educator and is responsible for teaching them how to be confident and how to live in this world (right path).

2. Where did you learn that these qualities encompass what a good mother is?

> Well, my mother was a great role model and really helped me in the area of self-confidence. She was always there for me and encouraged me to go for what I wanted in life.

3. How would you feel if you were unable to live up to your expectations of a 'good mother'?

> I would feel like a bad mum (worth-less) and that my kids were missing out on the best start to life (missing out). It's really important for kids to have a healthy view of themselves and to be able to live a comfortable life (right path).

Work

1. Why is work important to you?

> Work is my release. It's who I am (self-worth). I get to be someone other than just a mum (right/wrong path), so it's kind of like my time out. I love what I do, so I feel like there's still a bit of me alive when I'm working (self-worth). Also, I need to work, otherwise we couldn't have this house and the kids wouldn't get the lifestyle that they get to have (missing out).

2. How would you feel if you couldn't work?

> I'd feel a bit lost actually (worth-less). I would feel like my life didn't mean as much (worth-less). Also, we wouldn't be able to afford the things that we do. We'd probably be able to keep paying the house off on my husband's wage, but we definitely wouldn't be able to afford the luxuries that we do. The kids wouldn't be able to do some of the things that they get to do – such as get take out, go to play centres, get new clothes and shoes – and that wouldn't be fair (missing out).

Marital/partner relationship

1. What defines a successful relationship?

> Communication, respect for each other, love, understanding, a connection between one another

2. Where did you learn that this defines a successful relationship?

> Well, I learnt how not to have a relationship from my parents, and my husband taught me the rest. His parents are still together, so I guess he had some strong family values and we've figured it out along the way.

3. How do you feel when you are not meeting these expectations?

> I feel like I am fighting with my best friend (missing out). We have quite a close relationship and if it doesn't feel like we are on the same page then everything else kind of falls apart (wrong path). I am constantly monitoring how our relationship is travelling (note that this is congruent with the core belief behind anxiety – control and prevent – see page 90) because I don't want it to go down the same road as my parents did and end in divorce (wrong path). That would be terrible for the kids (worth-less).

Housework

1. What expectations do you have about the level of cleanliness that your house needs to be kept at?

> As long as it's hygienic and relatively clean, I'm pretty happy with that. We have a lot on at the moment and the kids keep messing it up anyway, so there's really no point in getting pedantic about it.

Chapter 12: Time out **203**

2. What events have contributed to you believing it needs to be kept this way?

> Well, my mum used to work a lot and she would clean once a week, but was never really one that needed to have everything in place 100 per cent of the time. I don't really hold it too high on my list of priorities. As long as it stays hygienic and generally clean then that's fine.

3. What happens if it isn't kept this way and how do you feel if your house doesn't meet these expectations?

> Sometimes I can get a bit stressed if it has been too messy for too long or if I don't have the time to make it to the standard I like it to be (wrong path). I think it's because I get annoyed that I have to make it a priority (should/could) in order to be a 'good mother and housewife' (self-worth). I get a bit annoyed that it is part of my role to look after the housework and I don't like that (wrong path). I have other more important things to do than clean, so it does bug me when I have to make it a priority to clean it sometimes (wrong path).

Me

1. What do you think your needs are outside of being a mum?

> To be interested in things other than parenting, to feel loved and accepted by my husband and my friends, to spend time with the people I love and enjoy being around

2. How do you feel if your needs are not met?

> I feel like all I am is a mum (worth-less) and that there is more to me than what I am currently doing. It's really important for me to be able to express who I am to the world (worth-less) and if I can't do that then I feel like my life is not as valuable (worth-less).

3. How do you feel when you take time out for yourself (for example, guilty, free, excited, ashamed, as though you are doing something 'wrong')?

> Most of the time I feel okay. I mean, I need to have a life too (self-worth). Sometimes I feel guilty if I'm not spending enough time with the kids (should/could), so I make a conscious effort to do more stuff with them, but at the end of the day, I don't feel guilty any more that I'm doing things for myself.

Exercise 4

The last two exercises were about gathering information about what your priorities are and the beliefs that are driving those priorities. In this exercise, let's analyse the last three exercises to see what we discover about our priorities and the beliefs that govern what takes priority.

Analyse your answers from Exercise 1, 2 and 3, and then answer the following questions:

1. Write down what the common beliefs were that stood out for each GYLR point in Exercise 3.
   a. Wrong path/right path
   b. Missing out
   c. Should/could
   d. Worth-less
2. Now that you have discovered that you hold these beliefs, review Exercise 1 and your list of priorities and state why you now think you make each one a priority.
3. What were the main beliefs that you felt you held with regard to your self-worth? What did you believe made you feel worth-less or that your life was of less value?

Let's look at Lucy's example to see what we can discover.

1. What were the common beliefs that stood out for each GYLR point?
   a. Wrong path/right path

Lucy felt that in order for life to be going on the right path she had to be responsible for teaching her kids self-confidence and how to live a comfortable life.

> b. Missing out

A lot of Lucy's answers centred around her kids missing out on something in their lives. But what also became dominant in her language was that Lucy was trying to avoid missing out on *her* life by wanting to work and be 'someone other than just a mum'.

> c. Should/could

While there was not a lot of should/could in Lucy's answers, she did feel like she should be the one to look after the household chores and that she should be doing something else with her time.

> d. Worth-less

In Lucy's answers there was a lot of language around being a good mum, but what was most dominant was Lucy's view on having a 'valuable' life by doing things outside of being a mum. It seems that Lucy has a lot of self-worth attached to being able to achieve certain things outside of her role as a mum in order for her life to have meaning.

> 2. Now that you have discovered that you hold these beliefs, review Exercise 1 and your list of priorities and state why you now think you make each one a priority.

Lucy makes her children her first priority because she wants to be a good mum and feels like she needs to be educating them on how to be confident and comfortable in life. It is her priority because she is the primary caretaker and it is important for her to provide the influence on her children that they might need in order to live comfortable and confident lives.

Lucy makes work her second priority because she has attached her self-worth to being able to express herself in this way and she believes it makes her life more meaningful outside of just being a mum.

Her relationship comes next because she is trying to monitor the health of her relationship in order to avoid going down the wrong path of getting a divorce like her parents did.

Lucy has made herself come next because she already views that she is making herself a priority in work, so she doesn't see that other extra curricula activities are as important. It has been vitally important for Lucy to be able to make her life valuable through her work.

Finally, she doesn't really consider housework too much of a priority and really only does it because she believes that it forms part of her role in the family.

> 3. What were the main beliefs that you felt you held with regard to your self-worth? What did you believe made you feel worth-less or that your life was of less value?

For Lucy, work is who she is. If she doesn't work then she doesn't get to 'be someone other than being a mum'.

When you look at the four exercises it is clear that lack of time out for Lucy could be a source of stress, particularly surrounding work.

Lucy holds the incorrect belief that her work defines her life as being more worthy, so if she doesn't make work her priority, or for some reason she is not able to go to work (for example, if the kids are sick), then she could start to become stressed or depressed or anxious around that time, particularly if she wasn't able to feel that her life had meaning outside of 'just being a mum'.

The answers to these exercises will be different for everybody but you'll be able to see a common thread and strong beliefs about how you prioritise the categories. You will also be able to notice that your priorities have little to do with time and more to do with what you have come to believe about each category and more so what these categories mean about your self-worth.

You are always acting in the best interests of yourself. What defined Lucy's priorities came from her beliefs about being a good mother so that her children wouldn't miss out, and also going to work, thus adding meaning to her life.

Step 2 (Reality)

Now that we have identified some of the beliefs that drive our priorities and linked them with the GYLR Model of thinking, it is time to upgrade these beliefs using the Personal Development Model of thinking. Remember that the GYLR Model of thinking causes stress, so we really want to practise becoming aware of these thoughts and upgrade them to view life in line with reality.

Exercise 5

> From the questions in Exercise 4, try to upgrade the beliefs you discovered on the GYLR Model to the Personal Development Model.
> 1. Life is a journey.
> 2. I am always learning and receiving.
> 3. I only know what I know at any given moment.
> 4. I am always worthwhile/100-per-cent worthy

Here's Lucy's example:

What were the common beliefs that stood out for each GYLR point?

1 Wrong path

Lucy felt that in order for her life to be on the right path she had to be responsible for teaching her kids self-confidence and how to live a comfortable life.

Upgrade: Life is a journey

Whether Lucy is able to teach her children self-confidence or whether they are able to have a comfortable life is irrelevant to the value of their lives.

Life is a journey of ups and downs. That is the reality of life. No matter what Lucy teaches her children they will experience ups and downs and sometimes they won't be comfortable with life and sometimes they won't feel confident about themselves. She is unable to control this. Although this doesn't mean that she will change her goal of trying to teach this to her children, she must become aware that they will still experience events where life doesn't go to plan and that these experiences do not make their lives less valuable – they are just experiences that add to their unique journey in life.

There is no right path where life has to be comfortable and we have to be confident in order for life to be successful. There is only one path and that is our life and all of the experiences within it.

2 Missing out

A lot of Lucy's answers centred around her kids missing out on something in their lives. But what also became dominant in her language was that Lucy was trying to avoid missing out on 'her life', but wanting to work and be 'someone other than just a mum'.

Upgrade: I am always learning and receiving

In every one of our experiences there is value. We are always learning new things from our experiences and this happens whether it is an enjoyable experience or not. Lucy's concern is that her children might miss out on some aspect of life (for example, money, certain experiences, and so on). However, they are always receiving lessons and experiences for their development so they are *never* missing out on what their lives need in order to progress through it. From every experience there is event learning (what we learn from the event) and life learning (our view on life and self-worth) and if Lucy's children don't get something that they wanted in their lives, they can either view it as 'missing out' (which causes stress) or they can learn something from it. If Lucy learns to view life this way, she can pass this learning onto her children so that they can practise it in their lives. With regard to 'just being a mum', Lucy needs to start looking at the value of being a mum and the learning and receiving that she gains from that experience too. She is not missing out on anything when she is 'just being a mum' because she is learning about life from being a mum and from being with her children. She learns new skills such as time management, negotiation with her kids, parenting skills, and she receives the experience of being a mum and knowing what this is like. *Motherhood changes her whole view of life and she receives the opportunity to redefine how she views life.*

It is often the case for women that becoming a mum gives them the opportunity to take a step back from life and review what is important to them and what they want from their lives. There is value within that. For Lucy, she needs to start seeing the value that has come from all events, which will enable her to view motherhood as just as meaningful to her life as going to work.

3 Should/could

While there were not a lot of should/could responses in Lucy's questionnaire, she did feel that she should be the one to look after the household chores and that she should be doing something else with her time.

> **Upgrade: I/we can only know what we know at any given moment.**

The household chores have become her responsibility because somewhere along the line it was agreed that this would be her role in the family. Whether that was directly or indirectly based on the information she and her husband had at that time, this is the decision that was made, so being in conflict with this reality is what causes her stress with regard to housework. It is her role at the moment because that was what was agreed and if she wishes to change it then she needs to make a new agreement.

With regard to doing something else with her time, Lucy must recognise that if she is doing the housework, or looking after the kids instead of 'doing something else with her time', it is because she has made it a priority in that moment. Due to her dominant beliefs in that moment based on all the information and experiences she has had up until this moment she has chosen to do the housework or look after the kids.

By reviewing your priorities and identifying the beliefs that drive them you can come to terms with the reality of why you are doing what you are doing in this moment. You can only know what you know in any given moment and your decisions are based on your beliefs and what is considered a priority in that moment.

4 Worth-less

In Lucy's questionnaire there was a lot of language around being a good mum, but what was most dominant was Lucy's view on having a 'valuable' life by doing things outside of being a mum. It seems that Lucy has a lot of self-worth attached to being able to achieve certain things outside of her role as a mum in order for her life to have meaning.

> **Upgrade: I am always worthwhile/100-per-cent worthy**

This upgrade is the core understanding for releasing stress in terms of time out. Often we feel that we are missing out on time out and that therefore our lives are of less value.

In Lucy's case, she felt that missing out on work (being her time out) would make her life less valuable and being at home with the kids makes her life less valuable in some way. Now, that doesn't mean Lucy doesn't like being at home with her kids; it just means that she has attached her self-worth to being able to work and what she does at work.

However, neither work nor being at home with the kids defines self-worth. What defines self-worth is the value in all experiences – that in all experiences you learn and grow and add to your development and knowledge of life and in all experiences you are contributing to the process of life.

When Lucy is at home with the kids she is learning and adding to her own development as well as contributing what she knows to her children and adding to their development. They are doing the same for her. When she is at work, the same thing is happening. She is learning and growing, contributing to others around her and learning from others.

Lucy's self-worth never changes. However, what has changed is how Lucy rates herself – that is, her self-esteem.

Because of her beliefs that her work gives her life meaning, Lucy rates her life as being less valuable whenever she's not able to work. She also rates herself as worth-less whenever she is not able to teach her kids self-confidence or facilitate a life that is comfortable for them.

In all experiences, Lucy is always learning, growing and contributing and is always 100-per-cent worthy.

> Now, in your own notebook, see if you can upgrade your own beliefs and find a different way to view your beliefs on time out.

What about life balance?

We are often told that we need to have our life in balance.

Particularly when we have children and go to work, there is a lot of emphasis put on the work/life balance.

When we talk about balance, we often think that each area of our lives (us, work, relationships, children and housework) must be equal, meaning that an equal amount of time and energy must be put into each area.

The reality is that sometimes we can't experience all parts of our lives equally. Sometimes we will spend more time on one area of our lives than others – and that's okay. It doesn't mean that our lives are out of balance. It just means that there is an area of our lives that's taking up a lot of time – that's all. It also means that it's an area that we have made a priority over others due to our beliefs – and that's okay too.

For example, when our children are between the ages of birth and three years, they take up a lot of our time. This doesn't leave a lot of time for favourite pastimes, household chores, relationships or work and that's just the reality of parenting. During this stage of our lives, we are simply unable to give all areas of our lives equal attention.

Life doesn't have to be in balance in order for it to be going correctly. Sometimes some things take more time out of our lives than others. However, if you are feeling stressed because one area of your life is taking up too much time over another, it's not because your life is out of balance. It's because you are rating this situation (based on your beliefs), possibly believing that you 'shouldn't' be spending so much time in this area and 'should' be spending your time elsewhere. However, there is a priority you have (also based on beliefs) for spending time where you do, so investigating these beliefs and upgrading them will reduce the stress.

Readjusting your idea of 'time out'

Sometimes the answer to time out and feeling like you're getting enough of it of it comes from a deliberate alteration of how we think about time out. Often we are in direct conflict with how we used to view our time out (from work, relationships, and so on) compared with how much time out we get now.

Before we have children, we are pretty much able to do what we want when we want and for however long we want – definitely with more flexibility than once we have children.

Unhappiness about lack of time out can come from an attachment to the way things used to be. Our idea of time out has its reference point in the past. Sometimes after having children, we are still trying to measure our current experience of this time out against our old reference point, which was before children. The reality is, this reference point just isn't relevant anymore. You simply can't expect to have the same amount of time available to pursue the projects and tasks that you spent time on before having children. It doesn't mean you can't have time out; it just means that it needs to be created in different ways.

You have to deliberately reset your mind to work within the circumstances of your current commitments. You have to get rid of the old picture that you have painted in your mind of how time out plays out in your life and create a new picture that fits with present-time reality.

Step 3 (Aim)

The different types of time out

Before we get into time out, it's relevant to look at the different types of time out so that you can be clear on exactly what you want your time out for. There are four different types of time out that I have identified, each with its own benefits.

The quick-fix time out

This type of time out is designed to give you a quick break from being a mother. Think of it as a morning-tea break or a lunch break. Quick-fix time out includes:

- doing housework without the kids. Okay, I can hear you all screaming at me saying that housework is not time out! However, it can sometimes be a nice, mindless job that allows you to think about life and gain perspective without having to participate in a planned activity, especially if you are doing it without the kids in the house. This can be an appropriate quick fix to a challenging and busy day and also helps make you feel on top of things again.
- running down to the shop to get some groceries without the kids. Again, this is not traditionally time out as it is still a chore, but it can give you some time to think and calm down if necessary.
- running down to the bank or the accountant or the solicitor, or any other errand that you slip into your day without taking the kids. It can make you feel organised and allow you to get those odd jobs out of the way that are just too complicated and stressful to involve the kids in.

A quick-fix time out is a very fleeting time out and not enough to generate a deep sense of peace and re-composure, but it has its place in your life when things are really crazy and you are looking for a spontaneous, quick fix to avoid feeling consumed.

Refreshing time out

Refreshing time out is about rejuvenating your physical self, which can make you feel better about yourself physically, affecting you mentally and emotionally. Examples are:

- catching up on sleep. This makes you feel physically better

equipped to handle the world and your commitments. If you are lacking in sleep, this kind of time out is a necessity if you are to cope with raising your children calmly and rationally. When we are tired, it affects us physically, mentally and emotionally. Taking this kind of time out is imperative if you have a baby or an unwell, unsleeping child. The world is a different place to a well rested mother.
- getting a massage, facial or manicure. This kind of time out is very relaxing and just what you might need to soothe away your troubles momentarily. You awaken from these kinds of self-indulgences a new woman physically, which has positive effects on you mentally and emotionally.
- reading a book or watching a movie. Sitting around idly and immersing yourself in fiction or someone else's story or words is very relaxing and quite enjoyable. It takes you away from your life and puts you into someone else's. For moments in time you are miles away from your own life and relaxing into the realms of somewhere else.
- having a long, hot bubble bath. This kind of time out is caring for the body. It relaxes you on the surface level of the mind and can give you a renewed sense of peace and readiness to get back into your day-to-day life.

This type of time out is quite enriching on a surface level and, again, has its place in adding peace to your life

Time out to be someone other than 'mum'

Time out of this nature helps you identify your connection to life outside of the home and after experiencing this time out, you will see that you are not 'just a mum' and that you also have other interests outside of that role that make up who you are. This type of time out includes things such as:
- taking time out with your partner. Reconnecting as a couple is a really important time-out activity. You are not just parents, but you are two people united as a team. Taking time out exclusively with your partner allows you to identify yourself as a couple in addition to being 'the parents' and

enjoy the relationship that you have exclusive of the one you have together as parents.
- coffee or lunch with friends. This kind of activity keeps you connected with adults and adult conversations and activities, particularly when it is uninterrupted. Incidentally, you also get reminded of what it is like to eat a meal in its entirety without having to get up. Taking the kids with you for play with other friends' kids doesn't count here. This is exclusively uninterrupted conversation that is purely about you and the people you are socialising with. Being with friends helps us feel accepted in the community and not isolated, which is how you can sometimes feeling when you are a stay-at-home mum.
- attending social events – alone. Having fun is an essential part of time out. Doing something that makes you laugh or smile or that clears your mind and helps you to reconnect to other parts of who you are. Being social helps you to be the person you are when you aren't thinking about your child's safety, toilet needs and meal times.

Time out such as this is about purely connecting yourself to your individuality outside of being mum.

Time out for the soul

Time out for the soul, in my opinion, is the most precious time out that you can give yourself. This time out will add more peace and calmness to your life on many levels.

When you participate in time out for the soul, you will find the time and importance to take all of the other types of time out for yourself. When you experience time out for the soul, your whole world feels more peaceful.

The kind of time out I am referring to in this area is self-exploration and meditation. Participating in activities that help you to get to know yourself, your habits and why you do the things that you do helps you to go easier on yourself and be patient and compassionate towards yourself and others. When you 'know thyself' you naturally gravitate towards a more peaceful existence.

Meditation is a valuable habit to get into because it really does calm you down and add some much-needed quiet time to your life. Being in a quiet place is so therapeutic for a mum who listens to noise pretty much all day. You will find vast improvements to your view of life and how you feel about events going 'wrong' when you invest time into meditating.

How do I want to spend my time?

Be specific

Before you begin creating a time schedule to fit in everything that you want to do, your first step is to be specific about how you want to schedule your time.

Consider the following five categories, and how much time you would like to put into each category in general.

Time out just for me

This is time where you get to do something for yourself, whether it's reading a book, participating in a sport, watching a movie or seeing friends. This category is about doing what you want to do, factoring in any of the types of time out just mentioned.

Quality time with the kids

This category is about spending some one-on-one time with the children, either individually, or collectively or both. There is no running off to put clothes on the line, or doing the dishes; this time is exclusively for them and you to have fun and connect with each other.

Quality time with my husband/partner

This category keeps you connected with your partner. Whether you are just conversing about your day or realigning your future, or whether you are planning a night away from the kids, you need to get specific about how much time you want to keep you connected with each other and on the same page.

Doing the housework or running errands

This category is where you can list all the things that you need to complete in a week when it comes to the housework or running errands. You can also list how much time in a week you are willing to spend doing these things.

Miscellaneous

This category is for all of the miscellaneous items that might come up, such as unusual appointments (doctor, bank, and so on).

Exercise 6

> Before we start trying to create a specific schedule for your week, try completing the following exercise.
>
> For the categories listed above, write down how much time you want to spend on each area. You can decide whether you will do it in days, weeks or months – it just needs to be what you're happy with. Remember to be specific about what it is you want.
>
> Don't worry at this stage about whether you will be able to spend the allocated time on each category; we will determine that later. For now, just list what you would consider as satisfying to you.

For example, your list might look like this:

Time out for me:
At least four hours by myself per week

Quality time with the kids:
At least one hour per day of individual time with each child; at least one hour per day of combined time with all children

Quality time with my husband:
At least half an hour per day of uninterrupted conversation and at least one to two hours a week of alone time together; one day or night out a month away from the kids just for us

Doing the housework or running errands:
About two hours a day of housework, which includes weekly cleaning, general day-to-day tidying up, washing and folding clothes, grocery shopping, and so on.

Miscellaneous:
I will just rearrange my schedule to fit these items in when required.

Why do I want this and is this aim in conflict with reality?

Take a moment to review what you wrote for Exercise 6 and test why you want to spend this amount of time participating in each category.

Be mindful of the story (self-talk) you tell yourself about what spending this amount of time on each category will add to your life. Why do you want to spend this amount of time on each category? Is it going to make your life 'better'? Will you feel more worthwhile? Check your thoughts with the GYLR Model and see if there are any thoughts you can capture that might need upgrading.

You might be consciously aware that spending time on a certain area makes you feel better about yourself, meaning that you rate your self-esteem higher when doing this. This is fine as long as you know this area of life doesn't define your self-worth. Our rating of ourselves goes up and down all of the time based on our beliefs. It is your beliefs that make you feel better about yourself (worth-more), not that you are actually worth more when you are spending time in this area of life.

Step 4 (Choices)

When it comes to your time out, now that you have lots of commitments as a mum you might just need to do a little planning, or 'plotting' – as my friend puts it – in order to get some time out. Sometimes you will need to steal your time out for a few minutes here, or a few minutes there or wherever possible.

Because we have covered quite extensively what drives our choices when it comes to time out, I don't need to discuss it here again. However, be mindful throughout this whole process that the decisions you make about taking time out will be rooted in what you believe your priority 'should' be.

You will give yourself more time out and fulfil the amounts of time you allocated in Step 3 when you make time out a priority; that is, when you believe that it's okay to take time out. You know that time out is beneficial, so now you just need to find a way to incorporate all the other things that you need to do with having time out.

The first solution could be that you begin to find out what other mums are doing, or you can look for books and information on time management and planning.

Here is a simple exercise that I created to help you identify how you're currently spending your time. In order to complete this exercise you must make it a priority first. Remember, if you tell yourself that you don't have time to complete this exercise, what you are really saying is that it's not your priority to complete this exercise – that other things are more important. However, if you complete this exercise you will learn how to fit in your time out as well as the other important tasks in your life.

Exercise 7

Step 1

Create a simple form that you can use for the next one to three days that lists, in as much detail as possible, what you are currently doing with your time in one-hour increments. Create a column to also complete Step 2. For example:

Time of day	What did you do?	Step 2
5.00–6.00 a.m.		
6.00–7.00 a.m.		
7.00–8.00 a.m.		
8.00–9.00 a.m.		

Step 2

In the Step-2 column, write whether you consider the activity to be:
- highly important to you
- of medium importance
- of low importance
- an outright waste of time.

Review this last exercise after the designated one-to-three days and consider which beliefs were driving you to spend time on the activities that you consider to be of low importance or an outright waste of time. This will help you to understand that we only know what we know in any given moment and that our priorities at that time are governed by our beliefs and the particular belief that took precedence over the others in that moment.

For example, you might have sat down and watched 'Oprah' while the children were having their day nap instead of cleaning up the house, which you consider to be of high importance. By being aware of your self-talk about the cleaning and 'Oprah' you might find that you were saying something like this:

'I've had enough of all this work that I'm doing all the time. I'm just going to sit and relax and enjoy the peace and quiet while the kids are asleep. Stuff it! I deserve a break sometimes too'.

You can see that the reason why 'Oprah' became a priority in that moment was because your time out and feeling that you deserved a break (wanting to feel more) became priorities over your housework, in that moment.

Even though you might normally consider housework a higher priority than watching 'Oprah', in that moment – due to the beliefs that you had about the housework – your priorities shifted.

When you create your own schedule, be mindful of this example because it illustrates that while it's great to have a guide for the day, sometimes our goals and priorities change due to how we perceive what has been happening in our day or because something unexpected has happened (for example, a phone call from a friend). For this reason sometimes our schedules won't be followed to the tee – and that's okay. Conversely, it's also useful to be mindful of the self-talk you have about events in order to consciously track your motivation towards achieving a goal and sticking to your schedule by checking your priorities and beliefs when you aren't following the schedule you set. Why aren't you following the schedule? What is the story you are telling yourself about why you aren't following the schedule? The answers will help you to consciously decide – with awareness of your beliefs – whether you are going to shift the goal posts, change the goal or continue with the original schedule.

Awareness of your beliefs and where you place your worth makes your life a lot more deliberate.

Step 5 (Action)

The final step in this chapter is to create your schedule so that you know what plan you are trying to stick to.

This schedule is going to incorporate your aim – being the five categories and how much time you would like to put into each category – with the knowledge you gained from the last exercise of what you normally do with your time.

The first point to remember about getting organised and being efficient with your time is to get into the practice of creating lists of all the things you need to do in order to achieve your goal.

Let's take household chores and running errands for example. There is so much that you need to remember to do that you need to get it all out of your head and onto paper. You are trying to remember everything, prioritise it and action what needs to be done all at the same time and this can be quite stressful, especially if you have your self-worth hinged on getting out the door on time or achieving your goals.

There is often so much to think about that you tend to get into brain overload and feel overwhelmed and disorganised.

For example, let's say that you are trying to get the kids ready for day care. In this scenario, while they are at day care, you have a doctor's appointment to show him some X-rays, you have an appointment with the bank manager to go over a loan and you need to do grocery shopping. In order to complete all of these tasks, there are many other things you need to do in preparation for these tasks. If you tried to organise all of this in your head, here is what you would have to remember all at once:

- Get the kids' lunches ready – morning tea, afternoon tea, lunch, drinks – what healthy food do I need to prepare?
- Pack the kids' bags – spare clothes, nappies, wipes, hats, sunscreen, sleep sheets and blankets
- Make the kids' breakfast
- Dress the kids
- Brush their teeth
- Brush their hair
- Remember to take the X-rays with you

- Grocery shopping – you need milk, eggs, breakfast cereal, bread, biscuits, meat, pumpkin, potatoes ... and so on
- The bank manager needs a list of things for the meeting:
    - proof of income
    - tax returns
    - proof of identification
    - quotation for the item you are buying.

If you don't write all of this down, you not only have to remember each and every point that I just made here, but you also have to try to prioritise this list and carry it out without forgetting any of it.

I haven't even mentioned any of the washing, dishes or cleaning up that may need to take place during this morning of preparation.

Then, throw the cranky, clingy or uncooperative child or children into the mix and you have the recipe for a disastrous morning.

It is quite difficult to remember everything that you need to do, then prioritise it correctly, handle the unexpected interruptions and complete each task effectively (without getting stressed and flustered) unless you write it all down.

Move the information out of your head and onto paper where you can see it, rearrange it where necessary, prioritise it more effectively and tick it off as you go.

You can also incorporate your lists into a schedule so that your schedule includes everything that needs doing when it comes to household chores. For example:

Daily housework

- a load of washing per day
- put washing on the clothes line
- fold washing and put it away
- make the beds
- general tidy-up
- sweep floors
- cook dinner
- wash dishes – breakfast, lunch, dinner and snacks

Weekly housework

- change sheets on all beds
- clean toilet and bathroom
- vacuum carpets
- sweep and mop floors
- ironing
- dust and polish furniture
- clean glass doors
- wipe fingerprints off doors and walls

Monthly housework or other long-term house chores

- clean windows
- sort though kids' old clothes
- de-clutter cupboards
- clean up outside
- clean carpets
- clean cupboards
- clean the stove
- clean the fridge

Day-care preparation

- kids' breakfast
- clean kids' teeth
- get them dressed and brush their hair
- make lunches and drinks
- pack bags – with sleep sheets, hats, sunscreen, nappies, wipes, lunch and drinks

These are just examples of the lists that you might like to create to remind you of all the things you need to do within one chore/task, or of all the things that you would like to achieve in a specified time – for example, weekly/monthly household chores. They will come in handy when you come to creating your own time schedule in Exercise 8.

Exercise 8

> On a piece of paper that you can keep handy, create your own lists according to your circumstances.

Creating your schedule

Following are two examples of schedules I have created that fit into my day. You might notice that I have started my day at 5 a.m. This is because I am using a schedule that I created when my children were very young and, sadly, I was blessed with children who would not sleep in, so 5 a.m. was when my eldest child would wake up. Your schedule should factor in your particular situation.

Example 1: a workday schedule

5.00 – 6.00 a.m.	Get up and have breakfast
6.00 – 7.15 a.m.	Get ready for day care and work Clean up if time (do a load of washing and put in dryer)
7.30 – 4.00 p.m.	Day care and work
4.00 – 4.30 p.m.	Return home from work and get kids' dinner ready
4.30 – 5.15 p.m.	Tidy up and do dishes Get kids' clothes ready for bed and dinner table ready to eat
5.15 – 6.00 p.m.	Pick up kids from day care
6.00 – 6.15 p.m.	Dinner
6.15 – 6.30 p.m.	Clean up after dinner
6.30 p.m.	Bath time – Steve (husband) baths the kids and Jackie to fold washing and put away
7.00 – 7.30 p.m.	Quiet time with the kids before bed
7.30 p.m.	Kids' bedtime

7.30 – 8.00 p.m.	Something from weekly cleaning list, e.g. sweep and mop kitchen floor
8.00 – 10.00 p.m.	Writing time or 'Steve and me' time

Example 2: a stay-at-home day schedule

5.00 – 6.30 a.m.	Get up and have breakfast
6.30 – 7.30 a.m.	Breakfast clean-up and get dressed for day, brush kids' hair and teeth Put washing on for the day and hang out or put in dryer
7.30 – 8.30 a.m.	TV off and Mummy playtime with kids
8.30 – 9.00 a.m.	Morning tea
9.00 – 9.15 a.m.	Clean up from morning tea
9.15 – 10.30 a.m.	Kids play by themselves. Change bed sheets; vacuum floors and couches
10.30 – 11.00 a.m.	Mummy playtime with kids
11.00 – 12.00 p.m.	Get lunch ready and eat
12.00 – 12.30 p.m.	Lunchtime clean-up
12.30 p.m.	Kids' nap time
12.30 – 2.00/2.30 p.m.	Writing time or time out
2.30 – 3.00 p.m.	Kids awake and afternoon tea
3.00 – 4.00 p.m.	Clean up afternoon tea, then outside time
4.00 – 4.45 p.m.	Prepare dinner
4.45 – 5.15 p.m.	Clean up with kids Fold washing and put away
5.15 – 5.45 p.m.	Dinner
5.45 – 6.15 p.m.	Dinner clean-up and get kids' clothes ready
6.15 – 6.45 p.m.	Bath (Steve to do)
6.45 – 7.30 p.m.	Quiet time with kids
7.30 p.m.	Kids' bedtime
7.30 – 10.00 p.m.	Writing time or time with Steve

These examples were created at a time when I felt that I was spending too much time writing and was compromising my values on time with the kids and time with my husband, causing me to feel stressed as I wasn't able to 'do it all'.

I needed to create a plan that I was comfortable with and that balanced my commitment to my family with my desire to pursue my personal goals.

This is the value of having a schedule. A schedule helps you to incorporate everything you want into a reasonable time frame. You will know what's next and you will be confident that you are going to be able to meet all of your needs, your kids' needs and the needs of a healthy relationship.

Exercise 9

> Using my personal schedules as a guide, incorporate your lists and your aim into your own schedule.
>
> Include all of the commitments you have and most importantly how you want to spend your time (that is, the five categories: time out for me, quality time with the kids, quality time with my husband, household chores and errands, and miscellaneous).
>
> Start by creating a schedule for the next week only and then each week you can revise this schedule as necessary. It might be useful to create this schedule on your computer so that each week you are not having to rewrite it all, but just making slight changes before printing it out.

Summary: Time out

The important thing to remember when thinking about time out is that you always have the time to take it, you just need to sort out why you believe that you can't and maybe re-organise your schedule a little so that it becomes a priority.

Once you've done this it's all a matter of organisation and following your schedule.

Be mindful that you do not attach your self-worth to achieving everything that is on that list, as sometimes things happen and life doesn't go to plan. Embrace these times too, as there is value in these moments and they are a natural reality of life.

Your schedule is a guide that will help you to experience all of the different areas of your life in alignment with your values and the amount of time you would like to invest in each area.

Sometimes this means that you need to re-evaluate how much time you can spend in one area or another and, again, this will be dictated by where you place your priorities.

One thing to remember is that there is no right or wrong way to parent. There is no right or wrong amount of time to spend in any one area of your life and it doesn't always have to be balanced. Try to be flexible in life and understand the reality that although we set goals to achieve them, success doesn't just come from reaching them, it comes from the journey we experience just by having them and moving towards them.

'Definition of madness: keep on doing the same things again and again, expecting different results.' – Einstein

Chapter 13

Relationships: You and your partner

> '... and Cinderella and the prince got married and lived happily ever after.
> The End.'

That's what relationships are supposed to be like right? At least that's what we were taught. From early childhood we are taught that relationships are meant to be happy, blissful, full of romance and exciting all the time. If there are troubles to overcome, they will always end in reigniting passion, lust and a 'happily ever after'. We've seen it in fairytales from when we were young and we've watched it endlessly portrayed in movies over and over again.

However, this is not always the reality in relationships, especially once the honeymoon period is over and we slot into a comfortable lifestyle with our partners. The lens of perfection we once saw the love of our lives through begins to lift and we start to see their 'true colours'.

Add a child or children into the mix and, especially during the early years, the fantasy relationship can seem like a million miles away.

The dynamics of your relationship

Regardless of whether you have children or not, there are certain dynamics that have been set up between you and your partner.

These dynamics are like agreements between you that determine how you treat each other, what the boundaries and deal breakers are for the relationship, how much time you spend together or apart, the agreements for living together and what your roles are within the relationship. The roles we play can be anything from the advice giver, the cook, the cleaner, the gardener, the affectionate one, the romantic one, the peacekeeper, the one who always gives in, the one who always wins the arguments, or the needy one, to roles where a parent/child dynamic has even been set up.

These dynamics are set up in the early stages of your relationship and reflect what you believe about yourself, what you believe about your partner and what you believe a relationship should look like.

When you have children, these dynamics can change somewhat and this can cause stress in an otherwise healthy relationship, or it can cause further stress in one that wasn't healthy to begin with.

It is important to be able to observe and identify these dynamics and the roles that you play and your partner plays before you can work towards making the changes that you need to make for creating a happy relationship.

'You teach people how to treat you.'

This is a famous quote coined by American talk-show host and psychologist Dr Phil.

Through your interactions with the people around you, you teach them an appropriate way of treating you. By responding to their treatment of you, you teach them what is acceptable by you and what is not. Here is a perfect example of a common dynamic that is often set up in the early stages of becoming a mum.

When the baby arrives, the mother usually handles most of the baby's needs. She feeds the baby the most, she gets up in the night because her partner usually goes to work, she looks after the baby all day, and she gets so good at the role of being the baby's mother that it becomes unspoken that the mother will attend to most of the baby's needs.

When a baby arrives, the mother can often push Dad away to a degree, fearing that he won't do things properly or that he won't know how to do something. She might even do everything herself because it's quicker for her to do it or just because she is so used to doing everything for the child that it becomes an automatic reaction to just do it, without thinking about giving her partner a turn.

Her partner might initially try to help, but is met with criticism that he is not doing it correctly and mum then takes over anyway – or she is already up and doing it before he gets a chance to.

So the dynamic has already started. You have already started to teach your partner that he is not needed and that you have got it covered. So he begins to stop trying to help and just lets you handle it like you seemingly want to, because you have taught him this.

Because you have it covered, he thinks that you will be fine and off he goes to do other things that maybe he likes to do.

Now, the first few times he does this you might feel happy for him to go out and have some fun. After all, he works hard and deserves a break, and you are quite happy to be at home with your baby and show him or her off to your friends anyway, so you don't really mind him doing his 'guy stuff', thus adding another link to the dynamic.

In contrast, sometimes the case is that your partner never really did anything from the beginning. Maybe he believes it is the woman's job, or he was too scared to try, and because you didn't encourage him or challenge the point, he didn't bother trying to do much and that's the way this dynamic was set up.

Either way, you can see how the circumstances have naturally evolved to an 'unhelpful' partner. It's not that he's inconsiderate; it's more that he's been taught by you not to have to consider that you might need his help a lot. You taught him that you've got it covered.

If the case is that he believes that this is a woman's job and he shouldn't have to do anything, then he believes that you accept and respect his belief, and therefore he doesn't need to change anything because you haven't voiced otherwise.

So now you have a partner who is just doing what has been indirectly agreed to by both of you. He's living his life interacting with you the way that you have taught him is acceptable by you and – incidentally – the way he has taught you to interact with him.

Meanwhile, you are sitting at home with your kids with this building resentment towards his freedom and your lack of it. He comes home from his little outing, all happy and refreshed and is suddenly confronted with a cranky, irritable wife who is snapping or giving him the cold shoulder, and he has absolutely no idea why.

He asks you, 'What's wrong with you?'. Mortified by a question where you think the answer is blatantly obvious, you blurt out how selfish he is and how he never helps you do anything, and how he's constantly running off doing this, that and the other and leaving you stuck at home, never getting any time to yourself ... and so on.

Your partner has no idea what has just hit him. The name calling gets his back up, he gets defensive, fights back, thinks you're just being a whingeing wife, or that your hormones are acting up and storms off, leaving both of you feeling bad.

Or, he begins to help you out of obligation and starts to simmer in his own resentment and anger towards what you've just said. The truth is, he has no understanding whatsoever of what just happened, and is trying to figure out what is so wrong with him going out and leaving you at home with the baby.

He doesn't understand because you taught him that this was okay, and all of a sudden you come out of the blue with indirect accusations about his character and how bad a father and a husband he is. If you can see it from this perspective, how do you think he's going to react to your seemingly sudden outburst?

Now, of course, there may be other things going on for both parties here, all along the lines of the GYLR Model of thinking. However, this is a basic example of how easy and unconsciously dynamics can be set up and how, when one or the other party is suddenly behaving in an unexpected way, it can cause all sorts of confusion and stress.

It is important for you to identify these dynamics and take ownership for your part in how these dynamics came to be. Remembering that you only know what you know in any given moment, so the choices you made at the time of setting up your relationship were governed by what you believed at that time.

Using the example above, the mum's priority at the time that the dynamics between her and her partner were set up (when the baby was born) was getting to know her new baby and being able to show her baby off to those around her. Her husband's priority was to go and do what he normally does because of the belief that 'she's got it covered' or 'it's her job', or whatever the belief may have been.

The reality, though, is that throughout our lives we are constantly changing, and our priorities also change based on new information and experiences that we have, so relationships need to be constantly changing and realigning with the changes that are occurring in the people that are a part of them.

The reality of a relationship

What we must become aware of is the reality of what a relationship is. In a marital/partner relationship there are two individual people who have two different belief systems. They have come together because of some kind of attraction with each other and because some of their beliefs and values align.

The intention of a relationship is to connect with the other person in love and peace and to live together harmoniously.

Now, when you take a person's individual belief system and analyse it, you will see that from their upbringing, experiences and observations they have created their own ideas about themselves, other people, relationships, goals and expectations about life, all of which define their specific wants and needs. In most cases, their self-worth will be incorrectly attached to some of these wants and needs too.

In order to create this harmonious, aligned connection between two people there needs to be a solid awareness that it's not just about one person anymore. We all have our own wants and needs (driven by our beliefs) and the challenge in a relationship is to work out a way that both parties can meet their wants and needs or support each other through the times when meeting them is not possible (sometimes life doesn't go to plan).

The reality of life is that we are all learning and growing and as a result of that we are changing who we are, and constantly re-evaluating our wants and needs because we have new information. This happens to everybody. When you look at this reality in line with relationships it is logical to see that relationships change as a result of this too and hence constant realignment, communication and negotiation are required in order to keep up with these changes, otherwise dynamics previously set up don't get played out and one or the other party becomes confused because expectations of behaviours and reactions are different. This can cause arguments, anger and disconnection from one another to varying degrees.

This can happen a lot for a woman from the second she finds out she is pregnant because sacrifices are made to her current lifestyle almost immediately and she begins to think differently about her life choices.

Parenting changes both parents' views on life to varying degrees and is a huge transition to make. This is the time where realignment and redesigning of boundaries, dynamics and roles are pertinent to a successful relationship because both parents are re-evaluating their wants and needs, and testing whether they are relevant anymore or whether they are realistically able to be met.

The blame game

'I'm always doing everything. He does nothing. All he ever does is come home from work and he does whatever he wants to without any regard for what I might need. He never does any housework. He leaves his stuff all over the house for me to clean up. As for affection, I never get any hugs other than a dig in the ribs and a "How 'bout it?" every once in a while. He's so grumpy all of the time. He doesn't spend enough time with the kids. He's not romantic. If he keeps going like this, we're not going to have a relationship. He needs to change his ways, or this relationship is going to go downhill and we'll end up splitting up, all because of his selfish ways.'

When things aren't going the way we would like them to in the area of relationships, it can be easy to start viewing all of the things that your partner is doing 'wrong' as contributing to the relationship's decay.

It's important to remind you here that any kind of blame, regret, anger and resentment is because of beliefs you have that align with Point 3 on the GYLR Model of thinking – should/could: I am or someone else should be doing something differently.

When we apply the upgrade to should/could – I/they only know what I/they know at any given moment – you will see that you are where you are right now because of everything that has unfolded up to this point and both of you have made decisions and reacted in the ways that you believed were best at the time (in any situation), based on your beliefs.

The reason you are at where you are in your relationship is because of your individual beliefs and how they guided each of your behaviours, resulting in the current dynamic.

It's also important to remember that there are beliefs behind every behaviour, and those beliefs are working in the best interests of the beholder every time.

This means that if there is a dynamic between you and your partner where you are being taken advantage of, not appreciated or even verbally and physically abused over a period of time, then there has been something in it for you too. There is a pay-off (priority) for you staying in that dynamic over this period of time and behind that priority is a belief that is serving you 100 per cent of the time.

This could be many different beliefs, such as: 'A good wife takes care of the kids and does all the housework.' 'My husband works, therefore he deserves to spend the money on himself.' 'I don't deserve extra money because I don't earn it.' 'He is a good dad and he looks after me, so I can't really complain about how he speaks to me'. There could be a million different beliefs depending on each individual's belief system and from where they got them.

Regardless of what the belief is, it has become the dominant belief that is driving you to accept what is happening in your relationship, even if you logically know that it's not acceptable or you don't like it.

There are many different beliefs, dynamics and situations that can bring a relationship into turmoil or uneasiness and I could spend an entire book addressing just the most common examples, so the best way to approach this chapter is to get you to begin applying your situation and your problems within your relationship to the Mind TRACK to Happiness process so that you can get a clearer understanding of your specific circumstances and how you can change and renegotiate your relationship to being one that you enjoy and feel fulfilled in.

Step 1 (Thoughts)

In Step 1, we want to first identify what your current view on your relationship is: why it is not matching the expectations you have of it and also what your expectations actually are of relationships.

Exercise 1

The following questions will help you to identify where your thinking is at in regards to your current relationship. Please answer these in your notebook.

1. Write at least one-half to one page of your view on what is going wrong with your relationship, why you feel it's not going the way that it should and what events have led up to this being a problem.
2. What ideals do you have of a relationship (that is, what should a successful relationship look like)?
3. What do you need to happen in order for this relationship to be better?

Exercise 2

Go back through the four questions that you just answered and identify all of the GYLR Model points:
1. Wrong path/right path
2. Missing out
3. Should/could
4. Worth-less

The following case study is an example of how one mum, Angela, might answer these questions.

Case study 9: Angela

1. Write at least one-half to one page of your view on what is going wrong with your relationship, why you feel it's not going the way that it should and what events have led up to this being a problem.

   My relationship is starting to go majorly downhill because my husband doesn't help me with housework or the kids, our sex life is virtually non-existent and we just don't seem to be on the same page anymore (wrong path).

   I mean, he wanted to have kids too, but all of a sudden now that we have children, I am the one who does all the work (missing out). I bath them, feed them, put them to bed, read them stories, teach them new things, as well as all of the housework (wrong path – in terms of her part in her relationship).

   He does work full-time and brings in a pretty good income that gives us quite a comfortable lifestyle, but it's like he thinks that just because he brings in the money and I'm a full-time stay-at-home mum that that's all he needs to do in the family unit – provide money (should/could). There's more to life than money.

The kids need him too. He gets so angry when the kids get over excited, too noisy or jump all over him and I keep trying to tell him that it's normal, but he doesn't listen. I feel so sorry for them. They just want to play with their dad (missing out).

He just looks so miserable all the time. Our sex life is virtually non-existent because I am just so exhausted (missing out) and quite frankly don't really want to be close to him because he is so miserable and cranky all the time (wrong path). It's hardly good grounds for lust and passion, is it?

Before we had children, we used to be so affectionate to one another, giving each other hugs all the time, speaking to each other affectionately and generally communicating quite well when something wasn't meshing right between us. We had a normal relationship (right path).

But since we've had the kids, I can see that he has been slipping away more and more from me. The only time I see him happy is when he goes for a boys' weekend or night out and is away from the family (missing out).

I should have a husband who wants to be with his family and enjoys our company (should/could), not one who finds it all too hard and just wants to live the 'golden' years (wrong path). Sometimes I think he would be happier if he was a single man.

I don't know. I'm just not happy being the stay-at-home mum who does everything with the kids and has to do everything to keep the house running (worth-less). I used to be a career woman with goals of my own and purpose to my life (right path). Now I just feel like I'm stuck in a 1950's movie scene where kids and housework are my life (worth-less) and I should be happy being the dutiful wife doting on her husband (should/could).

2. What ideals do you have of a relationship (that is, what should a successful relationship look like)?

My husband should be able to talk to me and tell me what is happening with him (should/could). Why is he so miserable all the time (wrong path)? Why doesn't he want to spend time with us (missing out)? A relationship should be one that is full of love and affection and we should want to be close to one another (right path). I know that we won't always be happy all the time, but we should at least be able to talk to one another and sort through our problems together (should/could). I want someone who is going to be considerate and share the responsibilities of the kids without getting cranky. I want someone who I can share my life with and communicate all my thoughts, dreams, likes and dislikes to and who will help me through life without judgement and criticisms (should/could). I want someone who values me (worth-less).

3. What do you need to happen in order for this relationship to be better?

My husband needs to step up and be the dad that he wanted to be in the first place (should/could). Our lives have changed and we can't keep trying to live life like we used to. He can't go out with his mates whenever he wants. He has family commitments now that he needs to get on board with (should/could).

He needs to start being a good husband to me by considering my feelings and what's happening in my life and helping me to do the things that I want to do too (should/could). I need to feel loved and appreciated and to feel like I'm more to him than just his housecleaner and the mother of his children (worth-less). I want him to recognise that just because I don't bring money into the home my contributions to the family unit are just as valuable as the money side of things too (should/could).

And I want to see him start being more patient with the kids and being happier around them too (right path) so that they don't think that their daddy doesn't love them or that they are doing something wrong or naughty when they are just being kids (missing out).

I just want to live a normal family life (right path) where I feel fulfilled and validated (self-worth).

Chapter 13: Relationships: You and your partner **243**

Completing this exercise will give you a firm idea of how you perceive your current relationship. You will most likely identify plenty of GYLR thinking, which we are going to analyse in the next step.

Step 2 (Reality)

One of the biggest challenges in relationship problems is to get both parties to recognise that they are both involved in how a problem came to be. It is too easy to get stuck in the blame game, believing that if only the other person would change, then everything would be fixed.

However, it is both parties who have participated in all of the interactions that have led to the problems within the relationship. The Fountainhead Method™ can be a useful tool for identifying the beliefs you have about relationship issues that are causing you stress (GYLR Model) and upgrading these beliefs (Personal Development Model) before addressing the issues with your partner.

Applying this method to your perception of the relationship first will help you in communicating with your partner because you will be looking at the reality of the relationship and how it has come to be the way it is. Before applying this method, however, we need to consider a couple of other events that can contribute to how you perceive the relationship and consequently the relationship breakdown.

My life has not gone to plan

Sometimes we can feel stressed that our lives are not going the way that we would like them to go. Because we feel this way, it can be common to start looking at the outside influences that have caused our lives to not go to plan.

For example, sometimes prior to having our children we can have experienced rewarding and successful careers, unknowingly attaching our self-worth to these careers or something about our jobs and feeling like the gratification, the challenges or the experiences of our careers defined who we were. Now that we have become mums, we might feel that our lives are somehow worth-less than they were.

What can sometimes happen is that we begin to search for someone or something to blame in order to make sense of why we don't feel so good anymore. We can also start to search for that same gratification in other external environments in order to increase the worth that we thought we were getting from our jobs.

When you look at Angela's story in case study 9, it is possible that due to her beliefs she is feeling worth-less now that she is a stay-at-home mum and is looking for validation from her partner that she is worth more. She begins searching for proof that he thinks she's worth more in order to improve how she feels about herself. However, she will never get enough proof from anything he does because of her own beliefs about being a stay-at-home mum.

Before discussing her relationship problems with her husband, she must first look at what is happening for her and upgrade her beliefs about the current situation by coming to terms with the reality of her life. Perhaps she too is in denial that things cannot be the same as they once were – that she neither has the physical or emotional energy left at the end of the day to be as affectionate or loving as she once was with her husband.

It is important, if you haven't done so already, to go back and read and do the exercises provided in Chapter 11 (Loss of identity), so you can see where you are attaching your self-worth and whether you might be in conflict with the current reality of the changes that being a mother brings. This is absolutely crucial to do before trying to negotiate an alignment with your husband or partner and will help you to be clear on what you actually want in this relationship.

Step 1: Personal Development Model upgrade

In your notebook, see if you can apply the Personal Development Model to the GYLR points that you identified in the previous exercise.

Here is a summary of an upgrade for Angela:

1. Wrong path/right path

... my husband doesn't help me with housework or the kids, our sex life is virtually non-existent and we just don't seem to be on the same page anymore ... before we had children, we used to be so affectionate to one another, giving each other hugs all the time, speaking to each other affectionately and generally communicating quite well when something wasn't meshing right between us. We had a normal relationship. A relationship should be one that is full of love and affection and we should want to be close to one another.

Upgrade: Life is a journey

The reality of my relationship's journey is that it is full of ups and downs. There are always going to be moments throughout it where I am more affectionate than at other times. This could be due to conflict, busyness, being caught up in my own problems, or just because I am feeling particularly passionate or not feeling passionate. That is the reality of relationships. Just as I feel excited about life sometimes and not at other times, I will also feel this way about my relationship. This Cinderella-Hollywood romance idea of relationships is just not realistic and will only cause me stress. In the dynamic that has been set up in my relationship, somewhere along the line it became accepted that my role was to do the majority of the household chores and the raising of the kids. Just because I now don't like this role, it doesn't mean it's going to magically change. I need to redefine and realign what works for both of us in order to change this.

2. Missing out

... he gets so angry when the kids get over excited, too noisy or jump all over him and I keep trying to tell him that it's normal, but he doesn't listen. I feel so sorry for them. They just want to play with their dad ... our sex life is virtually non-existent because I am just so exhausted ... since we've had the kids, I can see that he has been slipping away more and more from me. The only time I see him happy is when he goes for a boys' weekend or night out and is away from the family.

Upgrade: I am always learning and receiving

I am learning that my husband is learning how to transition into this new role of being a dad and having his whole life change too and that I can be more mindful of that in how I approach him about things.

I am receiving a faithful and hard-working husband who provides well for us and we have a history together of being able to work through our troubles. I am learning that being a parent means that I have to work harder at my relationship, especially in these early years when there has been such a dramatic change to our lives.

I have learnt that we need to keep the communication channels open during this time as we need to renegotiate some of the roles we've played and how we've interacted with each other in the past.

I am still receiving his commitment to the family. It's just that he views his commitment as being in a financial respect and I don't value that as much.

Because our relationship is also full of ups and downs and that's what's normal, I am continually learning how to work with another person and compromise and negotiate, thereby also teaching my children about relationships. I am also receiving the opportunity to make our relationship stronger with this level of communication.

The kids are also still learning about life and about interactions with family and that life is not all about being happy all the time. They are still receiving a father who does love them and does give them cuddles and kisses and provides very well for them. They are getting valuable lessons about life.

3. Should/could

... he thinks that that's all he needs to do in the family unit – provide money ... I should have a husband who wants to be with his family and enjoys our company ... I should be happy being the dutiful wife doting on her husband ... my husband should be able to talk to me and tell me what is happening with him ...we should at least be able to talk to one another and sort through our problems together ... I want someone who is going to be considerate and share the responsibilities of the kids without getting cranky. I want someone who I can share my life with and communicate all my thoughts, dreams, likes and dislikes to and who will help me through life without judgement and criticisms. My husband needs to step up and be the dad that he wanted to be in the first place. He has family commitments now that he needs to get on board with ... He needs to start being a good husband to me by considering my feelings and what's happening in my life and helping me to do the things that I want to do too ... I want him to recognise that just because I don't bring money into the home my contributions to the family unit are just as valuable as the money side of things too.

Upgrade: I/we only know what we know at any given moment

I am realising that there is a reason that he is behaving this way and it's very real for him. He obviously has certain beliefs that are playing out in his head that are in conflict with reality. My partner is a miserable man at the moment and that can't be very nice for him. His behaviour is because of what he knows at the moment and the priorities that he has based on his beliefs. I can understand from the work I have done that my behaviour has been driven from my beliefs about feeling worth-less now that I'm a mum and he must be feeling similar things. I need to discuss with him how he's feeling too so that we can talk about how we are going to help each other out.

I have not spoken to him about how I feel so how can I expect him to give me all these things that I want when he doesn't have that information? I have not given him that information and he only knows what he knows. He can't be a mind reader.

Both of us can only be the people we are with the information that we have and we have not been communicating our wants and needs enough in this relationship since the kids were born and not helping each other to get what we both want. We need to talk some more and each listen to how the other is feeling, not just about our relationship, but also about how we both feel about the major changes we've had since the kids and how that has affected us individually.

4. Worth-less

... I'm just not happy being the stay-at-home mum who does everything with the kids and has to do everything to keep the house running. I used to be a career woman with goals of my own and purpose to my life. Now I just feel like I'm stuck in a 1950's movie scene where kids and housework is my life ... I want someone who values me ... I need to feel loved and appreciated and to feel like I'm more to him than just his housecleaner and mother of his children ... I just want to have a normal family life where I feel fulfilled and validated .

Upgrade: I am always worthwhile

I have been attaching my self-worth to the person I used to be and feeling like I am somewhat worth-less because I am a stay-at-home mum. I have been in conflict with the reality that my life has changed and that's why I've been so mad that my husband believes his financial contribution is enough because I have been feeling like this belief further confirms that I am less valuable because I'm not bringing in any money.

I have wanted him to validate my self-worth through his behaviour, needing him to love and appreciate me in order to feel 'better'. I am always 100-per-cent worthwhile because I am alive and experiencing everything that I do in my life, learning and growing as a person and contributing to the lives around me. My husband is learning from me and my kids are learning from me and I am learning from them too.

I was not more worthy when I was working than now that I'm not. My husband is no more worthy because of the money he brings in. We are all contributing to the family unit and also to those interacting with our family unit.

Although I would still like to feel loved and appreciated, I am mindful of the fact that this does not determine my worth and will not feel completely worth-less if I don't get it sometimes. I feel like I can now talk to my husband from a different space in my mind because I realise where I have been feeling worth-less and now that I've upgraded this and understand my true worth, I can still ask for the things I want and try to negotiate the relationship I want, but not from this place of neediness.

When you begin upgrading your own story, make sure you take into account the current roles that you and your partner play and how they've been set up. Recognising and identifying the roles and games you play with each other that you believe could be defining you as worth-more or worth-less will help you to be able to make the changes that you need to make.

Step 3 (Aim)

Here comes the shift in thinking. Now that you have established the reality of the relationship, how it was set up, where you – or perhaps he – have been attaching your self-worth and how the dynamics have come to be set up, you can now begin to think about what you want in your relationship.

In this step, what you are priming yourself for is the conversation or maybe several conversations where you are beginning to discuss both of your wants and needs and how you can both negotiate and compromise in order to meet both your needs.

So, in this step you not only want to establish what you want, but you also need to establish what he wants. This is going to mean that you engage in conversations with him that are nothing to do with what you want (at this stage) but just gathering information about what he wants.

Exercise 3

Strike up an informal conversation with your partner about what he wants for his life or what the ideal scenario might be if you are having problems in one specific area. This will probably be an easy conversation for him to have as he is talking about what he wants, so there is little conflict (on his part) to be had. Try and keep a detached point of view and don't try and negotiate at this point. All you are doing is gathering information – that's it. You might find when doing this that you feel annoyed or reactive to some of what he is saying, but don't get sucked into an argument.

Stay detached by looking at him as a person, not your husband/partner who should be thinking and feeling according to your expectations. Treat him as though he is just a person telling you what his beliefs, feelings and experiences are, because that's exactly what he's doing. It doesn't mean anything about you – it's just his view of his life.

Remind yourself of this if you feel that you want to engage in an argument over what he is saying. Just gather the information and finish the conversation for now, as you have more work to do before negotiating new terms of agreement.

Take into consideration questions such as:

1. How have you been feeling about our relationship lately?
2. Do you think there are any problem areas that you would like us to fix?
3. How do you feel lately? Are you happy?
4. Is there anything that you would like to change in your life that you aren't happy with or are there any goals you would like to set that you've always wanted to achieve?
5. How do you feel about life since we've had the kids?
6. Why do you want these things?

Chapter 13: Relationships: You and your partner

You might need to have several conversations over time so that you don't look like you are interrogating him. Even if you want to tell him that you are trying to see what he wants so that you can figure out how you can help each other get what you want, that's okay. Be honest. What you are doing is no secret, but you aren't quite ready to have the negotiation and compromise conversation yet.

Write his answers of your questions into your notebook.

Exercise 4

Now go back and answer these questions yourself. Apply them to yourself and what you want and write your answers into your notebook.

1. How have you been feeling about your relationship lately?
2. Do you think there are any problem areas that you would like to fix?
3. How do you feel lately? Are you happy?
4. Is there anything that you would like to change in your life that you aren't happy with or are there any goals that you would like to set that you've always wanted to achieve?
5. How do you feel about life since you've had the kids?
6. Why do you want these things?

If you have the type of relationship that has strong communication anyway, answering these questions together may already be enough for you to negotiate and compromise and have this conversation at the same time – and that's okay.

Just make sure that you approach this conversation at a time when you aren't both tired or occupied (such as when he's watching the footy).

To help you further establish what your aims are with regard to your relationship, below are a few examples of some common issues that arise in relationships in a family environment. These questions will help you to be more specific about what you want in the context of your specific situation.

My partner works too much
- In an ideal situation, what hours would you like your partner to work?
- What is your budget? Does he have to work these hours to just pay the bills, or to maintain a level of lifestyle?
- Is the level of lifestyle important and necessary, as opposed to him being home more often?
- Is your ideal of this situation realistic or do you need to be a bit more flexible in your views about this situation?
- What is the real reason you want him home more often? Is it because you and the kids miss him, or because you want more help? If it's the latter, what other means of help can you think of implementing if reducing your husband's/partner's hours isn't an option (for example, a housekeeper; a babysitter)?
- What is your husband's/partner's view on how much he works? Is he happy about it, or does it distress him too?
- If your husband/partner is unhappy with his job, what other options does he have? Can he find another job? Can you sell something (for example, furniture, cars, a house or other assets) in order to buy some time until he finds a more fulfilling job with fewer hours?

Housework: I feel like I do everything or my husband/partner demands the house to stay at a certain level of cleanliness
- What is your ideal of the level of cleanliness that the house should be in on a regular basis?
- What is your husband's ideal of the state of the house?
- What are the discrepancies that you have between the two ideals?
- What are some compromises that you are willing to make to bring these two ideals onto common ground?
- What specifically do you want your husband to do more of?

- Create a description of everything that needs to be done in the household daily, weekly and monthly, and divide it up as you believe it should be divided.
- Can you create a roster that includes the husband and the kids?
- Go back over the list and decide whether you are willing to compromise on any area.
- Consider your husband's/partner's demands and roles and whether you are being realistic or fair about what you want him to do.
- How does your husband/partner already contribute to the family unit as a whole?
- Are you managing your time affectively to contribute as much to this as possible?
- Can you afford to outsource some of the housework?
- Is there an agreement that you can both reach as to who does what and how often?

Time out: I want some. He wants some

- How much time out do you want? Be specific. Is it one hour a day; is it one hour a week; is it a day a week, or a day a month? Be clear about exactly what you want at the time you are negotiating for it.
- What do you consider as time out? What do you want to do?
- Come up with a fair agreement that allows both of you the time out to be independent of your roles as parents.
- Are you willing to be flexible about this agreement when talking to your husband/partner about it?
- Why are you not getting your time out now? Is it because you don't ask? Are you waiting for your husband/partner to offer you the time out? How are you contributing to the time-out problem?

See Chapter 12 (Time out) for further information.

As you can see with the three issues above, you want to try and consider as many possibilities and viewpoints as you can and get very specific about what it is that you really want. If you enter into a conversation with your husband having an idea of what to align on and negotiate for, then you will be more likely to come up with a favourable result.

Men often find women very difficult to understand, and I believe it's sometimes because we don't actually know what we want ourselves, yet we somehow expect our husbands/partners to know and then offer it to us. We need to be more specific and actually communicate what we want so that we can both work out a solution as to how to get it.

There's no point in expecting the change to occur by itself. You need to be pro-active about challenging the issues and going for what it is that's going to improve your happiness.

You want to deliberately consider all avenues and the opinions and outcomes you would like on all accounts so that when you do discuss the issue with your husband/partner, you know what you want and how much you are willing to negotiate.

Why do/does I/he want it (the goals)?

In Exercises 3 and 4 you would have identified what is driving these wants and needs in both of you. You might already be seeing that his wants are associated with his self-worth and getting some insight into what he believes about what defines him.

Even though you know what defines real self-worth, unless he's willing to learn this method, you will just have to take it into consideration when negotiating that this is where he's at and some of the things he wants are because he wants to feel 'better' about his life or because he is trying to feel happy.

Exercise 5

> Write in your notebook why each of you want these goals.

Is what I/he want/s in conflict with reality?

Take a look at both of your answers to the questions and look at whether any of them are in direct conflict with reality.

For example, if you or your husband had down that you wanted to spend every weekend going out with the girls or fishing (respectively), then this might be in conflict with the reality that this just can't happen anymore. Yes, you can still go out and do these things, but there is a family commitment at play now and every weekend is just not something that can happen anymore.

However, these things are still on your and his lists of things that you want, so they will be brought to the negotiation table.

Exercise 6

> Write down any areas where either you or your husband's/partner's wants or needs are in conflict with reality.

This whole step has been about gathering information in order to create the plan for successful negotiation and alignment.

Exercise 7

> In summary to this step, write down what you want and what you will be aiming to negotiate when you discuss these issues with your husband/partner.

Step 4 (Choices)

Before we start looking at how you are going to negotiate with your husband/partner, I'd like you to reflect on how you have communicated in the past.

What I want to emphasise at this step is that our behaviours are driven by our beliefs. Think about your last argument with your husband/partner and consider what it is you were actually arguing about. What was each of you trying to do in this argument? What did each of you have attached to your self-worth in order to feel the emotions that were felt during the argument? Were you both trying to be right (feel worth more)? Were you feeling like what the other person was saying was making you worth less? Were you campaigning for something that you felt you were 'missing out' on, or that he 'should' have done differently? You can see that the GYLR Model of thinking would have been playing out in that conversation and this can be useful in identifying for the next time you have a discussion about something.

You cannot change his behaviour, but you can change yours and at least understand his. This can be very powerful in changing the way that you approach and carry out the conversations that you have with your husband/partner. You are viewing the interaction in a more detached way. The conversation no longer means anything about you (self-worth) and is merely about beliefs that you both have that are clashing and you need to find a common ground. It's a very different approach.

Strategies for communicating well with your partner

Now that you are armed with what you want, here are some strategies to use when communicating and negotiating with your partner to start implementing these changes.

1. Find the right time to hold the conversations

When your husband comes home from a hard day at work, the kids are in 'arsenic hour' and everything's crazy is not the time to be discussing emotional needs or asking your partner to do more housework.

Aim to set up a time when you are both relaxed and open to having a conversation such as this. Perhaps this is a time when you can get the kids baby sat and go out for dinner, or stay at home and relax with a few drinks to set the mood.

Maybe you need to literally tell him that you want to have this discussion too, so it's not a surprise conversation and he has time to prepare for it. If you have a partner who is in denial that there is even a problem, then your first step is to convince him that this is a problem for you and you have to discuss it. Sometimes this means being quite frank about the severity of its effects on you, especially if you are considering leaving the relationship. In this case, he has to know that this conversation is crucial.

2. Create an intention for the conversation before you start

What do you intend to achieve with this conversation? Are you just opening the discussion? Are you hoping to re-negotiate some terms of your relationship? Are you just getting a feel for your husband's/partner's viewpoints on the topic before you negotiate any changes? What attitudes are you determined to maintain throughout the conversation? Deliberately align yourself with your intention of the conversation and commit to maintaining your intended attitude regardless of what is said (for example, 'I intend to stay calm and rational').

3. Be flexible

While it's really important to know what you want, it's also important to be flexible and willing to compromise on what you expect. A partnership is exactly that: a partnership. You can't always have your way, and you need to align on an agreement, not just expect to have your way. Communication from this perspective, in my opinion, is about being able to effectively speak and voice your opinions and ideas, as well as being able to listen and interpret the reply from your husband/partner.

Knowing that no one person is right, but there are lots of different viewpoints to consider, helps you to avoid trying to make your husband/partner 'wrong' and you 'right'.

4. Ease into a conversation to avoid defensiveness

Before you initiate a conversation, deliberately think of ways to ease into it rather than getting straight to the guts of it and potentially catching your partner by surprise. If he's thinking to himself, 'Where the bloody hell did this come from?', his confusion might cloud his ability to give you concise answers, or he might automatically have his back up and become defensive.

Try a conversation such as, 'I was on this website the other day, and these dads were talking about how they feel about women's mood swings. One guy said that he had no idea what to expect from one minute to the next and had no idea how to handle it. Do you feel like that sometimes?'

This is a nice way to ease into how he feels about your relationship and for you to understand his perspective before you go into what you want. The conversation gets the chance to evolve into a direct discussion about what both of your wants and needs are and how you can find an alignment to create these.

5. Write letters

Some people find it more useful to write down their feelings, particularly when the issue is a highly emotional one. By writing down what you are feeling, you are able to look over and change what you have written and help yourself articulate your feelings accurately.

Doing this can keep you on track with what your intention of the letter is, and to avoid blaming, judging or trying to be right, hence improving the chances of your information being received a lot more amicably. You can even admit to your partner before he reads the letter that you have written it so that you can communicate your feelings without getting emotional and saying something that will come out the wrong way.

If he can read your letter first – before discussing it with you – he will get a clearer impression of what you are trying to say.

6. Be sensitive to your partner's wants and needs in this scenario

While speaking to your husband about your issues, remember to ask him what his ideal scenario is about this issue. How does he see that it can be improved? Remember, you are negotiating an outcome to this issue – not trying to get him to do what you want. Sure, you might end up getting what you want, but you want this to be an agreement between the two of you. You never know, your partner might have some valid points and ideas that could be the fair answer to the problem, but if you go into the conversation trying to be right, then you won't be open to his suggestions.

Try to understand his point of view and how he might have come to perceive things the way he does. What outcome is going to make him happy too, so as to avoid resentment and unsolved conflicts? If it is chore delegation that you are discussing, ask him what his idea of fair is, and why.

If you are discussing time out, then discuss his time out too. What is going to get both of you what you want that is fair? Factor his wants and needs into the conversation whenever you can; that way he feels that you are working together, rather than you just trying to get your own way. This is a team effort and you want to communicate it that way.

How to speak effectively when communicating with your husband/partner

- Listen well to what your partner has to say, and repeat what you have heard and how you have understood it. For example,

'So what you're saying/feeling is ...' This helps him feel that you understand him and that he really is being heard.
- Be 100-per-cent present when your husband is talking. Try to avoid thinking about what you are going to say next instead of really listening to what he's saying and feeling.
- Use 'I' statements such as 'I feel...' For example, 'I feel bad when you go to work without saying goodbye'. Here are two facts that cannot be argued with: the fact of how you feel, and the fact that he goes to work without saying goodbye. Stating comments such as this doesn't make any statement about his character, but simply states how you feel about what has happened.
- Avoid comments that serve to make your partner wrong, such as 'I hate it when you ...', or 'You always ...', or 'I don't want you to ...'
- Point out the positives as well as the negatives. Make sure you include as many positive aspects to the conversation as you can. Make comments such as 'I really like it when you wake me up so that I can have a shower before you go to work. That's really considerate of you'.
- Use genuine appreciation: 'I really appreciate that you work so hard to provide our family with the lifestyle that we have. You deserve time out too, so let's negotiate what's going to make both of us feel like we get enough time out.'
- Use 'wonder' in your statements: 'I wonder whether there is another solution to you working so many hours. Do you think there is another way that we can make money other than you having to work so much?'
- Turn complaints into requests. Instead of 'You never do the dishes when I always make the dinner', use a request such as 'If I make dinner, will you do the dishes?'

Common issues in marriages with young children and how to communicate for resolutions

My husband works too much

As mentioned earlier in this tutorial, this issue often makes a mum feel that she has to do everything with very little time out.

Let's revisit this issue with some suggestions on how to approach the topic. There are many issues within this issue that need to be ironed out in order for both parties to be satisfied.

- Why does he need to work so many hours? Is this because of financial commitments? Is what you are spending your money on something that you both want? Do you have an aligned goal? If you feel as though you are working towards something that you don't really see as important then you need to voice this in your conversation with him. It doesn't mean that you will get your way, but perhaps there can be a more aligned way for both of you to get what you want.

    For example, what if your husband feels that it's incredibly important for him to own his own house, and that is what he is working towards. On the other side, you value his time and being home with you and the kids as more important than owning a house. There needs to be some considerable negotiation to bring these extremes together.

    Be clear about what your ideal outcome is, and listen to what his ideal is. Is it possible for him to shift his ideas about when he needs to own his house? Is it possible for him to shift his idea of which house he has to own? Is the answer to downsize on the property he wishes to own so that you can have a smaller mortgage and he can work fewer hours?

    Discuss with him the idea of why he feels the need to own his own house by a certain time. Is this what he really wants or does he feel that it's what he 'should' do based on what he's been taught. How will he feel if he owns his own house? What does that mean for him? Find out what drives his desire to achieve the dream he has that causes him to work so long and see whether you can negotiate a change that gets you both what you want.
- Does he work because he loves his job and his career? If this is the case, the way I would approach this topic is to listen to how he connects with the passion for what he does. Get him to explain that passion and what it gives him on a spiritual level. Then, when he's really feeling that passion while talking, I would simply fit into the conversation, 'Wow, I

really wish I had something that inspires me like that. I'd really like to do "x". Do you think there is some way that we could negotiate the time for me to do "x"?'

Again, be specific with what you want in this scenario so that you can negotiate an outcome that you are both happy with.

- Does he work long hours to get out of having to handle the kids? This is sometimes the case and might be difficult for him to admit, but it happens. Sometimes it's easier to hide behind work rather than come home and have to help with what may appear as menial duties and facing the children when they seem to be at their worst (as they usually are in the evenings).

Try to understand your husband's perspective in this area. This is the impression that he gets of looking after the kids. He might mainly see them when they are at their most tired and crankiest and maybe that's the reason why he doesn't want to come home from work.

To begin tackling this reason for working late, the first conversation I would have is to try to discover the reason (from his point of view) why he works late.

Listen to what he has to say and discuss how reasonable it is. Try to explain how you feel about being with the kids for these long hours and how it impacts on your quality of life not being able to pursue your dreams. This can be a tricky one, but use the tips above on how to communicate with your husband. This is one conversation where you are teaching him how to treat you. You deserve to have time out and if there is no real reason for your partner to be working long hours other than his priority to avoid the reality of parenting, then this isn't really fair and you need to teach him that you expect there to be some alignment where you get a break too.

Make sure you are really certain that his reasoning for working long hours is that he doesn't want to handle the kids. Don't just assume this is the reason, as he may feel his reasons are very valid. Really listen to his viewpoint on why he works so long.

Regardless of the reason for your husband working long hours, there is always a way to negotiate different options that will make you both happy. If you find that you end up agreeing that the long hours have to stay, then you need to accept this reality rather than continue to complain about it.

For example, if you both agree that the house mortgage has to be paid, neither one of you is willing to move or downsize and hours must be worked to obtain this commitment, then that is the reality of the situation.

The key point with this issue is that your commitments within the family unit must be a team effort. You both must agree to the responsibility each one of you takes to the contribution to the family.

It cannot be assumed that you will just happily look after the kids during these long hours. If you can't align to why the hours need to be worked or can't align with looking after the kids for long hours then you must respect yourself enough to negotiate change where needed, or to change the way you think about the situation if you have agreed to accept this situation.

My husband doesn't help enough around the house

First and foremost, what do you want him to do? Be specific. Imagine that he offered to do anything you asked him to do, and you needed to tell him what would make you happy. What would you say? What do you consider to be fair? This is what you need to know before you even begin a conversation that tackles this issue.

Here is another suggestion of a procedure for negotiating this issue:
1. Negotiate a time to sit down with your husband and work out a fair distribution of tasks that make up the running of the house.
2. Make up a list of every single household duty that's required, daily, weekly and monthly. This list should include chores inside and outside.

3. Beside each chore, negotiate with your partner which one of you will be responsible for doing each chore and how regularly.
4. Decide which tasks the kids can get involved in so that you begin teaching them to help with household duties.

Negotiating chores in this way helps both of you to physically see if the chores are split up evenly. Your husband will be able to see for himself how fairly the chores are being distributed and could possibly come to the party in a way that you wouldn't expect when deciding who does what. If he is the one who participates in the agreement and doesn't fulfil his agreement, then you can talk to him about the broken agreement, rather than having to nag him to do something that you want him to do. This will make a big difference.

Your husband will feel that he has a say in his responsibilities, rather than feeling that you are being bossy and delegating work to him. I know personally that my husband hates it when I tell him what to do and is less likely to do it if it feels like a command from me. Let both of you decide what is fair and what is not, in terms of your own circumstances.

We never agree on how to discipline the children

This issue can be a major cause of arguments between couples. You may have both been brought up by your own parents in different ways, and this can come out in how you wish to discipline your own children. We know how we were raised and what that did for us on a very personal level, and this will dictate strongly how we treat our own children. For example, you or your husband might have had a very physical form of discipline while growing up and you might either feel that it worked for you because you turned out alright, or because of the way it made you feel, you have vowed never to allow that to happen to your kids.

For various reasons, you might find that you both feel very strongly about how children should be disciplined so there needs to be some deliberate conversation about what each of your standpoints are on this matter so that you can decide how to handle it before the situation presents itself. Here are some suggestions for tackling this issue.

- Get an understanding of the reasons why each of you believes your discipline method is the 'right' way. When you understand each other's points of view and can see where they might be coming from you might discover that the reason is from a past hurt that has been experienced, and compassion can be factored into the equation when discussing this issue.
- Educate yourself on specifically tried and tested alternatives to what you are both doing. Information on child discipline these days is huge. There are so many books and support networks around that can teach you a friendly way to discipline your children. Perhaps the way both of you are disciplining is not effective.
- Try one technique that you both agree on for an agreed period of time. If it doesn't work within that time frame, then agree on trying another one for another time frame. It may be that you need to try your husband's technique of discipline to really see whether it works, or that he might need to give your method a try for a while and wait for the results.
- Be very aware of why you are disciplining your children when you do. Are you trying to be right, or are you trying to control and get them to obey you? Or are you trying to teach them social and moral boundaries and respect for others? Discuss with your partner your intentions of administering your type of discipline. Discuss how your method effectively creates the education that your child needs in this matter and get him to do the same.
- Put yourself in your children's shoes. How do they feel when they are receiving this method of discipline? If you think they are feeling hurt, humiliated, not loved by either parent, or getting literally physically or emotionally scarred, then another method must be found.
- On another note, you as a parent must feel that your children are well loved and taken care of. If for any reason you

feel that your children are being abused either physically, mentally, sexually or emotionally then in my opinion, there is no negotiation. This is a deal breaker and you need to get your children away from that situation straight away. If you can't get your husband to change his behaviour from administering discipline in this way, then it's your responsibility to help your children get away from that cycle. At the end of the day, like everything in your relationship, you need to have a discussion and align on a decision. Try something different and see whether it works. This is not a right and wrong game. It's a trial and error one.

Every child is different, as we know, and you might go through a few discipline techniques before you find the one that works for your child.

The key is to stay aligned with each other. Discipline often fails when parents are not providing a united front for their kids. Never undermine each other, but if you have a problem, then fix it at a separate time when the kids aren't around.

In Step 4 (Choices), you really want to take into consideration what the possible solutions are that will help you and your partner to achieve your aims.

Consider:
- What compromises am I willing to make for him?
- What compromises am I asking him to make for me?
- Know that it's okay for the conversation to not go the way you expect. You are talking to another human being with his own beliefs and priorities so you can't control or predict the outcome of the conversation.
- Keep the conversation flowing towards alignment. If you're starting to venture into the right and wrong game, either put it back on track or postpone the conversation to another time, giving you both the space to digest what has already been put on the table.

Step 5 (Know your plan and action it)

Exercise 8

> In summary to all of these points, on a separate page in your notebook, put together your individual plan for discussing the problems in your relationship.
> 1. Jot down some key beliefs that you discovered that align with the GYLR Model and how you have upgraded them. This will remind you of what has previously been driving your behaviour and the way you've been interacting with your partner.
> 2. Write down specifically what you want and what you are going to be negotiating for.
> 3. Write down what you found out (through conversations with him) about what he wants and what you are willing to compromise on in order to give that to him. Remember that you're going to bring this to the table in order to show him that it's not just about you getting what you want.
> 4. Align with your partner an appropriate time when you can both sit down uninterrupted to have these discussions. This might be something you need to do regularly over a period of time until the issue or issues are resolved, so don't think that this has to happen over one conversation. There might be several issues that you need to address one at a time.
> 5. Before each conversation begins mentally align yourself with your intention for the conversation. It's like setting an aim for the conversation itself. It will help you to stay on track with what you are intending to achieve. For example, 'My intention for this conversation is to align with my partner how to set up some regular time out for me, for him and for us as a couple'.

Summary: Marital/partner relationships

The point to keep in mind when handling issues that arise within a relationship is that this is a team effort. You can't handle these issues in a selfish way, nor allow your partner to.

You are two individuals who are integrating your lives into a partnership that will allow you to be the individuals, the couple and the parents that you both desire to be.

Once you start practising communication without judgement, criticism, selfishness, 'Woe is me', 'I'm right, you're wrong', 'Give me what I want or else', and begin communicating with compassion, respect for another person's desire to be happy, union, fairness, compromise and flexibility about how you can achieve what you want, then you will start to see a more affectionate, united and happy relationship.

Before children, somewhere at the beginning of your relationship there was something that attracted you to each other: something that brought you together. Perhaps that something has changed and you need to rediscover what you love about each other now. The reality is that people change all the time and you need to continually redefine what is bringing you together and what attracts you to one another.

We change in our appearances, in our values and in our beliefs because we age, have new experiences and receive more information than we had before, which can upgrade or change how we perceive life.

This is happening to each individual person and being in a relationship means that you need to integrate these changes into your relationship too.

Our partners are not the enemy: they are our partners in life and in parenthood. We need to treat our marital relationships like any other partnership that you may have – one that has respect for the other person, negotiation, compromise, sharing, growth and development.

You want someone who is beside you in life, supporting you and helping you grow and achieve your dreams, not someone you feel is better than you or beneath you.

You are always two equal people living life together, trying to get what you want in life and living through the beliefs that you hold based on all the experiences you have had in your own individual lives. No one is better or worse because of that.

When we have our first child, our lives get turned upside down and the way we used to view life changes. What you must realise is that this change has occurred in your partner too and now is the time for each of you to step up and be a beacon of support for the other because this major change has affected both of your lives.

Talk to each other and help each other to handle these changes and make sense of the way life needs to be now that you are a parent and how different that is from your old, childless existence.

As Ghandi put it: 'Be the change you wish to see in the world'. Be compassionate, affectionate and loving to your partner and you will start to see some real changes to your relationship.

Chapter 14

Summary of Part B

Behavioural and developmental challenges

We will experience challenges with our children throughout the entire journey of parenting. This is the reality of being a parent. How we perceive these challenges will dictate how we feel about them.

Your child, in his or her journey to maturity and through life, will be observing, experiencing, learning, growing and contributing just as we are. He or she is behaving, acting and reacting in accordance to his or her beliefs and what his or her priorities are in each moment, just as we are.

Your child's behaviour is not a reflection of anything you are doing 'right' or 'wrong'. There are methods that work to ease these challenges and there are ways of handling these challenges that you will come across and learn from. However, whether you get your child to behave or not, your self-worth is always 100 per cent.

When you are experiencing challenging behaviour or developmental challenges that seem to be causing you stress, just take a few minutes to stop and observe your self-talk about the event. What you will find is a story riddled with thoughts that are in conflict with the reality of what is actually happening in front of you and more so a story about what this event means about your life, you as a person or you as a mum – and it will have little to do with the actual event.

Over time you will get better at recognising these thoughts and changing them in the moment so that you can become solution focussed about how you can help your child to move through this phase with a healthy mindset towards life.

You are an important teacher in your child's life, and mastering your own mind will become the most effective way of teaching your child how to master his or hers.

Anger and guilt

Emotions such as anger and guilt come about because a belief or beliefs have been activated that have produced a physical sensation in the body.

The most dominant beliefs associated with anger and guilt are covered in Point 3 on the GYLR Model: I/They should have done something differently.

The story we have in our minds of what should have happened creates the physical sensation that we feel as either anger or guilt.

We feel anger because of a conflict between the picture we held in our minds of how we expected something to be and the reality of what is actually happening. Because it has not happened the way we believe it should have, we perceive that our life has been negatively impacted (worth-less) in some way.

When we experience guilt we feel as though we should be doing or should have done something differently in the past and therefore we are or, in most cases, our child is worth-less or his or her life is worth-less in some way.

It's important to understand that in every moment we can only know what we know and our mind can only ever access the information it currently has stored to determine the appropriate response.

If anger is your habitual response to not getting what you expected, then this is likely to be your response until you are able to consciously change this response over time through repetition and experience.

Guilt often occurs mostly in mums because of the many different decisions that we have to make and areas that we need to tend to and take care of. We continuously have to prioritise and choose which area is more important than another. In each moment we are only able to access the beliefs we had about what's important in each moment and this is what dictates our decisions.

We can only know what we know, and in every moment we are simply deciding and acting upon the accessed beliefs and responses that our brains have assessed are the most appropriate *in that moment*. It cannot be any other way.

Loss of identity

You have not lost your identity. Your identity has changed and a large part of it is now being a mother. This is a reality that you have to accept and you then need to revisit your views on who you are and what defines you as worthy to this world.

All of the labels that you give yourself and that make you up are just that – labels. They do not define the value of your existence because the value of your existence lies in the mere fact that you are alive and contributing to how the world exists today.

As I stated in the introduction of this book, motherhood changes you physically, emotionally, mentally, morally and ethically and you cannot expect to be the same person you used to be.

This time in a woman's life is an opportunity to redefine herself and take a look at her values and what she has considered important in the past as she will inevitably begin to re-evaluate and recreate a new image of herself in alignment with this dramatic change in her life.

Just because life is different, it doesn't make it less valuable. Throughout this journey through life, change is constant and as we learn and grow our personality changes too. Allow yourself to change and grow with the experience of motherhood and say goodbye to the way you used to experience your life, for things have changed.

Motherhood is a new world and you need to allow yourself the time and space to get used to this new world by accepting the new experiences and challenges that arise. All of your life's experiences have brought you lessons and are always incredibly valuable. Motherhood will too.

Acknowledge that parts of you have changed and that your identity has changed too. Embrace the lessons and experiences that your new identity offers you because they also form part of your journey in life. Know that even once you get used to this identity, over time it will change again and again and again with new experiences and new information constantly influencing who you are. This is a natural and wonderful part of living and experiencing life as a human being.

Find the value in all events and it won't really matter what you label yourself as – you'll just enjoy the ride of life.

Time out

We all know that we need time out. We all know that taking a break from our kids makes us happier and more rational parents. But we don't take it, because we don't make it a priority.

Become aware of the story you tell yourself about why you can't take time out and you will find that the real reason for not taking time out is because something else is a priority and your beliefs are making that more important than your time out.

I remember a girlfriend saying to me once that she had plenty of time out but never felt like it was enough. It is possible to feel this way if you are in conflict with the reality of your new life now that you are a mother. You are limited as to how much time you have away from the kids, especially when they are under five years of age, when they need you the most.

We need to change our reference point of when and how we do things from the way it used to be to the reality of how it is now.

Having children doesn't mean that we have to give up our lives and devote them only to raising our children. You can still do anything that you want to do. However, you have to be flexible on the timing for what you want to achieve and 'plot and scheme around your kids' in order to do it.

You are not worth more as a person when you take time out and your life is not worth-less when you are at home with your children. All of your experiences with or without the children hold value and add to your journey through life. Your rating of what you do, which is governed by your beliefs, is the only thing that makes you feel that your life is worth more or less.

Time out is needed to help you feel independent and to enable you to experience things that are also an extension of who you are, including being a mum. It helps us to feel excited about our lives and motivated to try and learn different things.

If your kids, your family or other things are more of a priority than taking sufficient time out for yourself then there is a belief that you hold which is stopping you from taking time out.

When you discover what this belief is you can get a new understanding of yourself and maybe allow yourself to be important too.

Marital/partner relationships

The transition into motherhood and the huge changes it brings to your life has its effect on even the strongest of couples.

The dynamics that have been set up in the past as a result of the two people you were before becoming parents are often changed and redesigned and if communication becomes limited then it can cause stress, confusion and conflict between you.

It is important to understand that you are two individual people with unique belief systems that have been formed from each of your journeys through life so far. You are joining your lives together and integrating these beliefs together to create harmony, love and support for each other.

Because we are forever changing and adding to who we are in our lives, it's vital that the communication between couples stays open, especially when becoming a parent, for this is when the most dramatic changes occur to both Mum and Dad.

We have to look at our partners as human beings just like us – they have their own wants and needs and are only trying to make their lives happy, just as we are. They are also transitioning into this huge change of life and trying to accept that life is no longer as self-indulgent as it was before.

Alignment, commitment, compromise and negotiation are what will make a relationship stay strong during these early years of being a parent. Recognise that you are not the only one experiencing changes and your partner has his own beliefs and pressures about being a 'good dad'.

When you understand this and connect with compassion that he has the same basic desires that you have, you can communicate with him about how you can both get what you want and align ways that you can achieve this together.

I believe that relationships are about supporting one another to grow as people and to help one another in achieving what you want to experience in life. I believe it's about respecting each other and acknowledging that your partner is always changing and learning new things that over time change who he is and how he behaves.

We can understand our husband's or partner's behaviour by remembering that our behaviour is always governed by our beliefs. Learning the specific beliefs that are driving your husband's or partner's behaviour can be very powerful towards negotiating how you can communicate with him and work out a new agreement that works for both of you. All in all, the key to a successful relationship is understanding that it too has its ups and downs because two belief systems have to integrate and because personally we are each going through our own highs and lows in life that affect how we feel, who we are as people and consequently how we respond to those we love.

When you can really view the trials in your relationship to be a result of how you have both contributed to the relationship, then you can begin to solve the conflict by also both contributing to its solution. Remember the old saying, 'It takes two to tango'?

Chapter 15

Summary to changing your mindset

The way you think about your role as a mum, your role as a person outside of being a mum and your role within your relationship is the key to your happiness.

Becoming a parent takes you on a journey where you've never been before and no one can ever really understand this journey until they are living it.

Intense emotions such as immense love and affection for your children and strong desires to give them the very best in life combined with anger, frustration and possibly mourning the loss of your old life and the freedom you once had can take you on a whirlwind ride that no other experience could ever replicate.

Everyone experiences this parenting ride differently because of what they believed about their life, their self-worth and parenting before they even began experiencing it. It's these beliefs that can easily lead us to experiencing major stress, depression or anxiety, which has a major impact on our lives and the ones we love.

It's important to remember that because of our own upbringing, our observations and experiences and how our lives have unfolded to date, we have formed beliefs in our minds that drive the behaviour, actions and reactions that we have on a daily basis and form how we perceive life events.

Happy people aren't just lucky people or people who have never experienced upset or hardships; they are happy because of the mindset they have adopted towards life.

We have often heard it stated that parenting is one of the toughest jobs that we can ever have and so it becomes even more crucial to be able to develop a mindset that can handle this tough job and all the challenges that it involves so that you don't have to experience pain and suffering and so that you can enjoy your children as much as possible.

The Mind TRACK to Happiness process

The Mind TRACK to Happiness process was created as a tool to use to help you create this mindset with the aim of being one of those happy mums.

T – THOUGHTS

By becoming aware of your thoughts about how you perceive the challenges in your life, you open up your conscious mind to seeing what is actually causing your stress, for it's never the event that causes you stress, it's the way you view the event and what you perceive this event to mean about you.

The Fountainhead Method™ Get Your Life Right Model of thinking is always at play when dealing with any form of stress and you can always align your thoughts to the following three assumptions, followed by one core belief:

1. My life is on the wrong path.
2. I am missing out (on what my life needs).
3. I/they should/could be doing something differently.

Core belief:

4. I am/my life is worth-less.

R – REALITY

All stress is a conflict between belief (your thoughts) and reality.

Reality, for the purposes of the Mind TRACK to Happiness process is an accurate view of the current situation, of life and of your self-worth. It is finding an acceptance of now by understanding how your thoughts are in conflict with what's happening right now and with the reality of your life and your self-worth.

It's accepting that whatever you are experiencing right now is happening because of how your life has unfolded in the past (which has led up to now). All of your experiences, actions and beliefs that were formed prior to now have dictated how this current event has played out and *that* is the reality about everything you experience.

The Fountainhead Method™ Personal Development Model of thinking relates to each point on the Get Your Life Right Model to help you upgrade your beliefs from being in conflict with reality to becoming aligned with reality. They are:

1. Life is a journey.

Life is a journey and it is our unique journey – our story. We are on a journey, our child is on a journey, our husband/partner is on a journey and we are all experiencing different events and learning and growing throughout this journey. There will always be ups and downs – that is the reality of life. It doesn't mean that you are on the wrong path when life doesn't go to plan; it's just another experience along your journey in life.

2. I am always learning and receiving.

Throughout all of your experiences there is always value and something to gain. We are always learning new ways of doing things and receiving lessons about life. Finding the value in events helps us to stop viewing them as good or bad. Some of our most valuable lessons have come from some of the worst moments in our lives. Whenever you feel like you're missing out on something, ask yourself, 'What is this experience teaching me? What am I getting from this situation?'

3. We only know what we know at any given moment.

At any given moment we only ever have the knowledge we have gained from life so far to draw upon. Information and experiences have formed our beliefs and this is what governs the priorities that we have in each moment. All of our behaviours, actions and reactions are driven by accessing the beliefs we have in each moment and which belief holds the most importance in this moment. This is the reasoning part of the brain, which sorts through all information about past experiences, habitual responses, thoughts and actions and determines what the best scenario is in this moment based on all the information it is receiving from this moment through the senses.

You can only ever draw upon the knowledge that you have in each moment. You cannot know more than you do until you've received and been convinced of new information that changes or adds to your current knowledge. When looking at past events you couldn't have behaved any differently for this is the information you had at that time and that was the priority your brain determined was appropriate at the time, according to your current beliefs.

4. I am always 100-per-cent worthwhile.

Self-worth comes from your very existence. You are here in life contributing to the day-in, day-out process of life. Everything you do affects people around you and contributes to their development and the way their life unfolds and to your development and the way your life unfolds. You are learning and growing and also teaching and helping other people to grow just by being alive and living in this world. You are always important and valuable for this very reason alone and your worth cannot be added to or taken away. We are all valuable because we are all adding to life in our own ways.

Self-esteem is the rating system we have that comes from our learnt beliefs. We rate ourselves and others based on what we have been taught to believe.

I have heard it argued that someone such as the Dalai Lama is more valuable because he has contributed so much to so many compared to someone who sits at home and won't leave the house. However, it is still your beliefs that dictate the Dalai Lama's contribution to being this significant. You rate his contribution as significant, due to your beliefs. Others might not, due to their beliefs. What someone has learnt from the person who doesn't leave the house may be more significant and valuable to them than the Dalai Lama's contributions. It all depends on your beliefs and how you have been taught to rate life.

The reality is that we are all significantly contributing to each other's lives and to the development of our own life and that is what defines us as 100-per-cent worthy.

A – AIM

- What do I want?
- Be specific.
- Is what I want in conflict with reality?
- Why do I want it?

Here is where the mind starts to shift in a different direction. Rather than looking at the past, our attention becomes interested in what is wanted for the future, while still testing the beliefs that are driving the desire to achieve this as a goal.

C – Choices

- What are the options/solutions available?
- What beliefs are governing my choices?

'How do I achieve this aim?' becomes the next line of thought. What are the options available to me that will help me to achieve this goal?

Also, an understanding of what drives our choices is governed by our beliefs and what beliefs take priority over others, for we are serving our best interests 100 per cent of the time.

If we become aware of the beliefs that make us choose one decision over another we can test whether they fall on the GYLR Model, which will cause more stress and whether, after upgrading these beliefs on the Personal Development Model, we might just choose a different option or solution than we first thought.

K – Know your plan and action it

Now that you have come to terms with reality, have decided on an aim that is not in conflict with reality and have consciously weighed up all the options while continually testing and checking the beliefs driving your choices, you need to create the plan that you're going to use to move towards your aim and away from the stress that you feel.

However, in this step you must always keep reminding yourself of the purpose of goals. While we set goals in order to achieve them, achieving them is not the valuable part of having a goal.

The true purpose of goals is to experience life. Throughout these experiences, we are not only learning and growing, but are also contributing to the life process and to other people's development, just by completing each step along our road towards the goal.

Whether you get the goal or don't get the goal, while you are on the journey towards the goal you are always learning, growing and contributing to your and others' lives.

Chapter 16

Be the change you wish to see in the World

The Happy Mum Handbook has been written to give you a somewhat different approach to being a Happy Mum by helping you to recognise the reality of life and all the challenges and fun times that it entails, with parenting being no different.

Your mindset is going to be what makes you enjoy your life and feel fulfilled and valued, and no external event is ever going to change this for you. Your beliefs are always there waiting to steer you in the direction that you believe you should go and you are always perceiving life in accordance with your beliefs.

If you have found within this book that you have identified some beliefs in your mindset that have been causing you stress (which I'm sure you would have), then know that you can change these beliefs through repetition, consistency and experience – the exact same way that you learnt to hold them. Once you are convinced that these are the correct beliefs, they will become long-term memory and thus your new habitual responses.

So hang in there and keep bringing these thoughts, these perceptions and these stories that are causing you stress into your awareness so that you can consciously practise this new mindset.

Keep practising the Mind TRACK to Happiness process so that you can become solution focussed about the challenges that you come across and how you can move through them.

Remember, no fairy godmother is going to wave her magic wand and make you happy, nor is she going to make your kids behave or make you enjoy motherhood more. Your mindset and the way you perceive this role is what is going to make the difference towards how you experience being a mum.

Finally, I know that you want to enjoy your children. I know that you love your children dearly and would die for them, so why not try living for them instead?

Learn to treat yourself well and know that you are worthy and beautiful just the way you are. You are such an important part of your children's lives because you are their mother and you have been blessed with the wonderful opportunity to be an influence on your children and to teach them what you know.

Please teach them to love themselves and to embrace the value in all of their challenges in life and that you don't always have to get life right in order to have a successful life. Teach them that whatever they are doing is contributing immeasurably to those around them and to their own development. Teach them that every step of the way they are living their journey. They are creating the unique story of their life.

Teach them this by teaching yourself, loving yourself and respecting yourself and knowing the true value of yourself and your life.

Our societies need you, as you can be the beacon of change that influences your children and teaches them this deeper, more profound understanding of self-worth and the true purpose of goals, rather than the old values of achievement, success and 'right' and 'wrong' dictating our worth.

You are always important. You are always influential and you have the power to shape lives and future generations just by being the mum you are.

Enjoy your journey and may love be the light that drives you.

Best of luck
Jackie Hall

Afterword

Many issues that we all seem to suffer from during our lifetimes seemed to have had no new effective solution offered for many years.

As the psychotherapy industry has expanded, so has mental illness. When we look back in 50 years' time, I feel the Fountainhead Method™ will have gained its place in history by identifying that so many of these issues are in need of an educational program and not a therapeutic program.

The Fountainhead Method™, though originally developed as an educational method of alleviating stress, is now being applied to depression, anxiety, fears and phobias.

In this book Jackie Hall brings the Fountainhead Method™ and its application to mothers to help them to deal with the everyday challenges and emotions that can arise through the experience of motherhood.

I remember my first meeting with Jackie at the Fountainhead Retreat quite clearly. Here was a passionate lady who really wanted to make a difference to people's lives. All she lacked, as evidenced by her prior stress levels, were the right tools.

Here we are only a relatively short time later and she has taken The Fountainhead Method™, re-interpreted it and applied it for a whole new audience, and is getting fantastic results every day.

On a personal note, I now see a young mother who has learnt to learn from her own stress levels and who is enjoying her own life so much more because of it.

I commend Jackie on her honesty, passion and dedication to the cause of alleviating stress in motherhood.

Wayne Parrott
Honorary Chairman
Anti-Depression Association of Australia
www.adaa.org.au

Acknowledgements

Just by being who you are, you are always influencing and contributing to the life of someone else. We are all shaping and moulding each other's lives just by being human, living in this world and interacting with one another.

Through these experiences with others, they either reinforce what we already know, or they teach us to look at life differently.

In all of our lives, as I'm sure you have experienced too, there are always those few special people that leave an imprint on us that can change us forever. These are the people that form part of your life either briefly or for a long time and they encourage us to stretch past our limitations and experience life in a way that wouldn't be possible without them.

I could not send this book to be published without publically acknowledging and thanking those special people that I have been so fortunate to have had as part of my experience in this life.

Chronologically, the first person who has contributed the most to my love of personal development is my mum. Since I was a teenager she has introduced me to my spiritual side and allowed me the freedom to explore who I am. She has been incredibly influential and inspirational in teaching me to have a 'can do' attitude and to never let anything get in the way of what I want.

Through my experience of my mother, I have learnt that when I want something, all I have to do is search for how to do it. Anything is possible. You will find within this book, this very lesson that I am now passing onto you. So if you get anything out of this book, then it is because she has been my role model in life and allowed me to learn this valuable information.

The next person that has been a huge support in my life and helped me to grow as a person is my life partner of 14 years, Stephen. I am enormously grateful that this man has come into my life and I couldn't imagine being without him. He is such a calm, gentle, caring and genuine soul and has taught me from the word go how to be calmer, relax and have fun. He has always supported everything that I've ever wanted to do and there is nothing that I cannot share with him.

Most of what you read in the chapter on relationships is there because Stephen has taught me how to listen, communicate, say sorry and understand the other person. He has been my teacher in how to have the most rewarding and successful relationship and marriage that I could ever have hoped for.

He has a very kind nature and loves to see other people happy and get through their adversities. We have big dreams and I cannot wait to fulfil our dream together of helping kids at risk on our remote cattle station one day.

In the same category of family, I must also thank my two beautiful boys – Cody and Ryan. Becoming a mother has helped me to grow in ways I never thought was possible. I have always wanted to have children but never knew that this part of my journey would reward me with enormous personal growth and change. My boys are a gift to me and I treasure their energy, their love and their presence in my life. I could not be the person I am today without them and I love them 'to the moon and back and to the stars and back'.

As I move through my list, I find an influential person that completely inspired me and helped me to follow my passion. He is also someone that I've never met. His name is Steve Irwin – The Crocodile Hunter. His passion for conservation matches my passion for helping people to learn to love themselves and learn a 'can do' attitude like I've been taught.

He has taught me that just one person can make such a difference to people in the world just by being yourself and standing tall with conviction over what you are passionate about. I have a quote of his that sits on my desktop and it reads:

"If there is one thing that I'd want to be remembered for, it's passion and enthusiasm. Conservation is my joy, my life, my whole being".

This is how I feel about helping people love themselves and love their life. His ability to live with passion and integrity, push past what people think is possible and be such a huge contributor to changing the beliefs of mankind for the better is what I aspire to do. His influence on me has touched me to my core and I'll never forget this extraordinary man.

Last, but certainly not least, is my most recent influence in my life – Wayne Parrot. He is the founder of the Anti-depression association of Australia and has found what is for many people the cure to stress, depression and anxiety.

After experiencing his own mate with depression and being told that he could not be helped, he decided that was not good enough. He began to search for his own answers and has been relentless in the last 10 years about coming up with the answers to help people overcome this debilitating illness.

This mission to help his mate and other people with these illnesses has resulted in The Fountainhead Method, used in this very book.

What I love about Wayne is his passion and 'can do' attitude. I have never heard him say that we can't do something and whenever I've wanted to achieve something, he has thought of a way to make it happen. I have been incredibly fortunate to have him as my mentor and teach me that if you want something then you just have to think about how you can do it.

The most important lesson I have received from Wayne though, was to never take someone else's word as gospel, even if they are a professional. Seek your own answers and keep striving and searching until you find what you are looking for. Never listen to people who tell you that you can't and when you have found the answers that no one thought you could find – share them with the world and help other people.

These influential people in my life have shaped who I am, who I will be and how many people I am able to help in this lifetime. They have taught me to be passionate, help others, love myself, and believe in myself and to stand strong in my determination to make a difference.

This world that we live in is in pain and through the help and influence of these people and what I have learnt in this lifetime so far, I know that I have some answers that can make a big difference to other people's lives.

Teaching people to have love and compassion for themselves and others is my joy, my life and my whole being and I would like to publically thank all of those special people in my life that have made it possible for me to be a writer and facilitator of change.

When it comes down to our life's final hours, everyone you've cared about and shared your life with combined with the wonderful memories of your life are all that matter. Already, in just 32 years I have been blessed with a rewarding life full of love and I am extremely grateful for everything that I have received.

So thank you to those who have been there for me and to those that will be there in the future.

Jackie Hall

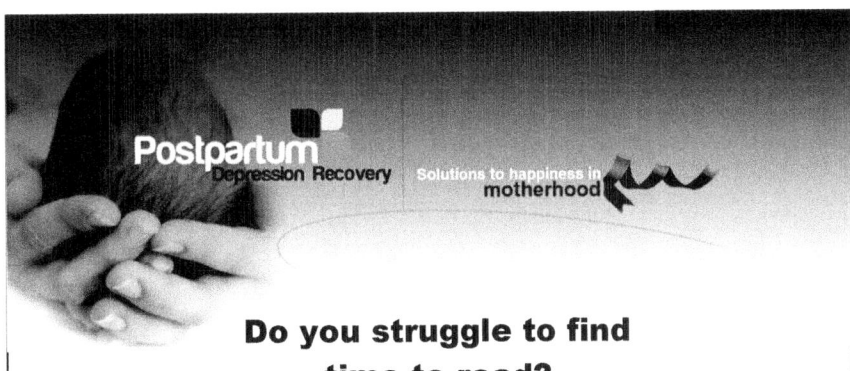

Postpartum Depression Recovery — Solutions to happiness in motherhood

Do you struggle to find time to read?

Are you looking for more support?

Jackie Hall - Author of
The Happy Mum Handbook introduces...

The Postpartum Depression Recovery Program

An online 12 week personal development program specifically for mums to help them STOP motherhood stress, depression and anxiety.

Step-by-step, daily lessons that take no more than 15-20 minutes of your time

You get full support through our exclusive membership Q&A Forum– ask for help on how to apply the tools you are learning to your life and interact with other mums. You are not alone!!

Let us hold your hand and guide you towards being the happy mum you want to be!

www.postpartumdepressionrecovery.com

Self Help for Mums
Free yourself from motherhood stress

www.selfhelpformums.com

The Home of
The Happy Mum Handbook

- Sign up for our Monthly newsletter

- Read our blogs

- Read more helpful articles

- Find out about Author - Jackie Hall's public speaking appearances, book signings, seminars and workshops

Find us on Facebook
For daily tips and inspirational quotes

www.facebook.com/pages/Self-Help-for-Mums/143962378957916